ECONOMY AND SELF

ECONOMY
AND SELF

Philosophy and Economics
from the Mercantilists to Marx

NORMAN FISCHER

Contributions in Economics and Economic History, Number 24

GREENWOOD PRESS
Westport, Connecticut • London, England

Library of Congress Cataloging in Publication Data

Fischer, Norman, 1943-
    Economy and self.

    (Contributions in economics and economic
history ; no. 24 ISSN 0084-9235)
    Bibliography: p.
    Includes index.
    1. Economics. 2. Marxian economics. 3. Self
(Philosophy)   I. Title.
HB72.F48   330.1   78-73799
ISBN 0-313-20888-3

Library of Congress Catalog Card Number: 78-73799
ISBN: 0-313-20888-3
ISSN: 0084-9235

First published in 1979

Greenwood Press, Inc.
51 Riverside Avenue, Westport, Connecticut 06880

Printed in the United States of America

10 9 8 7 6 5 4 3 2 1

To the memory of my father,
John Francis Fischer

Contents

Preface

This book examines the interconnections between philosophy and economics in the late eighteenth and nineteenth centuries, including the economic ideas of philosophers and the philosophical ideas of economists. For the most part, the philosophers and economists studied here wrote within a period of about a century—from the early synthesis of free-enterprise theory found in Quesnay and Smith in the latter half of the eighteenth century, through Kant and Hegel writing within the tradition of German idealism, to Marx attempting to synthesize both traditions in the latter half of the nineteenth century. Insofar as these thinkers form a historical tradition, it exists between and shades into mercantilism on the one side and late-nineteenth-century opposition to subjective value theory on the other. The philosophers and economists studied are tied conceptually by the way they relate questions of the self to problems of individual and holistic explanation in economics.

I would like to thank those who have heard and commented on the ideas in the book over the last several years: participants in the social theory program and colloquium at the University of Washington; my classes and colloquia at Kent State University; the Institute for Marxism and Culture held at St. Cloud University; and the second and third annual Conferences on the Current State of Marxism held at Athens, Ohio, and the Red Feather Institute in Colorado.

I am particularly indebted to those who have read and commented on the manuscript: Alok Bhalla, Tom Dubis, Peter Fuss, Wayne Grytting, Robert Hall, Lyman Legters, James Mish'alani, Govind Naidu, Lou Patsouras, Melvin Rader, and Dawson Schultz. Kenneth Calkins, Jack Schillinger, and Simone Georgopoulos helped with some difficult passages from German and French. For encouragement while I was working on this book, I would like to thank Sue Berkey and my colleagues in the Philosophy Department at Kent State University: Ted Bickley, Chuck Burlingame, Bob Dyal, Nenos Georgopoulos, Jim Parmenter, and Art Wheeler. Special thanks are extended to Arlene Lawson, who typed the manuscript, and to N. Georgopoulos, Lew Fried and Teodros Kiros for help in the final stages.

Norman Fischer

Introduction:
The Self and Alienation

The most general concept of alienation is that there is division in the self. Although this definition does not cover all aspects of the word "alienation" as it is now used, it does seem to encompass much of what comes from psychology, philosophy, and sociology as well as literature, art, and popular culture. For all of these contemporary modes of expression, alienation seems to be equated with lack of self-unity.[1] Division or lack of unity in the self, however, can take so many forms that alienation must be arguable for in many different ways, an observation which gives a clue for further clarification of the concept. Alienation exists when there are good arguments for holding that the self is divided; the better the arguments are, the more justified the claim of alienation.

The large number of possible arguments does not mean that they do not fall into general groupings or types. One type of argument is over conflicting descriptions of the self. In this case, arguments for alienation arise out of problems in knowing the self and how to describe it.

In some cases, there are no arguments over ways of describing the self. It may be agreed that several descriptions are correct, but there still may be an argument. What could it be based on? Perhaps the elements of the self that are described prevent the full realization of each other. It may be agreed that both P and N describe x, but that P and N will ultimately prevent each other from existing or developing. They cannot exist together harmoniously.

A slight variation on this second type of argument is that there are disagreements about the self because its parts do not coalesce into one unified system. However, this is probably not the usual way for accounts of alienation to develop. Arguments about the unified nature of the self ordinarily tend to draw their power from arguments about its division. There are many ways in which aspects of the self can be divided. Thus, the one who holds an ideal of self-unity will perhaps not positively state in what this nondivision consists, but rather will argue that in a particular case where self-division has been upheld, this claim is incorrect. But the upholder of nondivision or unity must always be prepared to take up the argument against the one who urges division.

The first type of argument may be said to be less valuational, the second more. Yet if that distinction is pursued, it does not seem so clear. The second argument does stress harmony and system. Yet, harmony as value may rest on an order which is not so clearly valuational, and a system may seem to be unified because of both factual and valuational claims. Furthermore, it is not clear that the first type of argument, which depends on knowing whether a description is true or not, can ultimately be separated from knowledge of a value order. The search to end alienation is the search to find order in the self, an order which can be conceived of as value laden or not. Indeed, the theory of economy and self developed here stresses the search for both moral order in the self and factual order in the economy: economy and self.[2]

Although explicit arguments for alienation have been increasingly stressed in the nineteenth and twentieth centuries, it is an old concept. The problem is to figure out where the new concept begins and the old ends. Historically, accounts of alienation can be divided into several overlapping stages. The first stage is the premodern or timeless. Here are described certain problems of the individual or the individual and society that may naturally occur whatever the historical, social conditions. Even though they may be said to be premodern in origin, that cannot be stated with as much confidence as that they are timeless, in the sense that they could arise out of observations of eternal characteristics of man or philosophical reflection upon such characteristics. Many psychological and social theories of alienation may be timeless in this sense, probably premodern in origin, and yet continuing to the present. Such psycho-logical accounts may arise from the fact that any individual may have specific divisions within himself which can be argued about in different ways. In contrast, social accounts may arise from the fact that there is always a potential conflict between the claims of the individual and those of society. Greek tragedy gives examples of psychological and social division as easily as the most expressionist painting, from Grosz expressing social alienation to Munch express-ing psychological alienation.[3]

The second general stage is when alienation becomes used in a more reflective way by economists and social contract theorists in Western Europe, particularly in the seventeenth and eighteenth centuries. In the third stage, alienation becomes incorporated into what is sometimes called classical German philosophy, particularly Kant, Hegel, Feuerbach, and Marx.[4] Finally, in the fourth stage, alienation enters into that popular and psychological usage of the twentieth century when the state of alienation often seems almost synonymous with all of mankind's ills.

As can be seen from the preceding sketch, accounts of social alienation develop simultaneously with accounts of alienation in general, which includes both social and psychological alienation:

Alienation in General	Social Alienation
Premodern or Timeless	Premodern or Timeless
Social Contract	Social Contract
Classical German	Classical German
20th Century	20th Century[5]

These social accounts exist implicitly in the premodern period as claims of division or potential division between social and individual aspects of the self. For our purposes, the easiest way to characterize these premodern accounts of social alienation is in terms of what they are not. They are not accounts giving rise to the concept of a socialist economy that pays attention to the imperatives of economy and self discussed in this book. For it is one characteristic of the economy and self theory that, when linked up with certain ideals of freedom and ethics, the theory allows us to create imperatives for ending some (though not all) aspects of present-day social alienation in capitalism.

The second stage of the social theory of alienation is more capable of giving rise to something like these imperatives. Here, in the social contractarians and economists of the seventeenth and eighteenth centuries, the division between individual and social self takes the form of positing a society which both rigidly follows social laws beyond the individual and yet appears mysterious to him. Thus, it can be argued that the social or communal aspects of the self both belong and do not belong to the self; so that there are good arguments for thinking that the self is divided and thus alienated. This community, which can be held to both belong and not belong to individuals, is divided.

In the third stage, this social account of alienation intersects with a similar problem, of a community which belongs and does not belong to individuals, as interpreted by classical German philosophy, particularly Kant, Hegel, and Marx. This intersection of classical German and the economic and social philosophies of the seventeenth and eighteenth centuries is the clearest expression of an account of alienation arising from reflections on economy and self. In this account, two types of arguments, one primarily economic and the other primarily philosophical, complement each other in showing how man's community and common actions are divided from him.

This account of alienation lives on in the twentieth century in the works of Hegelian Marxists, such as Lukács and Goldmann. The intersection between economy and self also occurs a number of times in nineteenth- and early twentieth-century Germany, e.g., Tönnies, Schmoller, Simmel, and Weber.[6]

The political economy that does not intersect with classical German philosophy, or some other form of humanism, goes, for the most part, into the route sketched by Jevons, Walras, Marshall, and Keynes. Such a political economy is not interested in the self and thus ultimately constructs a thing-like image of the self.[7] At the same time, other thinkers, such as the existentialists, have constructed an account of self which, because it does not often touch on a broad economic or social foundation, from the start limits both its concept of self-alienation and the possibility of ending it.

There remains a conceptual connection between the often seemingly autonomous developments of economy and self in the late nineteenth and twentieth centuries. For the skepticism of technical economists about bringing the self into their analysis could be the reverse side of the disinterest of some existentialists in society and objectivity. In the one case, self-order would have to be discovered simply as an afterthought after the economic laws have been analyzed. In the other case, self-order would have to be created outside of the order of society and economics. In contrast to these poles, the intersection between classical German philosophy and political economy found in Hegel, Marx, Lukács, and Goldmann allows a concept of self-order which is both created and discovered. In order to understand how this is possible we must pay special attention to the genesis of the concept of alienation in classical German philosophy.

A number of interconnected themes in classical German philosophy make it capable of interpreting alienation, both social and nonsocial: freedom, God, values, community, and, the theme that cuts across all of them, the nature of the self. Classical German philosophy's attitude toward such topics is that one must not be prematurely certain about them. This critique is expressed most succinctly in Hegel. For him this premature certainty was characteristic of rationalism.[8] As opposed to this kind of certainty, Hegelian idealism gives an account of these themes which doubts itself and also believes in itself. This double attitude is probably not resolved by showing that the doubt is basic or the belief is basic. Goldmann was right in connecting Pascal with classical German philosophy and saying of him that he both believes and does not believe—that he says both yes and no.[9] Part of this yes/no syndrome is Marx's ridiculing of certain uses of the theme of alienation in the *Communist Manifesto*, coupled with his failure to use the concept in public speeches, at the same time that some of his published writings, and even more his unpublished writings, depend heavily upon it. The difference between Marx and Marx, Hegel and Hegel, Feuerbach and Feuerbach, Lukács and Lukács, is not just between different parts of their careers. It is also found in the very same book, as will be suggested later in the analysis of *The Philosophy of Right*.[10]

Classical German idealism, then, has this peculiarity: wherever it sees community, it also sees it broken; where it sees freedom, it also sees its lack; where it sees God's presence, it also sees His absence; where it sees value, it also sees no value; finally, where it sees mind, and purpose and unity of the self, it also sees lack of mind and purpose and division in the self. All of these factors lead classical German philosophy to talk of a self behind the self, a self which is united rather than divided, a true self. This true self behind the self is in tune with God, with values, with community and freedom. However, the divided, alienated self, the self in front, says that this is not the case—that there is no community, no freedom, no value, no God. This concept of a true self opposed to a false, nonalienated self links up with an old method of treating one of the key themes of classical German philosophy: freedom.

The point was first tentatively formulated by Plato who argued in the *Republic* against the notion of freedom as following desires. His argument was that although this made the desires free, it did not make the self free, since it had no control over the desires.[11] Such an account can logically lead to a self behind the self, a concept which can then present itself as an alternative to some modern formulations of the determinism/freedom debate. The debate leads to an opposition between following the laws of science, in which case one is determined, and not following the laws of science, in which case one follows chance. But what is free about following chance? As Plato noted, that only makes one's desires free, not the self. The self does not control which chance desires are able to manifest themselves. This suggests that the self must be able to impose an order on itself. But this must not be done arbitrarily. Thus, there must be an appeal to a self behind the self, intuition, or knowledge of which will tell what kind of order to impose. Calling the imposition of this order freedom seems to conform to certain basic intuitions about freedom. Who is free, the mountain climber who acts according to his orderly principles and rescues his fellow in distress, or the mountain climber who simply acts according to chance and might do it or might not? The Platonic theory says the former; similarly with the judge who follows his rules and makes a decision which is thus relatively predictable, as opposed to the one who acts by chance by simply following the latest fashion.

The question becomes, then, how can this self-order be attained and also known? We now see how the problem of freedom relates to that of alienation. The upholder of freedom as self-order must also seek a self behind the self, an order which is not simply identical with everything that the self does. For Plato, that order was found in a transcendent world, but at the most the classical German philosophers only believe ambiguously in such a transcendent world or God. Insofar as the theory of freedom as self-order ties into a world which is both infused and deserted by God, the existence of the self behind the self can neither be totally asserted nor totally denied.

Classical German philosophy, at the same time that it was doubting the existence of God in the traditional sense, was also using God or His disappearance as a central focus of its account of self. Present, God gives the self unity by giving it a soul; absent, He gives the self division. Yet, God could never play the role, as in earlier religious thinkers, of showing that the part of the self that was unified into a system could be elevated above the part that was not. In the nineteenth century, the self behind the self, the true self, was something which could not be asserted with total confidence, as opposed to the medieval period when belief in God allowed one to assert the reality of the true self over the false. Since for classical German philosophers God was neither completely there nor completely not there, they could never be absolutely sure or unsure about the ability to achieve the self behind the self. The self was caught between the world of reality and the world of the ideal, but neither could adequately define it. A God could, but such a God no longer clearly existed for much of classical German philosophy.[12]

The concept of the self behind the self also arises out of classical German philosophy's search for value. Again, there is something both old and new in this concept. In the history of ethics from Plato through the Middle Ages and the modern period, there is concern with how the self orders itself.[13] That order was frequently said to be the result of a natural law and thus discoverable by knowing the natural law. As we will see, however, the economics of physiocracy was one of the last echoes of this old naturalistic ethics. After that, the order had to be both created and discovered.

The question of whether value is created or discovered is connected with the themes of God, community, and self.

The self behind the self can be created and discovered only if it already has some qualities before the search for this self is begun. But these qualities are only possibilities. Not everything can be created out of them; on the other hand, it is not a matter of simply discovering qualities which have already been actualized. The concept of potential qualities of the self is connected with the interpretation of God as community in classical German philosophy. This idea was stated by Feuerbach as the notion that many of the attributes of God were the attributes of human nature, which because it projects *(entäussert)* itself in God has become lost to itself. The human community had been lost or made ambiguous and needed to be retrieved. All attempts to retrieve this community, however, are not simply discoveries but also creations. Feuerbach, for example, finds the human community in religion but alienated from itself. He shows how mankind can create a new human community out of this old religious community, but it is not the same as the old one. Similarly, Marx discovers a self in political economy which will be refurbished on a new level in communist society.[14] This refurbishing involves a creative act as well as a discovery of the deformed potentials of the self under capitalism. The discovered human community as it exists in capitalism both belongs and does not belong to the individual, and is thus alienated. When it can be said to belong truly to the individual, then it will have been both created and discovered, and the alienation of both asserting and denying the existence of community will have been ended.

An alternate interpretation to that of Marx and Feuerbach, who stressed that the self behind the self must be both created and discovered, was the right-wing interpretation of Hegel which held that community was already in God and just had to be looked for. According to this interpretation, the self behind the self could be attained simply through discovery and contemplation of what is discovered. This was a very conservative route because the discovery would mean going back to the old forms of community as found in the church and the state.[15]

It is sometimes held that the left Hegelians gave a truer interpretation of Hegel, one which led directly to Marxism. The truth is, however, that Marx opposed the interpretation of Hegel's thought by the left Hegelians (his opposition to right-wing Hegelianism goes without saying). For the left Hegelians, the self was often simply created. In the case of some members of the *Freien* (the left Hegelians whose papers Marx sometimes rejected when he was an editor of the *Rheinische Zeitung*), this concept of pure creation of the self involved a rejection of the notion of the human community.[16] Indeed, in many ways the left-wing interpretation of the death of God was merely the mirror image of the right-wing interpretation of His life. The right Hegelians held that God gave all meaning to an otherwise alienated human existence. The left Hegelians agreed that human existence was alienated, but, since they were unable to see a way of ending that alienation through the rediscovery of the human community, they were forced to posit, as against the void left by the death of God, the void created by men who can only find meaning by arbitrarily creating it. Ethics becomes egotism, freedom becomes the arbitrary creation of self; the path is begun to nihilism.

The whole tradition of economy and self outlined here stands against this nihilistic interpretation of alienation. The nihilistic theory, where the self is simply created and not discovered at all, leads to the concept not just of a self behind the self, but of a self stripped bare, a self which has no qualities, or rather, has so many qualities that it does not know what to do with them. But there is a problem in the notion of a self stripped bare, a self which is totally created rather than discovered as well. This problem can be found in thinkers such as Nietzsche and the early Sartre, who have sought such a self. For the self which thinks the self stripped bare is not itself stripped bare.

Nietzsche strips the self bare and calls it the overman. Yet, Nietzsche himself talks of the misunderstandings of his concept of the overman. He tries to resolve them by saying that the overman may be closer to Cesare Borgia than to Parsifal. But the misunderstandings that Nietzsche tries to resolve only show that his overman, supposedly stripped bare of cultural forms, is spoken of and understood against the background of cultural forms. How can one separate the image of Borgia as murderer from the image of Borgia as non-alienated man?[17]

Sartre strips the self bare and yet, when he tries to deal with the question of whether the self stripped bare can be both progressive and fascist, he introduces an element from classical German philosophy's search for community, namely, Kant's moral law, to show that the liberated self cannot be fascist.[18] The social theory of alienation, on the other hand, denies that the self can be totally stripped bare, and its ability to make this denial is predicated on its ability to connect factual order with valuational order. One way of making this connection is to link economy and self.

The economy and self account also utilizes a final theme of classical German philosophy: community as an epistemological category. We have seen how a social theory of alienation arises out of the concept of a communal self which is both discovered and created, whereas a nihilistic and nonsocial theory arises out of the notion that the self is simply created. Is there, however, a connection between belief or disbelief in the social theory of alienation and acceptance or lack of acceptance of communal categories of epistemology? The whole tradition of economy and self suggests that there is and that an account of the self which involves both creation and discovery necessitates stress on communal and objective categories of thought.

In the social-economic theory of alienation arising out of the intersection of political economy and classical German philosophy, conflicting claims about what the self is become interpreted as doubts about the communal nature of the self. The communal aspects of the self are seen both in political economy and classical German philosophy to involve lawlikeness and common aspects of actions which no individual can control, and thus which are said to both belong and not belong to individuals. This analysis is descriptive and evaluative—descriptive in that the reality of the communal self challenges the reality of the individual self, and evaluative in that, even if both aspects are seen to be real, they do not fit together in harmony. This concept of alienation is connected with freedom, in that freedom leads to the notion of the self behind the self. This self behind the self must be ordered, and for the social theory this ordering must be in some way communal. Since this ordering of the self is partly evaluative, it is related to classical German philosophy's search for value. The ethical notions which most naturally interpret this communal ordering of the self are connected in turn with epistemological categories. Furthermore, those epistemological categories that stress the communal nature of knowing and thus the ability of the individual to get beyond his subjective limitations are the ones most likely to lead to social theories of alienation. It is this stress on objective categories of knowledge that will allow the self to be both discovered and created.

A specific social theory of alienation can be constructed by connecting the problem of the unity or order of the self with the problem of explaining the self's action in relation to the whole of economic society. This social theory concentrates on common economic actions like owning property, producing for the market, or selling. Alienation is argued for, then, by showing that common economic actions are such that, if performed, there are arguments for saying that the self is divided or not divided; or by showing that there are good arguments for holding that the self is divided or not and then showing how this division results in certain types of common economic actions. The pre-Marxist economists give examples of the former move, as thinkers primarily concerned with relating the individual to the whole of economic society, but who also gave hints for a possible theory of self-order. Kant and Hegel give examples of the latter move as thinkers primarily concerned with the order of the self, but who were forced to come to grips with the problem of how to relate the self's actions to the whole of economic society. Marx, on the other hand, can be approached with equal ease from both perspectives. The advantage of the economy and self account is that it allows one to approach the problem of self-order from the general idea of a social self and also from the standpoint of stress on the whole, as well as on a communal account of knowledge emphasizing common rather than particular elements of action. The stress on the whole is found in both the economists and the classical German philosophers. The stress on common elements rather than particulars is found especially in the philosophers, where it is tied to the problem of universals.

The common actions of society raise the same problems as common elements have always raised in the traditional problem of universals. What is more significant, the particular exemplars or the common features they exemplify? This problem becomes connected with economics when the particular elements studied are economic actions. Relating the problem of universals to economics leads to questions about the common features of various economic actions, e.g., the ability to own property or to create goods that will sell on the market. These common features are not, of course, as universally present as whiteness or triangularity, but such universality is not needed for the problem of universals to arise. Fifty thousand common actions limited to Western Europe at a certain juncture in history can raise the problem just as easily as actions found in all parts of the earth's surface or, if there were such things, actions which were found everywhere.

Even though the political economists and Kant and Hegel start at different points, there is a connection between the one account which tries to connect a concept of the social aspect of action with a concept of the self and the other which tries to connect a concept of the self with the social aspect of action. In Kant, for example, the problem of the self is foremost, and this leads to an analysis of common action. In the economists, on the other hand, questions about the nature and cause of common actions are foremost and this leads to or implies a concept of the self. Unlike Kant and Hegel, Smith and Quesnay do not give an explicit analysis of the concept of common actions. Nevertheless, they study social aspects of actions such as obeying property laws. Thus, any account of the self which could come from what they say about the coherence and unity of an economic society must be one of the self which acts according to economic rules that others follow as well. Similarly, the account of the self elaborated by Kant, since it has implications for common actions, is also an account of the self following rules that have to do with the coherence and unity of society.

There is a link, then, in the economy and self account of alienation, between two concepts of holism: as an explanatory and as a moral concept. For moral holism, the ethical self should justify its acts within the context of social rules and claims; for explanatory holism, the individual self and action must be explained within the context of society and social rules. The economy and self account of alienation uses both concepts of holism, and in both cases the individual is related to the whole of society. The historical connection between holistic explanation and moral holism developed gradually and probably reached its peak in the intersection between political economy and classical German philosophy. The most distinctive feature of this intersection is the self-conscious connection between the concept of the whole of society, and the concept of common or universal features of action. Prior to that intersection, there were accounts of holism which did not always make its connection with universality explicit, even though it was often implicit.

For those concerned with the individual's relation to the whole of society one of the basic problems was the impossibility of explaining regularities in the economy simply as a result of a series of individual decisions and causes. This problem was found, among the economists, in both Smith and the Physiocrats. However, there was an ontology developing in classical German philosophy which was capable, to some degree, of elaborating on this problem. There was a hidden economic content in the classical German philosophers suggesting that it was no accident that they could develop such an ontology. Kant certainly begins with concern about the ethical self as opposed to, say, Smith's concern about social and economic actions. However, Kant's ethical self can only come into being when it acts according to universal moral principles that tie its actions to the actions of others.

Thus, for Kant, beyond the individual self there is a social self bound up with common actions. This social self is beyond the individual, but is located in an ambiguous space. Similarly, the social self remains ambiguous in Smith and Quesnay when they try to explain how regularities occur in society, even though no one intends them. When Smith feels the need to explain these regularities, he invokes an invisible hand. Quesnay talks of a natural order and uses metaphors drawn from his study of the circulation of the blood to illuminate that order. Where does this ambiguity about social existence come from? From the fact that social existence is seen to have power but no visibility. This social reality cannot be seen, and yet it affects people. It is posited to explain regularities, and yet itself cannot be grasped.

The problem of regularities in the economy entered the discussions of the theoreticians of capitalist economies because economic institutions had to be connected in some way or other with the actions of individuals. The first three schools of modern economics dealing with capitalism—the mercantilists, the Physiocrats, and classical British political economists—handled the problem differently.

In mercantilistic economics, two types of actions were particularly important: those defined in the context of the legal code of society, and those defined in terms of the individual desires that helped bring them about. Only the first type required analysis of common elements in actions, in relation to the common legal code. Without such actions, there could be no regularity or unity within economic life. In mercantilism, the problem of common actions was approached through consciousness. The state represented the conscious way of creating order and universality in actions that otherwise lacked these features. Insofar, then, as the common aspect of action was stressed, the self tended to be defined in terms of the state.

However, there was another model of political economy growing, culminating in classical British political economy and physiocracy, which deemphasized consciousness and the state. In this model, common actions and communal order were achieved more spontaneously or unconsciously than in mercantilism; the concept of economic value developed in order to explain this process. For theories of economic value arose as theories of moral and political right became theories of political economy.

Indeed, one of the epistemological problems of political right and the social contract, namely, the understanding of the individual's action in relation to the common legal and state definitions of action, is dealt with by value theory as a way of analyzing the common as opposed to individual aspects of action.

The epistemological problem of understanding common aspects of actions appears in social contract theory when, in definitions of the meaning of action as just or good, actions are looked at alternatively from the standpoint of their uniqueness or of their relation to what others are doing. In the state of nature, before society, a given action may be just if looked at by itself, but in the realm of the state, the same action may be unjust when considered in relation to all other similar actions. There are common and individual meanings of action, and the person is often at a loss as to which is most important.[19]

This problem of individual and social meaning of action is similarly expressed in physiocracy and Smith's price theory. Both stress the unconscious creation of common actions and at the same time further the growth of the value paradigm as opposed to the state paradigm.

For the Physiocrats, the individual and common aspects of action were unified through what they called natural law. This natural law theory asserted harmony between the individual and society to such an extent that the actions of the individual would rarely be in conflict with the needs of society to have certain goods. The meeting of these needs necessitated common actions. The difference between mercantilism and physiocracy is that mercantilism concentrates on the relation between the legal code and the state, on the one hand, and the individual on the other, whereas physiocracy concentrates on the relation between the individual's and society's need for goods. This need for goods in turn necessitates certain regularities in the production and distribution of goods. These regularities must then be connected with the actions of individuals.

Smith and the classical British political economists began to transform the problem of the relationship of the individual to social regularities and common actions. They did not stress the regularities associated either with the state or with social production and distribution as much as those associated with the market and with the practice of buying and selling goods for a price, what they called the realm of value. The most striking thing about the institution of the market, as opposed to the institutions of the state and of social production and distribution, is that it is not as clearly perceived as an institution as they are. As a result, common elements of action associated with it are not as easily picked out as are those associated with the state or with social production and distribution. The reason why the realm of buying and selling on the market does not, at first, seem to present as many regularities as the realm of the state or of social production and distribution is that the prices of goods which are sold on the market appear to vary according to each individual situation. Thus, neither the mercantilists nor the Physiocrats thought that this arena of human activity was as important as others for investigating the problem of the relation of individual activity to social regularities and common elements.

Adam Smith, however, representing classical British political economy, in his theory of economic value presents the view that individual prices do not simply vary according to each particular situation, but rather that here, too, there are regularities. The basic regularity is that there is a tendency for goods to be sold at prices which are proportionate to the labor time that went into producing them. The importance of this theory is twofold. First, it gives people some criterion for predicting prices. Contemporary American theorists of capitalism have concentrated almost exclusively on this aspect of the theory. Second, it allows regularities in action to be seen in places where they were not seen earlier.

Since the latter aspect of the theory of value is ignored by most professional economists today, it is natural that they should also ignore the possibility that the question of common economic actions in Smith could become connected with a theory of the self.

In Smith, the problem of understanding the connection between individual and common aspects of action is given nonmoral expression when he explains the connection between individual and societal meanings of work. The individual's action has a meaning in terms of personal suffering, sense of time, and so forth. His action also has a societal meaning in terms of supply and demand and how many other people are producing the same thing. The first would allow the laziest person to give his good the highest value based on the time spent in producing it. The second would evaluate the meaning of work totally in terms of whether the product of the work was sold. Smith's account mediates between these extremes. The ultimate meaning of x's work is defined by the way it relates to other work of the same type. The meaning of x's making a shoe is not his personal sacrifice or whether it will sell on the market, but the relation between the time he spent producing it and the time others spent producing similar goods.

Hegel and Marx expanded the concepts of common actions and communal order and developed a theory of the self out of them. For Hegel, the aspect of Adam Smith's theory of value which allowed the possibility of predicting prices was not of particular interest. What interested him was the theory of value as an account of regularities or similarities in human action.

As for Marx, he recognized that one of his major discoveries was his elaboration of the account of common actions implied by the concept of value. He thought that one of his three great discoveries in *Capital* was that he advanced Smith's theory of value by recognizing that the distinction in Smith between use value and exchange value must be backed up by a parallel distinction between the kinds of labor that produce use value and exchange value. Concrete labor produces use value and abstract or common labor, exchange value.[20] Marx's claim, that one of his major discoveries was to recognize that these two kinds of value necessitated two different kinds of labor, shows his central interest in the theory of value as a theory of common actions. It is quite clear, throughout Marx's economic writings, that abstract labor refers to social similarities in actions and thus in some sense to the problem of universals.

In both Marx and Hegel, the connection between common actions and self-unity changed, because of the move from the concept of property, stressed by the mercantilists, to the concept of economic value, stressed by the liberal British political economists. In the case of property-holding actions, similarities were more easily grasped than in the case of actions associated with the economic value. Thus, for the mercantilists there was a sense in which an action was seen to be similar to another simply because it follows a legal code written down on paper. For Smith, on the other hand, there are regularities in the actions that create economic value, but they are not regularities which can be reduced to the conscious following of a legal rule written down on paper. This aspect of value, as opposed to property, was seized upon by both Marx and Hegel, and is basic to their accounts of alienation. It allows them to stress that alienation results when common rules for action are followed, even though they are not totally clear or understood. However, coming from the epistemology of classical German philosophy, they were able to express this problem in a clearer philosophical form than were the English and French economists.

Thus, from the analysis of order in the economy, the self can learn something about the nature of its own order. Similarly, the idea of order in the self can help discover order in society. When the study of economy and self are combined, the self judges the economy and the economy judges the self. The two paradigms of classical German philosophy and political economy meet and fructify each other by merging two questions: what is the unity of the self, and what is the nature of the common, social aspects of the individual's action.

From the Mercantilists to Hegel

PART ONE

CHAPTER ONE

Mercantilism and Political Economics

Attempting to characterize mercantilism, some writers have occasionally contented themselves with setting historical parameters, e.g., that it lasted from the Reformation to the French Revolution, or that it began with the growth of modern states.[1] These parameters are very rough. Mercantilism is not medieval political economy, nor is it the laissez-faire philosophy that began most clearly in the latter half of the eighteenth century with Quesnay and Smith.[2] It is something in between. Of course, it is easy to go beyond this historical characterization and stress some of mercantilism's basic themes: its identification of money and wealth, its willingness to utilize state intervention in the economy in such areas as taxation, limits on wages or prices, tariff laws, granting of charters to companies that conduct economic activity abroad, making sure that no more money leaves the country than comes into the country, and, finally, the creation and maintenance of property laws.[3]

Yet, if mercantilism is characterized thus loosely—a time span and stress on state intervention and identification of money and wealth—writers on natural law, politics, and ethics between the Reformation and the French Revolution must also be seen as utilizing it in highly personal ways. To truly understand mercantilism, especially in relation to philosophy, we would need studies like "social contract theory and mercantilism," "natural law theory and mercantilism," "the altruism-egoism debate and mercantilism," as well as more specific studies of how elements of mercantilism entered the thought of Hobbes, Pufendorf, Cumberland, Locke, and so forth. Furthermore, such studies would cover only one side of mercantilism, the literary side. But mercantilism is also a set of practices which often may have had only a tenuous relation to written expression of mercantilism.[4] We need, then, to understand the peculiarities of mercantilism within its historical time span, but these peculiarities themselves give rise to a search for more general features of mercantilism.

There is one conceptual element in mercantilism which, in a narrower sense, keeps it within the historical parameters of the Reformation and the French Revolution, and yet, in a broader sense, allows it to be seen as a perennial type of thought about economic activity in the capitalist era. The mercantilists began to observe economic laws as they functioned in modern states. For the mercantilists, these laws were closely tied to the legal system and were open to inspection by human consciousness. They deemphasized that lawlikeness found in the market which often seemed to Smith and Quesnay to function like an unconscious and unplanned system.[5] With its stress on legality, mercantilism is akin to any economic system which stresses law and politics, from Aristotle to Keynes.

To see mercantilism as political, legal economics is the broadest possible way of approaching it. However, in a narrower sense, mercantilism is concerned with the law of modern states and with the increasing interaction between that law and the market system.[6] This last concept of mercantilism is not as broad as the characterization which would include Aristotle and all politial economics, nor as narrow as the one which would limit it to the period between the Reformation and the French Revolution, the narrowest definition.

For our purposes, the intermediate characterization of mercantilism, as stressing the interaction of law and economics in capitalism, is preferable to the broad definition as political, legal, economics, and to the narrow definition in terms of time span from the Reformation to the French Revolution. It will help to classify works of political economy which oscillate between the two paradigms of the market and the state and its laws. These various attempts to merge the market and the state may offer different ways of combining holism and individualism. What is holistic in relation to political policy may be individualistic in relation to the market. What is holistic on the market could also be less holistic in the state, simply because the hidden, unconscious patterns of the market might seem less engulfing to the individual than the more overt patterns of legality.

In a larger sense, then, our topic is neither political economics in general nor mercantilism in its strict historical parameters, but rather political economics which, however it may be abstracted from the capitalist market, can always be integrated back into it. Indeed, it is this integration, this bridge between political and non-political capitalist economics, which particularly illuminates the path from mercantilism in its narrower historical parameters to Marx. Yet, it is a path which has presented barriers for reconstruction.

The connection between politics and economics was fairly clear with the Physiocrats, but Smith destroyed the notes for his planned work on jurisprudence and only in May 1978 has the critical edition of Smith's lectures on jurisprudence seen the light.[7] There have been hardly any studies of Kant's economics, and those have not concentrated on the relation between politics and economics. As for Hegel, the two major studies of his economics, by Chamley and Lukács, significant as they are, have somewhat obscured the interpretation between the political and the economic in Hegel. Lukács claimed somewhat onesidedly that Hegel attacked Steuart's mercantilism and followed Smith, whereas Chamley claimed too one-sidedly that Hegel followed Steuart over Smith in almost all matters. But Hegel's originality as an economist seems to have been his ability to find a place between Steuart's version of mercantilism and Smith's free-enterprise theory.[8] Finally, only with the publication of the *Grundrisse* has Marx's political economics been brought to light. It must be pointed out, however, that such a nondogmatic Marxist as Gramsci was able to see the interpenetration of politics and economics long ago when he interpreted the Russian Revolution as the revolution against *Capital*, i.e., as the revolution against the exclusively nonpolitical interpretation of Marx's economics.[9]

The political element in modern theories of capitalism has been abstracted from in different ways at different times. Classical British political economy represents one such abstraction, which is only relative compared, for example, to the abstraction sought by the subjective value theorists after 1870.[10] Indeed, it can be argued that it was the extreme abstraction from political considerations found in Menger's version of subjective value theory which began the German reevaluation of mercantilism in the work of Schmoller. Furthermore, such reevaluation often had a practical side. Schmoller's association with *Kathedersozialismus* (socialism of the chair, or German academic socialism), for example, made him more open to the necessity of state intervention in the economy. Similarly, Keynes' praise for Malthus and List cannot be separated from his desire to have the state enter into the economy. Likewise Sen, the author of a recent positive reevaluation of Sir James Steuart, both stresses his relevance for contemporary economics and sees him as presenting a third way between laissez-faire and socialism, which he sees as particularly important for India's mixed economy. Myrdal, author of one of the most cogent critiques of a nonpolitical free-enterprise economy, wound up being an economic advisor for that same mixed Indian economy.[11]

Perhaps the integration of theory and practice is a key to mercantilism's attitude to politics. Although Heckscher has been criticized, e.g., by Viner, for overstressing the purely political power-seeking elements in mercantilism, the final sections of *Mercantilism* suggest that Heckscher was aiming at a logical critique of nonpolitical economics of the sort made by his countryman Myrdal. Thus, in his critique of Heckscher's attempt to reify a mercantilist doctrine that may never have been as unified as Heckscher thought, Judges recognizes that it is partly because of Heckscher's influence that people are seeing that something like mercantilism represents a logical aspect of all capitalist economics:

In the history of nations the brief episode of economic individualism may prove to have been a unique experience. The word neo-Mercantilism is already appearing with ominous frequency in serious discussions. . . . I can only suggest that such simple expressions as *national policy* would have more meaning if they could be applied without inward misgivings to all and every chapter in the history of a nation.[12]

The difference between myself and Judges is terminological. He wants to get rid of the term *mercantilism*, whereas I prefer to keep it in its two senses of referring to state intervention between the Reformation and the French Revolution and to the necessity (varying in degrees) of political intervention in almost all (if not all) periods of capitalism. (Judges also stresses this necessity with his idea that economic individualism may have been a "unique experience.")

This is not to deny that the idea of an autonomous market has been very important in understanding the structure of capitalism. Indeed, one theme stressed throughout this book is the far-reaching consequences that the concept of an autonomous market has had for the holism-individualism debate. The theme of the autonomous market often paradoxically stresses the role of the individual at the same time that it stresses the powerlessness of the individual in the face of impersonal forces. It stresses that the individual should work on his own at the same time that it stresses that he is also working for others.

One of the most insightful analyses of the human consequences of the idea of the autonomous market is found in the work of Karl Polanyi, which indirectly sheds light on the idea of mercantilism as a type of political economics. Polanyi calls the economy based on the autonomous market a disembedded economy. An embedded economy, on the other hand, is integrated into a political system.[13] Polanyi's disembedded/embedded dichotomy utilizes Maine's opposition of contract to status and Tönnies' *Gesellschaft/Gemeinschaft* contrast. For both Maine and Tönnies, the realm of contract, *Gesellschaft*, because it was disembedded from political and other social institutions, is a whole which the individual can neither understand nor control. On the other hand, *Gemeinschaft*, status, was a whole in which the individual felt more at home.[14]

The concepts of embedded and disembedded are valuable because they help us place mercantilism within the context of a political economics seen as a norm as opposed to the abnormality of a non-political, nonmercantilist, disembedded economy. We can then see Polanyi's discussion of Aristotle as the theoretician of the embedded economy as an attempt to put political economics in a larger context. His demonstration that Aristotle was mistranslated in order to fit him into the disembedded economy paradigm could probably be complemented, for example, with studies of other thinkers, particularly in the modern natural law tradition.

Nevertheless, if the modern capitalist economy is often political, it is political in a different way than earlier economies because it exists as embedded alongside a part, the market, which at least seems to be disembedded and is so in some respects. Indeed, it may be that the prime difference between mercantilist aspects of economists who came after Smith and Quesnay, and mercantilism in the narrowest historical sense as preceding laissez-faire is that pre-free-enterprise mercantilists kept thinking that the market could be totally controlled politically in the way that Aristotle thought the economy was controllable, whereas after Smith and Quesnay it was no longer possible to believe this. Post-eighteenth-century mercantilism is concerned with more or less intervention into an economy which always has some autonomy, although not perhaps as much as it appears to have.

If this is the case, then Chamley's reference to Hegel as Aristotelian in utilizing Steuart to put politics in command of economics has to be shaded somewhat.[15] The modern capitalist market was never as embedded as Aristotle's economy may have been, but neither was it as disembedded as Tönnies' *Gesellschaft*, Maine's contract, and Smith's idealized free market. It is an irony that the myth of the totally disembedded capitalist economy may have resulted from too literal a reading of *The Wealth of Nations* and *Capital*, both of which systematically abstracted from politics. Yet, both Marx and Smith had grandiose plans for writing a political theory to fit into their economics. Neither got to write it, although it can now be partially reconstructed from Marx's *Grundrisse* and Smith's *Lectures on Jurisprudence*.[16]

Some antidotes to the overly sharp separation of embedded and disembedded economies have been provided recently in two books dealing with the penetration of capitalist ideas prior to Smith: J. G. A. Pocock's *The Machiavellian Moment* and Albert Hirschmann's *The Passions and the Interests*.[17]

Pocock contrasts an economy based on inherited wealth in land and a citizen army to an economy based on credit, trade, and a professional army. In the debates during and after the English Civil War, the first economy, roughly analogous to the embedded economy, was defended by the country, and the second, roughly analogous to the disembedded economy, was defended by the court.[18] What did the court, which wanted to stress trade and credit, argue for?

They saw trade and commerce generally as a softener of the harsh spartan norms associated with citizen armies and inheritance of land. They opposed commerce to what they viewed as the selfishness and inhumanity of the country. Pocock notes that their view of the country is symbolized by the boorish Squire Western in *Tom Jones* (shown in the movie version sleeping with his dogs). Here the older economy of citizen armies and inherited property in land is seen to lead to individualism, and the new stress on the market and trade is seen to lead to sociability and integrating the individual into society—what we have called moral holism.[19] The country, however, argued that the trader and merchant could not provide for or understand civic virtue. Thus, trade and credit were seen to lead to individualism, and the older forms of property to integrating the individual into society. Pocock notes that the ideal squire for the country was not the slovenly Western but the honest Allworthy.[20]

Pocock does not, however, see the court and country sides as totally opposed. He notes that, for Defoe, for example, land was good, but it was dependent on trade; and that it was credit that was often attacked rather than the "virtuous tradesmen."[21] Furthermore, even credit could be transformed into a virtuous commerce, but only with great difficulty. Politics had to more and more control this "volatile" element, credit.[22]

It is through this account of the interpenetration of court and country ideas that Pocock and Hirschmann make their primary contribution to what I have called mercantilism as the political element in modern capitalist economics. Mandeville and Steuart, for example, are seen by Pocock and Hirschmann as thinkers who mediate between the state and the market, who want the state to give some social virtues to an economy which has the beginnings of such virtues but cannot fully realize them by itself.[23] For Steuart, the statesman promulgates trade, but then trade takes on an autonomy of its own:

Trade and industry . . . owed their establishment to the ambition of princes, principally with a view to enrich themselves, and thereby to become formidable to their neighbors. But they did not discover, until experience taught them, that the wealth they drew from such fountains was but the overflowing of the spring; and that an opulent, bold, and spirited people, having the fund of the prince's wealth in their own hands, have it also in their power, when it becomes strongly their inclination, to shake off his authority. The consequence of this change has been the introduction of a mild, and more regular plan of administration. When once a state begins to subsist by the consequences of industry, there is less danger to be apprehended from the power of the sovereign.

The point is that the state that introduces trade becomes very powerful, but then becomes limited in its power by the very fact of having introduced trade. For Hirschmann, the explanation for this paradox of power begetting lack of power

lies in the distinction, implicit in Steuart, between "arbitrary" abuses of power, that stem from the vices and passions of rulers . . . and the "fine tuning" carried out by a hypothetical statesman exclusively motivated by the common good. . . . According to Steuart, modern economic expansion puts an end to the former type of intervention, but then creates a special need for the latter kind if the economy is to move along a reasonably smooth trajectory.[24]

For Pocock, however, the two languages of court and country ultimately do not quite mesh, and he suggests that Rousseau first grasped the alienation in this fact when he saw the tension between the social and individual views of the person, a tension between "individual self-awareness on the one hand and consciousness of society, property, and history on the other."[25] The problem was that the person involved in landed inheritance, who participated directly in the commonwealth and himself fought for it,

was permitted the leisure and autonomy to consider what was to others' good as well as his own; but the individual engaged in exchange could discern only particular values—that of the commodity which was his, that of the commodity for which he exchanged it. His activity did not oblige or even permit him to contemplate the universal good as he acted upon it, and he consequently continued to lack classical rationality. It followed that he was not conscious master of himself.[26]

This difference in self-perception was based on the difference between the reality of property and the imaginary existence of trade.[27]

It was the task of the court to show that trade and credit did not have just an imaginary existence. However, the more the court attempted to show this, the more it had to stress that good comes out of selfishness—public benefits out of private vices. For Pocock, this means that "social morality was becoming divorced from personal reality and from the ego's confidence in its own integrity and reality."[28] Thus, even though the court tried to integrate man into sociableness, "its ethical vocabulary was thin and limited by the lack of any theory which presented human virtue as that of a *Zöon Politikon.*"[29] The defenders of trade could not attain moral holism.

Pocock's and Hirschmann's accounts, concentrating as they do on the interval between mercantilism as a narrowly defined historical epoch and free enterprise when it is usually conceived to have emerged victorious, shed light on a mix of political and nonpolitical economic forms. These accounts are especially important for my reinterpretation of Smith, Hegel, and Marx as thinkers for whom the mercantilist element (in the broader sense, as the political element in capitalist theory) has been neglected. Hegel in particular, who unlike Smith and Marx manages to present the world with a finished version of his political economics, fits into the peculiar mix of free enterprise and state control they have uncovered. It is the peculiar integration of market and state forms found before the triumph of free enterprise that sheds light on Hegel, and Smith and Marx as well. Although they were writing during or after this triumph, they nevertheless commented on the self's social and individual nature partly through their own integration of politics and the market.[30]

CHAPTER TWO

Quesnay and Physiocracy

The Physiocrats are said to be among the founders of macroeconomics because of their concept of the reproduction of economic society, which includes three processes: (1) the production of goods, (2) the distribution of goods among the various classes, and (3) the distribution of division of labor, i.e., the notion that a certain amount of labor has to go into each section of the economy. By considering how all these tasks were performed on a yearly basis, the Physiocrats introduced to an unprecedented degree the concept of nonplanned regularities among economic actions.[1]

Unfortunately, the Physiocrats are often remembered simply as the group of economists who, along with discovering macroeconomics, thought that agriculture was the source of all wealth. The Physiocrats did not concentrate simply on economic regularities and thus certainly did not accept the concept of a disembedded economy. Another important regularity was in the political actions of people seen as members of classes, estates, or social groups.

Thus, the king acted in a way associated with certain political prerogatives, and these actions were connected with the amount of goods distributed to him every year. Similarly, the farmers, merchants, and landlords had a certain place in society and the state which was connected with the way goods were distributed to them. The physiocratic system thus connects economics and politics and is concerned not only with material wealth, but also with the social, political, and moral system in which that wealth is distributed and produced. An observation of one Physiocrat about the nature of kingship and agriculture displays, for example, the relation between agriculture, political relations, and divine providence. He notes that the king of China was the perfect physiocratic king because he was the son of a god and every year during spring planting he put his hand to the plow.[2]

The interaction displayed here among godliness, kingliness, and farming suggests a great deal of unity in the economy and society, a unity of great importance for the concepts of the self and explanation of action. Concern with this unity is displayed in a medical metaphor running through Quesnay's writings, including the famous *Tableau Economique* (loosely translatable as "economic display sheet") The *Tableau Economique* depicted graphically the way labor was distributed to various segments of economic society, the way wealth was distributed among the classes, and the inter-relations between these two processes of distribution.[3] The metaphor found in the *Tableau* and the writings connected with it suggests that the economy has the same sort of unity that had been discovered by Quesnay's fellow doctor, William Harvey, to operate in the circulation of the blood. Special emphasis is laid upon the connection between the concepts of circulation and distribution, both suggesting the flow of elements in an orderly fashion.[4]

Whether the analogy between the circulation of the blood and circulation in the economy be strict or loose, it is still just an analogy. However, it goes beyond this when Quesnay makes a connection between the circulation analogy and a philosophical analysis of causality. The reconstruction of the relation between the economic theory and the theory of causality is made particularly easy by the fact that within a period of two years Quesnay produced both his most famous economic treatise and his only full-fledged account of his metaphysics and epistemology: Quesnay apparently wrote the *Tableau Économique* in 1758; "Évidence" had appeared in 1756.[5]

A theory of economic causality can be gleaned from these two works and an earlier book dealing with problems in the philosophy of medicine, the *Essai Physique sur l'Économie Animale.* Jean Sutter has characterized this work as being "haunted by the [idea of] circulation."[6]

Akiteru Kubota has argued for the close connection between the theory of causality developed in the article on evidence and in the

Essai Physique where Quesnay talks of God as "The efficient cause, the driving cause, the first impulsion, the only driving strength, the true driving cause."[7] Kubota argues that for Quesnay this terminology is bound up with the idea that the parts of the body are only occasional causes and that the true cause of the movement of the body is God. Occasional cause is a concept developed by Malebranche whom, Kubota argues, influenced both essays. Occasional causes in the Malebranchian system are called causes only because they are in conjunction with effects. They do not really have the power to move anything. Only God is the true cause in the sense that He can actually move things.[8] If Kubota is right, then the true cause of that movement of the body which is circulation is also God. Indeed, Kubota argues that, through the use of Malebranche, Quesnay was able to construct a general theory of causality, based on the idea that "a body does not act on another body."[9]

Kubota's analysis is borne out by the following passage from "Évidence":

We are assured by our sensations that these sensations themselves, . . . that all the effects and all the changes which happen to the body, are produced by a first cause; that it is the action of this same cause which vivifies all living bodies . . . that the essential and active form of man, as a reasoning animal, is not an interdependence of the body and soul of which he is composed. For these two substances cannot act by themselves on one another. Thus, one must not search either in the body or in the soul, nor in the composition of the two . . . for his liberty, for his moral determination. . . . These attributes result also from the act . . . of the supreme being.[10]

The specific argument here is that the interaction of mind and body is caused by neither mind nor body but by the first cause, God. The general point is that God causes all things to act: "It is the action of this . . . cause which vivifies all living bodies."

For our purposes, however, the negative doctrine that individuals do not cause things is more important than the positive doctrine that God does cause them. For to say that God causes and individual elements do not cause implies that particular parts are not as important as the whole context in which all the parts move. When stripped of its reference to God, the holistic ramifications of such an account stand out clearly. Thus, the animistic holism associated with the analogy between the circulation of the blood and distribution in the economy is supplemented by a holistic theory of causality.[11]

This account of the import of Quesnay's doctrine of God as cause could be said to parallel, in at least one respect, Mach's transformation of Berkeley's theory of God as the ultimate cause of all events. For Mach, Berkeley's claim of God causing particular events was transformed into the idea that when we examine causality we should stress regular connections rather than the idea that one thing actually moves another.[12] One reason why the claim that God causes could be connected with the claim that causal analysis involves discovering regularities rather than particular causes is that since the activity of God is not immediately visible, it must be deduced from these regularities. Thus, the idea of God as cause brings us to throw out the idea that particulars have causal efficacy; and the evidence for God as cause brings us to emphasize regularities.

Like Mach, then, I want to emphasize the general connection between a theory that denies individual causes and stresses the causality of God, and one that stresses regular causal patterns as a basic element in causal analysis. This is not to say that for Quesnay the idea of God causing is simply shorthand for the idea that causality is regularity. Rather, it is shorthand for explanatory holism in the sense that the particular is only explained in the context of God's manipulation of the whole.

Quesnay's analysis of the knowledge we can have of causation also suggests this connection with holism. Quesnay distinguishes two kinds of knowledge: evidence and faith. "The first cause and his activity," he says, is "evident to us, but . . . the intimate rapports between this action and our souls are inaccessible to our natural lights."[13] Basically, Quesnay uses "evidence" to refer to our knowledge of particulars. It does not grasp the cause of the movement of particulars. Faith, however, gives us knowledge of the first cause: "faith teaches us that the supreme wisdom is itself the light which brings light to all men . . . coming into this world."[14]

The doctrines of faith and evidence work in different ways. Evidence limits the individual to what he can actually see. Faith allows him to grasp the workings of the whole. For example, evidence allows knowledge of the parts of the blood, and faith allows knowledge of the total final plan of the blood's circulation.[15]

From the standpoint of epistemology, the utilization of evidence and faith involves combining the empiricism of a Locke or Condillac with the rationalism of a Malebranche. Quesnay follows the empiricists in stressing that a priori ideas cannot replace the "evidence" that we get through our sensations. Nevertheless, he still agrees with Malebranche that ultimately these sensations are linked together in a whole by God; and knowledge of this whole comes through faith. The fact that evidence is stressed as well as faith means that there is an individualistic as well as a holistic element in knowledge.[16]

For Quesnay, the individual's knowledge is thus extended much more than his causal power. Faith allows him to understand the movement of the whole, even though he is somewhat passive in relation to that whole. The maxim *laissez-faire, laissez-passer* catches some of the sense of being bound up in a larger whole without actively pursuing one's relation to it. In contrast, for Smith, as we will see, the individual's knowledge is limited as much as his power is.[17] For Quesnay, however, the individual has to act according to the evidence he has as an individual, but acting according to evidence, which does not grasp the whole, must be coordinated with acting according to faith, which does grasp the whole. Faith gives knowledge of how God is working for all in the economy, whereas evidence only gives knowledge of one's own interests.

There is a structural parallel between Quesnay's attitude toward holism in explanation and his holistic attitude toward the self and its values. This parallel emerges in his theories of natural law, the social order, and property. His defense of the individual right of owning property as a partial way of attaining the good of the whole parallels his stress on individual evidence as a partial way of gaining knowledge of the whole. In the first case, moral holism is coupled with a kind of individualism; in the second case, explanatory holism is also coupled with individualism. To see this parallel between Quesnay's ethics and his account of explanation, we must examine Quesnay's concepts of natural law and property.

The ethical theory of natural law stresses, first, that there is no sharp distinction between matters of fact and matters of value, and, second, that man will usually be in harmony with his environment. The first claim implies that what man should do arises out of an understanding of what he is, what his human nature is like. The relation between the two claims is that the analysis of the nature of man and of what he should do shows him to be basically in harmony with his environment. "Natural law" is also used by the Physiocrats in a more physical and scientific sense, where natural laws are seen to guide and depict what happens in the world. Thus, the circulation of the blood and the distribution of wealth and labor are discussed in terms of natural laws. Nevertheless, it must be remembered that the Physiocrats did not always make a sharp distinction between the two types of natural law and, when they did, often it was made only to collapse later. This collapse is well demonstrated by the following attempt on Quesnay's part to distinguish between the two aspects of natural law: the moral law and the physical law. "I am here taking physical law to mean the regular course of all physical events in the natural order which is self-evidently the most advantageous to the human race. I am here taking moral law to mean the rule of all human action in the moral order conforming to the physical order which is self-evidently the most advantageous to the human race." Furthermore "for us all is physical and the moral derives from it."[18]

All this strongly suggests that the moral and the physical laws are not in fact sharply distinguished. The physical laws are characterized as being the most advantageous to the human race; and advantageous seems to be a moral idea. Similarly, the moral laws are defined as simply being in conformity to the physical laws.[19]

This blending of physical and moral laws is in tune with the blending of facts and values. For it is easy to extend the claim that there is no sharp separation between facts about human nature and human values to the further claim that there is no sharp distinction between facts about human nature or nature in general and values for humans. Indeed, the tendency to collapse moral laws into physical laws represents denial of alienation, for it assumes that there is no problem with translating our most important intentions into actions. One reason is that all humans have a basic human nature, and thus one possible source of alienation is eliminated: society is not seen as hostile to the individual and does not prevent his intentions from being adequately translated into actions. For Quesnay to go one step further and identify moral laws with physical laws is to make the point that nature is also no barrier to translating intentions into actions.

This natural law viewpoint is basically in opposition to any theory of alienation based on some dichotomy between self and world. It does not imply that there is any opposition between the intentions of individuals, the material conditions of the world, and actions which are based partially on those material conditions. It implies rather that there is harmony between man's most important intentions and the conditions of the world. This account should not be reduced to its most absurd form where every intention can automatically translate itself into an action that conforms to it. Rather, the most important types of intentions can easily translate themselves into what have been called nonalienated actions. Thus, the intention to produce food and shelter, although it will not always meet with conditions favorable to it, will meet with them for the most part.

This systematic denial of alienation, this certainty that neither society nor nature is hostile to the self, emerges very clearly in a passage from "Natural Law" which sounds like an explicit criticism of Hobbes' theory that in the state of nature people will always be fighting each other. "In the state of pure nature men who require urgently to satisfy their needs, each through his own endeavors, will not waste their time by uselessly engaging in a mutual war which would only set up an obstacle to their engaging in the occupations necessary to provide their subsistence."[20] Yet, although Quesnay attempts to deny alienation, it continues to exist in the form of a tension between moral holism and moral individualism, similar to the tension we have already seen between epistemological holism and epistemological individualism. Both tensions are displayed in his theory of private property. Moral holism cannot justify private property because the selfishness involved in attaining property seems to deemphasize the good of the whole to which Quesnay appeals. Yet, a complete moral individualism is foreign to Quesnay. Explanatory holism cannot explain private property because, again, the property-seeking action and the inequality which Quesnay admits accompanies it are never demonstrated by Quesnay to fit in necessarily with the natural whole where everything has its place. Yet, for both general epistemological and specific economic reasons, Quesnay cannot give a purely individualistic account of property.

Apropos Quesnay's intermediate position between holism and individualism, we might recall that in 1851 Baudrillart argued that Quesnay successfully steered between individualism and socialism.[21] Yet, when Quesnay states that our freedom involves using intelligence to follow natural law and "is less an active faculty than a light which illuminates the way that we ought to follow," this seems to take all autonomy from the individual. But Quesnay also criticizes the view that the soul does not have the power to bring about changes in its situation, and here Quesnay's empiricism seems to lead him to give the individual some autonomy.[22]

The coupling of individual autonomy with the notion that man is free when he follows his duty seems to involve the compromise that it is one's duty, revealed by natural law, to own things, which will then "belong to him in accordance with natural law." Yet Quesnay also arrives at the point of constructing his theory of property, with his more holistic side telling him that property can only be realized by following "the legitimate conventions established between men who live in society." Such conventions are scarcely a good basis for an overly individualistic theory of property.[23]

One must remember that two general types of analyses of property were available to the Physiocrats. The first was that each individual supplied his own unique criteria for what made something property. The second was that a number of people must agree on the same criteria in order for there to be property.[24] Those who chose the second set of requirements for property said that the first only gave possession. Quesnay seems to have chosen the second and it is easy to see why.

The society in which Quesnay was living made a distinction between theft and ownership, but the extreme individualistic account of property could not make that distinction. For the thief could be said to be simply operating with his own unique criterion for what makes property. Furthermore, if property is defined by shared criteria, then talk about property is not just about the physical object; it is also about ourselves and our institutions. To say that something is mine is not to say that it has the physical quality, mine, along with having the physical qualities of being hard and being yellow. Rather, it is to say that in the social milieu in which I live most people will not take this from me, and that if they do, people will help me recover it.[25]

Quesnay indicates that he also accepts the distinction between possession and property: "the form of societies depend on the greater or less quantity of property which each possesses, or may possess *(posède, ou peut posséder)*, and in respect of which it wants to assure for itself protection and property *(proprieté)*."[26]

Furthermore, he indicates that property is associated with the state and that natural law naturally manifests itself through a state. Does this, however, mean that natural law itself will dictate the nature of property? Only in an extremely limited sense. The state implements the natural law theory of justice, but Quesnay simply says of justice: "If I am asked what justice is, I reply that it is a natural and paramount rule, recognized through the light of reason, which self-evidently determines what belongs to oneself or to another."[27] Nowhere, however, does Quesnay tell us how to determine what belongs to someone. Thus, property is not explained either individualistically or by the natural law. Quesnay explains property, just as he justifies it, with something between holism and individualism. Quesnay simply assumes that the good of the whole can only be attained the way it was attained in the French society of his time—in a private property system where different and unequal groups carry out the production and distribution of goods. "The foundation of society," Quesnay says, "is the subsistence of men and the wealth necessary to provide the authority required to defend them." This is best accomplished under a government which regulates "the particular rights of subjects relative to their different situations *(états)*."[28]

Quesnay never shows that social production has to occur through classes and property; he just assumes that this is the working of natural law. Here the doctrine of faith, which supposedly allows Quesnay to see the whole, simply becomes a blind belief in dogma. As we have seen, faith allows us to see God and nature working for the good of all relatively independent of our will. But here faith tells us that a certain property system is natural. This naturalness of the present economic and social order is expressed with particular clarity in Quesnay's attitude toward inequality. Quesnay notes that men are unequal and that "this inequality admits of neither just nor unjust; it results from the arrangement of the laws of nature."[29]

Inequality is thus simply part of the natural workings of society. There is a natural harmony in the world. How can there be disharmony between self and society or nature, when both are passive and await the causal activity of God? Never mind that this passivity is coupled with a seemingly contradictory stress on the active procuring of private property. Thus, Quesnay's oscillation between holism and individualism leads, ultimately, to a divided view of the self.

CHAPTER THREE

Smith and Classical
British Political Economy

Before we turn to Adam Smith's analysis of self and explanation, he should be placed in context as a representative thinker of classical British political economy. As we have seen, one respect in which Smith, especially in *The Wealth of Nations*, differs from mercantilism and the Physiocrats is his attitude toward the relationship of politics to economics. Indeed, he often polemicizes against the mercantilist emphasis on the importance of the state and its laws for the market. Smith's basic paradigm is the market, not social reproduction, which is the Physiocrats' basic paradigm, nor is it state intervention, which is the mercantilists' basic paradigm. This is not to say that Smith fails to utilize these other paradigms. After all, for Smith the market ultimately brings about social reproduction, and his opposition to what he identifies as the mercantilist tradition is partly a matter of degree. Smith recognizes that the state aids social reproduction; he simply does not see it as the prime factor.[1]

How does the market bring about social reproduction in its three aspects: (1) distribution of labor, (2) production of goods, and (3) distribution of goods? Smith's concept of exchange value, as opposed to use value, explains how this is accomplished.

The use value of a good is the use that people can make of it, which may be different for each individual. Thus, by studying use values we do not come up with regularities in the prices for which goods are sold. Smith argues, however, that there must be some standard which is more generally accepted than use and that standard is what makes the exchange value of the good. The standard that he fixes upon is labor. It is important to recognize that these two concepts of value, use value and exchange value, are very different and do not necessarily represent the ordinary conception of value as something worthwhile. Use values are worthwhile to the individuals involved. Exchange values, however, are simply the tendency that a good has to sell at a price which is proportionate to the labor time necessary to produce the good. Thus, exchange value should not be thought of as something intrinsically worthwhile; exchange value is defined within the context of a theory of price. For Adam Smith, if there was no price, then there would be no exchange value. Yet, we can think of many things that would still be worthwhile even if they did not have a price.[2]

The concept of exchange value explains how the market brings about social reproduction, which includes the division of labor and the distribution of goods. Whenever there are just enough use values of different types to meet the desires for them, then goods are sold at their exchange value, and goods and labor are distributed in a way that meets society's needs. However, if there are not enough use values of a certain type to meet demand, then the goods will be sold for more than their exchange value. Conversely, if there are too many use values of a certain type in relation to demand, then they will be sold for less than their exchange value. Adam Smith admits that oftentimes in a market economy there is disequilibrium between supply and demand. Thus, he does not hold that all goods are always sold for their exchange value.

When they are not sold at their exchange value, however, there is no equilibrium between the supply of and the demand for use values; yet that equilibrium constantly tends to be reattained because of job mobility. Thus, the concept of exchange value helps explain the division of labor.[3] Adam Smith holds that when there are too many use values of a given sort in relation to demand, then some people will move from producing those use values to producing different use values. Furthermore, if the supply of use values in a given area is too small for the demand, then other people will move into the production of those use values. The lack of equilibrium between supply and demand leads to a tendency to reestablish that equilibrium. Thus, the concept of exchange value helps explain the distribution of goods. Smith believed that this process of movement toward equilibrium in distribution of goods and labor was brought about by individual action and by a kind of harmony in society which he called "the invisible hand." Goods only sell for their exchange value when there is such equilibrium, but that equilibrium always either exists or is in the process of being reestablished.[4]

A central problem in this model of how exchange value and the market bring about social reproduction is a failure to distinguish adequately between how it works in petty commodity production and capitalism proper. In petty commodity production, individuals produce by themselves; in capitalism, they produce working for the capitalist. Smith seems to be more concerned with petty commodity production in the first five chapters of *The Wealth of Nations* and with capitalism in the rest of the book. The problem is that Smith sometimes ties the reestablishment of equilibrium between supply and demand to the model of petty commodity production with its characteristics of job mobility on the part of the sellers of use values; equality in ability and talent; lack of connection between political and economic advantage; no monopolies which artificially keep prices up or down; and the worker getting what he produces. Many of these points are denied at one point or another in Smith's description of capitalism after the first five chapters. Since Smith never faces these inconsistencies squarely, petty commodity production, which exists as a paradigmatic idea in the first five chapters, often exists as a confused utopia in the rest of the book.[5]

A second problem in the model of how exchange value and the market bring about social reproduction is found in Smith's various statements of the labor theory of value and the theory of wages connected with it. Smith complements his failure to clearly separate petty commodity production and capitalism with a tendency to intermingle a version of the labor theory appropriate for the petty commodity production with another version more appropriate for capitalism.

One possible implication of Smith's theory of economic value, as presented in the first five chapters, is that, in periods of equilibrium between supply and demand, the worker should get as wage the equivalent of everything he produces. Indeed, this follows logically from the theory that the value of the good is equal to the labor necessary to produce it, if the following premises are added: first, that the worker sells the amount of time that he works, his labor time; and second, that that which measures something else can also measure itself.[6]

The first premise establishes that what he exchanges is his labor time. From this it can easily be inferred that what he exchanges is equal to the value of what he produces. Suppose that A stands for the value of the good and B stands for the labor time necessary to produce the good. It has already been established that A is equal to B. However, if A is equal to B, then B is equal to A. Thus, what the worker exchanges is equal to the value of what he produces.

It still remains to be established that the *value* of what the worker exchanges is equal to the *value* of what he produces. This is where the second premise comes in. Labor time measures value, but does it itself have a value? The second premise suggests that it does have a value, since that which is used to measure something can also be used to measure itself. Take the case of a yardstick. A yardstick can be used to measure a yard of land and, thus, to assign to that land a numerical value. Can it also be used to measure itself? The second premise says it can. The value of the yardstick is also one yard. If this can be accomplished with the yardstick and if the case of labor time is analogous, then the value of the labor time is equal to itself. The value of eight hours of labor time is equal to eight hours of labor time.

Thus, with these two premises added to the labor theory (interpreted as the idea that the value of the commodity is equal to the labor time necessary to produce it), the conclusion becomes inescapable. The worker works eight hours to produce goods valued at eight hours of labor time. His eight hours of labor time has the value of eight hours of labor time. He exchanges his labor time for a wage. Since the value of his labor time is equal to the value of the good and since values are traded for equal values, it therefore follows that if supply and demand are at equilibrium, then he trades his labor time for the equivalent of everything that he produces. However, in capitalism, the wage of the worker is always much less than the value of the goods he produces, even in periods of near equilibrium between supply and demand. Thus, the labor theory of value does not apply to capitalism. This is a problem since its purpose was to give an account of the regularities of price in a capitalist society. Adam Smith does not explicitly recognize this problem in the labor theory, although it was explicitly recognized by certain of the English followers of Smith and Ricardo in the early part of the nineteenth century.[7]

Nevertheless, there is reason to believe that Smith was aware of the problem, since he creates a new theory of price in the sixth chapter of the first book, a theory which contradicts this implication of the labor theory of value. He now claims that the price of all goods is distributed among three different groups of people: those who own stock, those who work, and those who own land.[8] This theory is very different from the original one, and it is inconsistent with the implications of the original theory that the worker should get the full exchange value of everything that he produces. The first theory seems to apply to petty commodity production, and the second to capitalism. The relation between the two theories must of necessity remain confused as long as the relation between petty commodity production and capitalism is not clarified.

A third problem in Smith's model for the attainment of social reproduction through exchange value and the market is that Smith is never able to present an adequate argument for why social reproduction must be accomplished through the market. He claims that the fact that the one is brought about by the other is the "consequence of a certain propensity in human nature . . . the propensity to truck, barter, and exchange one thing for another."[9] He never establishes, however, that this propensity is anything other than its actual manifestation in a market society. If it is simply its manifestation in market society, then the problem still remains of determining whether it is basically a part of human nature or whether it arises from conditions outside of human nature—conditions which could possibly be changed. The question is what causes the common actions of market society. For Adam Smith, this question is answered by his claim that human nature has a propensity to exchange. Thus, common economic actions are explained by a prior unity of the self.

In the *Early Draft of The Wealth of Nations*, Smith gives a more political interpretation of the division of labor. There he suggests possible resolutions of the three problems in his own account of how social reproduction is brought about by the market: (1) the relation of petty commodity production to capitalism, (2) the inequality/equality dichotomy of the labor theory of value, and (3) the origin of the exchange economy.

In the first few pages of Chapter 6 of the published version, Smith indicates that there had to be some historical transition between the time when all people were workers and the time when the owners of stock and the owners of land joined in. When all people were workers, "the whole produce of labor [belonged] to the labourer." In the latter case

the whole produce of labour does not always belong to the labourer. He must in most cases share it with the owner of the stock which employs him. . . . As soon as the land of any country has all become private property, the landlords, like all other men, love to reap where they never sowed, and demand a rent even for its natural produce.[10]

In the *Early Draft*, the point is stated much more strongly:

In a civilized sociey the poor provide both for themselves and for the enormous luxury of their superiors. The rent which goes to support the vanity of the slothful landlord is all earned by the industry of the peasant. The monied man indulges himself in every sort of ignoble and sordid sensuality, at the expense of the merchant and tradesman to whom he lends out his stock at interest.[11]

In these passages, Smith seems to recognize the implications of the labor theory interpreted as holding that the value of the good is equal to the labor necessary to produce it. He also seems to recognize that those implications do not hold when the owners of land and stock demand their share of the goods. Yet, he avoids the conclusion that if the implications of the labor theory of value do not hold, then there must be something potentially wrong with that theory.[12] Furthermore, he avoids explaining the ability of the owners of land and stock to take part of the product of the labor, in terms of their relationships to political power. Such an explanation would be in conflict with one of the basic presuppositions of the first five chapters: that the activities of the market can be explained in general without reference to politics.

In the *Early Draft*, Smith seems much more sympathetic to the view that extraeconomic coercion influences market relations. He talks of how

In a society of an hundred thousand families, there will perhaps be one hundred who don't labor at all, and who yet, either by violence or by the more orderly oppression of law, employ a greater part of the labor of society than any other ten thousand in it. The division of what remains, too, after this enormous defalcation, is by no means made in proportion to the labor of each individual. On the contrary those who labor most get least. The opulent merchant, who spends a great part of his time in luxury and entertainments, enjoys a much greater proportion of the profits of his traffic, than all the clerks and accountants who do the business. These last, again, enjoying a great deal of leisure, and suffering scarce any other hardship besides the confinement of attendance, enjoy a much greater share of the produce than three times an equal number of artizans, who, under their direction, labor much more severely and assiduously. The artizan, again, tho he works generally under cover, protected from the injuries of the weather, at his ease and assisted by the convenience of innumerable machines, enjoys a much greater share than the poor labourer who has the soil and the seasons to struggle with, and who, while he affords the materials for supplying the luxury of all the other members of the common wealth, and bears, as it were, upon his shoulders the whole fabric of human society, seems himself to be pressed down below ground by the weight, and to be buried out of sight in the lowest foundations of the building.[13]

These lines suggest some answers to Smith's three logical problems. They suggest an analysis of the difference between petty commodity production and capitalism, based on the idea that although petty commodity production may be connected with an unpolitical ideal, capitalism is connected with a political and violent reality. They suggest that the labor theory cannot ultimately be interpreted in an egalitarian way because such an interpretation would conflict with facts about the unequal distribution of power which gave rise to capitalism and allowed some, "either by violence, or by the more orderly oppression of law, [to] employ a greater part of the labor of society." Finally, they also suggest a political and social answer to the problem of how the market came to be the means of bringing about social reproduction. In other writings, Smith tells us that it is because of man's innate propensity to barter. This psychological explanation, if it is meant by itself to explain trade, conflicts with the sociological explanation offered in the *Early Draft*.

In the published version of *The Wealth of Nations*, why did Adam Smith not more rigorously pursue the point about the market and the division of labor being explained partially by violence and law? One main reason may have been that between the *Early Draft* passage and *The Wealth of Nations*, Smith discovered what he thought was an alternate principle for explaining the division of labor: namely, the extent of the market, the extent to which one's ability to buy and sell has penetrated into a given geographical area.[14]

One problem with this explanation is that the extent of the market does not explain the division described in the *Early Draft*, between those who control labor and those who do not. It may explain how the market works once people are utilizing it, but it does not explain why people utilize it in different ways—whether, for example, they utilize it as buyer or seller of labor. A second problem is that the extent of the market principle disagrees just as much with the human nature explanation as does the political violence explanation, since one cannot explain by human nature something like the extent of the market, which in large part reflects physical circumstances.[15]

Furthermore, in the *Lectures on Jurisprudence*, which according to Meek and Skinner were given after the *Early Draft* but before *The Wealth of Nations*, Smith utilizes his extent of the market principle to supplement the violence and law principle rather than to supplant it.[16] In the *Lectures on Jurisprudence*, Smith also talks of how "They who are strongest and in the bustle of society have got above the weak, must have as many under as to defend them in their station; from necessary causes, therefore, there must be as many in the lower stations as there is occasion for. There must be as many up as down. . . . But it is not this which gives occasion to the division of labour."[17] The context in which Smith introduces this discussion is peculiar. He is considering, only to reject, the possibility that laws such as that of Sesostris, that people should follow the professions of their fathers, may have caused the division of labor. Smith rejects this possibility in favor of the psychological explanation of the division of labor. Yet, what is the necessity that Smith speaks about of having some people at the bottom? It seems that it can flow neither from the extent of the market principle nor from the psychological propensity to exchange, for neither of them tells us that those who are up are the strong and those down, the weak. Rather, in his discussions of these two principles, Smith usually takes pains to tell us that people are basically equal, and that differences and inequality between people come from the division of labor and the market. Here, on the other hand, he seems to be implying that the market and the division of labor come from the differences and inequalities between people.[18]

We must remember, of course, that Adam Smith justified the inequality that results from the division of labor on the basis that the total utility resulting from the division of labor made it worthwhile.[19] However, he never explicitly justified an inequality which did not arise from the market and division of labor but rather gave rise to them. According to Cropsey, even in those passages in which Smith speaks harshly of them, the division of labor and the market are still justified both because they are seen as natural as opposed to artificial, and because their bad effects are coupled with good effects. Even a passage like the following is not to be taken as a condemnation of capitalism.

In the progress of the division of labour, the employment of the far greater part of those who live by labour, that is, of the great body of the people, comes to be confined to a few very simple operations, frequently to one or two. But the understandings of the greater part of men are necessarily formed by their ordinary employments. The man whose whole life is spent in performing a few simple operations, of which the effects too are, perhaps, always the same, or very nearly the same, has no occasion to exert his understanding or to exercise his invention in finding out expedients for removing difficulties which never occur. He naturally loses, therefore, the habit of such exertion, and generally becomes as stupid and ignorant as it is possible for a human creature to become. The torpor of his mind renders him, not only incapable of relishing or bearing a part in any rational conversation, but of conceiving any generous, noble, or tender sentiment, and consequently of forming any just judgment concerning many even of the ordinary duties of private life. Of the great and extensive interests of his country he is altogether incapable of judging; and unless very particular pains have been taken to render him otherwise, he is equally incapable of defending his country in war. The uniformity of his stationary life naturally corrupts the courage of his mind, and makes him regard with abhorrence the irregular, uncertain, and adventurous life of a soldier. It corrupts even the activity of his body, and renders him incapable of exerting his strength with vigor and perseverance, in any other employment than that to which he has been bred. His dexterity at his own particular trade seems, in this manner, to be acquired at the expence of his intellectual, social, and marital virtues. But in every improved and civilized society this is the state into which the labouring poor, that is, the great body of the people, must necessarily fall, unless government takes some pains to prevent it.[20]

Cropsey, however, fails to mention even those passages in the published version of *The Wealth of Nations* which suggest that the division of labor and the market are bound up from the start with inequality among people.[21] These passages, especially when coupled with the more powerful *Early Draft* statement about violence and the more orderly oppression of law (originally published in 1937, twenty years before the appearance of Cropsey's book), refute the egalitarian origins of the division of labor and leave only the utilitarian idea, that production of a greater amount of goods justifies inequality, as the justification for an unequal division of labor.

The underground current in Smith's thought about the importance of violence and law in the economy can also be traced in his attitude toward property. In his 1763-1764 *Lectures on Jurisprudence*, Smith had stated the interconnection between property and political power. "Till there be property there can be no government, the very end of which is to secure wealth, and to defend the rich from the poor." This idea is stated even more strongly in the recently published 1762-1763 lectures:

But . . . when . . . some have great wealth and others nothing, it is necessary that the arm of authority should continually be stretched forth, and permanent laws or regulations made which may ascertain the property of the rich from the inroads of the poor, who would otherwise continually make encroachments upon it, and settle in what the infringement of this property consists and in what cases they will be liable to punishment. Laws and government may be considered in this and indeed in every case as a combination of the rich to oppress the poor, and preserve to themselves the inequality of the goods which otherwise would soon be destroyed by the attacks of the poor, who if not hindered by the government would soon reduce the others to an equality with themselves by open violence. The government and laws hinder the poor from ever acquiring the wealth by violence which they would otherwise exert on the rich; they tell them they must either continue poor or acquire wealth in the same manner as they have done.[22]

There is a striking ambiguity in this passage. Although the rich are seen to oppress the poor, they are also seen as potential innocent victims of the poor. Yet, in his *Edinburgh Review* letter of 1755, Smith had examined, although not clearly espoused, a stronger analysis which saw the rich as simply oppressors.

Smith had noted Rousseau's and Mandeville's view that the "laws of justice, which maintain the present inequality among men, were originally the inventions of the cunning and the powerfull."[23] It is true that Smith did not explicitly accept this Rousseauian analysis. But neither did he ever explicitly offer the alternate analysis that we have seen in Locke and Quesnay—to the effect that property is a basic natural law, in harmony with man's social nature and existing before the state. It must be admitted that there is something vaguely Lockian about the formulation which begins the lectures of 1763-1764: "Property and civil government very much depend on each other. The preservation of the property and the inequality of possession first formed it, and the state of property must always vary with the form of government."[24] It is vaguely Lockian, however, only because it does not explicitly say, as Rousseau and Hobbes did, that there is no property until there is a state. On the other hand, neither does it affirm clearly, as Locke did, that there is property before the state. This question of whether property existed before the state is a touchstone. On the one hand to hold that it did so exist usually entails the view that the property system is harmonious and natural and, thus, not the cunning invention of the rich against the poor. On the other hand, the analysis of property as a conspiracy of the rich against the poor entails that property be manmade by state or political power.

The closest Smith comes to revealing his position on the question of whether or not property existed before the state is in his analysis of the history of jurisprudence.

The next writer of note after Grotius was Mr. Hobbes. . . . Before the establishment of civil society mankind according to him were in a state of war; and in order to avoid the ills of a natural state, men entered into contract to obey one common sovereign who should determine all disputes. Obedience to his will according to him constituted civil government, without which there could be no virtue, and consequently it too was the foundation and essence of virtue. The divines thought themselves obliged to oppose this pernicious doctrine concerning virtue, and attacked it by endeavoring to show that a state of nature was not a state of war but that society might subsist, though not in so harmonious a manner, without civil institutions. They endeavored to show that man in this state has certain rights belonging to him, such as a right to his body, to the fruits of his labor, and the fulfilling of contracts. With this design Puffendorf wrote his large treatise. The sole intention of the first part of it is to confute Hobbes, tho it in reality serves no purpose to treat of the laws which would take place in the state of nature, or by what means succession to property was carried on, as there is no such state existing.[25]

This seems to be an argument against both sides: Pufendorf (and Locke) who held that property existed before the state and Hobbes who held that it did not. Yet, in reality it seems to support Hobbes. For who really wins if one cannot talk about the state of nature? The one who says there is no property in the state of nature, or the one who says there is? Clearly, the former wins because the concepts of property and state then become logically tied together, since there is no way of analyzing property without the state.

The material in the recently published lectures of 1762-1763 does not resolve this question. Smith notes that "The only case where the origin of natural rights is not altogether plain, is in that of property."[26] The origin of property is still not plain after his discussion. It is true that his willingness to utilize the moral concept of the impartial spectator to justify property suggests that property may receive a purely moral justification outside of the state. In this case, then, Smith would be following the tradition of Locke and Pufendorf.[27] However, his tendency at the opening of the lectures to define justice and property simultaneously seems to follow Hobbes' approach. This impression is bolstered when Smith seems to suggest that the state creates both justice and property: "The first and chief design of every system of government is to maintain justice; to prevent the members of a society from encroaching on one another's property or seizing what is not their own."[28] Thus, there continues to be a tension in Smith's mind between the view that property originates in harmony and that it originates in violence.

If this analysis of the importance of violence and law in determining the division of labor and property is correct, then Cropsey's hypothesis of a dichotomy in Smith's thought between the morally best and the attainable can be extended considerably.[29] The tension is between virtues like equality and selflessness on the one hand and industrial progress on the other. The former can be attained only at the expense of the latter. Another way of putting it is that moral holism is connected with lack of progress, and moral individualism with achievement of progress. Moral holism would condemn the oppression found in property and the division of labor, whereas moral individualism would accept it because it leads to progress.

The tension between seeing the individual in the perspective of moral holism and seeing him in the perspective of moral individualism allows Smith's ethics to be fit into a framework of alienation. We may find further evidence of such a tension in Colletti's reconstruction from Smith's *Edinburgh Review* letter of a new attitude toward progress and virtue. This attitude says, essentially, that progress is good but depends on selfishness, whereas selflessness is good but depends on lack of progress.[30]

It is true that Smith's attitude toward this paradox is somewhat ambivalent. In the *Edinburgh Review* letter, he notes that the society that lacks progress but has selflessness is conceived of as good by Rousseau and as wretched by Mandeville. In both *The Theory of Moral Sentiments* and *The Wealth of Nations*, Smith also holds that the society without progress is wretched. However, he is not as sure as Mandeville or Rousseau that the path out of primitiveness is in complete selfishness. Nevertheless, there must be a measure of selfishness:

It is not from the benevolence of the butcher, the brewer, or the baker, that we expect our dinner, but from their regard in their own interest. We address ourselves, not to their humanity but to their self-love, and never talk to them of our own necessities, but of their advantages.[31]

In parallel passages in *The Theory of Moral Sentiments* and *The Wealth of Nations*, Smith argues that the individual who wants to do good for the whole of society does not contribute as much to that end as the one who follows his own enlightened self-interest.

Thus, once again moral holism is shown to be inconsistent with progress.

In *The Theory of Moral Sentiments*, Smith distinguishes between justice and beneficence. Although we are forced by the threat of punishment to be just, beneficent acts are motivated by the love of society, not by the fear of being punished. Beneficent acts by themselves could bring about that cooperation between individuals which is necessary to keep society going. But they are not a necessary condition for such cooperation, which can also be brought about by the fear of being punished, thus by justice. It would indeed be an "ornament" to society if beneficence prevailed, but society would still hold together without it as long as there was justice.[32]

This distinction between beneficence and justice leads Smith to speculate about the causes of action in society. He notes that everywhere in the universe we observe parts working together in order to produce a larger end and how in "the mechanism of a plant or animal body, [we] admire how everything is contrived for advancing the two great purposes of nature, the support of the individual, and the propagation of the species."[33] However, Smith notes that in all these cases the efficient cause is distinguished from the final cause. The meaning of this distinction is made clear by the examples Smith gives. The efficient cause has to do with the circulation of a particular part of the blood, or the movement of a particular part of the watch; the final cause, with the purpose for the body of the circulation of the blood, or the purpose that the watch has of pointing the hour.[34]

Smith notes that we would do well to apply this analysis to actions in society. It is men's particular fears of punishment that bring about the cooperation that keeps society going. This is justice, which can be analyzed in terms of efficient causes. The final cause, which is the purpose of keeping society going, is not something that should be attributed to men but to God.

This analysis implies that there is a separation between the cause of social action and the effect. The cause is the motives of men desiring to avoid punishment. The effect is the creation of the cooperation necessary to keep society going. It is God's final cause which allows this effect to occur, but this final cause seems almost totally hidden from men, who are often led by an "invisible hand."[35] If this final cause were not hidden from men but clear to them, they could be conscious moral holists and act according to beneficence. Smith does not say that conscious moral holism would be bad, but simply that it would be impossible to maintain with enough regularity.

There is a structural parallel between this discussion of justice in *The Theory of Moral Sentiments* and the discussion of the division of labor in *The Wealth of Nations.* In *The Wealth of Nations,* the invisible hand is also invoked, this time to explain the division of labor. For Smith, as we have seen, the division of labor has to do with the fact that people produce different things and that this helps preserve the good of society. It is just that now the good of society is not defined so vaguely in terms of the cooperation discussed in *The Theory of Moral Sentiments.* Rather, it has to do with social reproduction in general: division of labor, and production and distribution of goods. The reproduction of society, however, is never the intention of the individual who is producing or selling goods, just as the achievement of cooperation in *The Theory of Moral Sentiment* was not the intention of the individual in the moral life. And just as in his moral system Smith introduced God or the invisible hand as the final cause of the social effects of self-oriented intentions, so too in *The Wealth of Nations* he is led to imagine that an invisible hand is responsible for bringing order into the chaos of individual aims. For the individual "neither intends to promote the public interest, nor knows how much he is promoting it . . . he intends only his own gain, and he is in this, as in so many other cases, led by an invisible hand to promote an end which was no part of his intention."[36]

Some have argued (e.g., Viner and Bitterman) that this appeal to an invisible hand is not necessary to explain what can be explained either by self-interest or political institutions.[37] However, for Smith, could appeal to self-interest explain the way in which the total division of labor in society works? There are several obstacles to such a view. Smith talks of "the certainty of being able to exchange all that surplus part of the produce of his own labor . . . for such parts of the produce of other men's labors as he may have occasion for."[38] This, however, suggests that men must be able to know something about the totality of self-loves, i.e., that Smith has tendencies toward Quesnay's position that men need knowledge of the whole. As

Hasbach has noted, the order of the whole tends to be more conscious in the minds of people for Quesnay and more unconscious for Smith.[39] That is why Quesnay talks about faith giving knowledge of the whole, whereas Smith begins with the idea that the individual is simply concerned with himself. Then, as we have just seen, Smith slips in the idea that the individual perhaps needs to know more about the whole and, finally, he winds up with the view that the individual can remain ignorant and passive as long as the invisible hand has both knowledge and power over the whole. So in relation both to justice and to the division of labor, the individual is to a large extent cut off from the social world in terms of knowledge and power. He does not see or control the relationship between what he does and the final result of his economic action.

In both Smith and Quesnay, providence, conceived of as an invisible hand or a natural law, relates the individual to the whole. For the Physiocrats, providence or natural law gives the knowledge to each individual that allows him to know the relation between his act as individual cause and its social effect. But providence is responsible for the ultimate relation between cause and effect. For Smith, providence or the invisible hand reserves for itself both the knowledge of the whole and the power over the whole. In each case, however, the concept of the invisible hand or natural law seems to work against the more individualistic assumptions of Smith and Quesnay. In particular, it undercuts the view that individuals owning property by themselves without any other knowledge could account for social reproduction.

Social reproduction, for both the Physiocrats and Adam Smith, is explained only when either (1) the individual is given knowledge of the whole, or (2) another source of knowledge and power, the invisible hand, natural law, is posited. Thus, Smith, who has put much more stringent limitations on moral holism in economic society than Quesnay, is in certain respects as willing as Quesnay to utilize explanatory holism in understanding society.[40]

In what sense, however, could Smith be considered an explanatory holist, other than in his appeal to the invisible hand? Given the destruction of Smith's own manuscripts, it is doubtful that his precise stand on epistemology will ever be uncovered. The interpretations of it are simply too divergent, ranging from Halévy's claim that he was a natural law realist, to Bittermann's claim that he was a type of logical empiricist, to Skinner's argument that he anticipated Kuhn.[41]

Bitterman's essay, written in the heyday of logical empiricism, makes a good deal out of Smith's friendship with Hume. Unfortunately for Bitterman's thesis, the recently published complete Smith correspondence, which contains all the letters between Hume and Smith, reveals practically nothing about their stands on epistemology. There certainly are passages in Smith's early writings suggesting Humean, empiricistic themes, and Bitterman uses them to the full. However, on the question of Smith's attitude toward Hume's theory of causal explanation, Bitterman inadvertently supplies negative evidence that no passage in Smith shows clearly that he adopted the Humean view that "experience provides the basis for causal connections which may be established only through repeated observations of similar events."[42] Bitterman is unable to back this up with a quotation, even though the series of observations on Smith's empiricism in which it is included are all documented. Hume's theory of causal explanation is usually thought of as individualistic, and the fact that Smith never clearly affirms it means that an opening is made for a possible holistic account of explanation.

In addition, Skinner's account of Smith's early writings on philosophy opens this possibility even further. He scrutinizes Smith's comment that philosophy is the "science of the connecting principles of nature" and that

Systems in many respects resemble machines. A machine is a little system, created to perform, as well as to connect together, in reality, those different movements and effects, which the artist has occasion for. A system is an imaginary machine invented to connect together in the fancy those different movements and effects which are already in reality performed.[43]

The meaning of these passages, Skinner argues, is that:

the mechanistic analogy . . . provided him with means of organizing the argument as a whole. . . . For example if we regard society as a single unit or whole; as a great machine, then if its elements are to be explained, we must break into the system at some point. . . . Looked at in this way, the *Moral Sentiments* and *The Wealth of Nations* are both concerned with the common problem of order and equilibrium with regard to complete systems.[44]

We must be careful, however, because if we push Smith's thought too far in the holistic direction, we run into the obvious ways in which he is an individualist and empiricist, such as his stress on empirical perception and his defense of the English tradition against the Cartesian viewpoint in his *Edinburgh Review* letter.[45]

One way of trying to resolve this question of holistic and individualistic elements in Smith's theory of explanation is to speculate about the historical and logical connections between Smith, Hume, Berkeley, Malebranche, and Quesnay. It is curious that Smith and Quesnay, the originators of free-enterprise theory, each had a close connection with a leading philosopher of causality: Hume and Malebranche, respectively. We also know that both Berkeley and Hume were influenced by Malebranche; and we have argued that Smith and Quesnay needed a holistic epistemology for at least part of their economic systems.[46]

Given this complex of facts and requirements, we may ask whether it is possible that Smith could have interpreted Hume as providing a theory of explanation somewhat like the holistic one that Malebranche apparently provided Quesnay; and that he did this the more readily in that he needed a sense of the whole for his account of economy and self? After all, Berkeley, who was presumably much more important to Hume than Malebranche was, was very much an explanatory holist; in a little known work, Berkeley even applied this holism to society.[47]

Is it possible that Malebranche's philosophy itself had a tendency to oscillate between stress on holism via God keeping track of the whole and stress on individualism via the particulars which awaited the action of God? If this were the case, perhaps Hume, borrowing from Malebranche what he wanted, could have appeared Janus-faced to Smith, giving rise to both holism and individualism.

If the Malebranchian theory of causal explanation had both holistic and individualistic tendencies, this would explain why Kant, who, as is argued in the next chapter, constructed a new version of holism, had to react not only against Hume, with his stress on particulars, but also against Malebranche, for whom particulars were atomistically separated, only to be connected by God's activity: ". . . there is a general *harmony* of things. But from it there does not follow the *pre-established* harmony of *Leibniz*, which in truth introduces only *concordance* and not *mutual dependence* between substances . . . nor do we here admit the action of substances by the *occasional causes* of *Malebranche*."[48] For Kant, holism, the "general harmony of things," the "mutual dependence between substances," is bound up with stress on universals or common elements much more than is the case with either Smith or Quesnay. The development of the Kantian concept of holism ultimately allowed classical German philosophy to oppose both empiricistic individualism and the ambiguous holism of Malebranche.

CHAPTER FOUR

Kant

In Kant's architectonic plan for his corpus, there is a parallel between a holistic concept of community as a way of approaching causality and a holistic ethical concept of a community of selves. Unlike the holism found in the economists, these holistic concepts do not arise primarily out of economic concerns, even though they are ultimately connected with them.

Both the causal and ethical concepts of commuinity are holistic in the way the parts are related to the whole. Causal community is the mutual causation of things that exist at the same time. Ethical community deals with the relation of one person to the situation of another, presumably in the same time span. Thus, both forms of community, causal and ethical, stress synchronous events.[1]

Causal community involves simultaneous interaction of cause and effect and is thus much different from the more ordinary notion of causality which does not assume simultaneity in time but rather assumes the opposite, i.e., that the cause is prior to, and thus temporally separated from, the effect.[2] The simultaneity of causal community, however, with the aid of Newtonian physics, becomes connected with a second characteristic—reciprocity. Kant borrows from Newtonian physics the principle that for every action there is an equal reaction. For the theory of community, this comes to have the meaning that in a simultaneous cause and effect relation if a is a cause and b its effect, then it is also true that b is a cause and a its effect.[3] According to this conception of reality, parts are seen as interdependent.

Just as the holistic concept of causal community stresses the interdependence of the parts of the world, so too does its holistic ethical analogue, community of persons. However, ethical as opposed to causal community rests not on the interdependence of parts of the world, but on the interdependence of persons. This notion emerges most clearly in the third formulation of Kant's basic ethical norm, the categorical imperative, which is said to rest on a "relation of rational beings (persons) to one another." The categorical imperative is also seen as "the idea of the will of every rational being as a will giving universal law." All these wills or persons are connected in a legislative body. "Morality, therefore, consists in the relation of every action to that legislation . . . which must be found in every rational being."[4] Thus, in both causal and ethical community, the parts are interdependent because of their relation to the whole.

Does this interpendence of wills in the ethics, however, mean that when the individual constructs the moral law he must have in mind the possibility that each will in the community of wills can potentially make the same law? Or does it mean that each individual will must actually make the law along with every other individual? If it were the latter, then there would actually be an interpendence of wills in an existing legislative body. In the former case, this interdependence would only be a potentiality. However, since in the theory of causality the interdependence of the world is actually present, if it were only potentially present between wills, there would be an asymmetry between the interpendence of the world and that of persons and their wills.

Since Kant is not entirely clear about this subject, I will have to show that other pieces of evidence imply an actual interdependence between wills. Even then, however, the analogy between the ethical and the causal points will not be totally clear. It must also be shown that the actual connection of wills is similar to the actual connection between the parts of the world. This means that the interconnection between wills must be shown to have two features that specifically are present in the interconnections between parts of the world: there must be reciprocity and simultaneity. To show these points, however, I am going to make a long detour. I am going to argue that the connection between causal community and ethical community depends on their mutual relations to the concept of universality. When we understand how universality is connected with causal community and with ethical community, then we understand how the two types of community are related to each other, particularly in their use of simultaneity and reciprocity.

Traditionally, as we have noted, the problem of universals at least expresses philosophical puzzlement about the mind's ability to compare particulars as, for example, when the mind observes an object and compares it to other objects. This puzzlement is sometimes followed by the claim that this comparing power allows the mind to grasp, for example, the object in general as opposed to particular examples of objects. According to this view, the comparing power is not only a power but also an element of knowledge. Acceptance of this notion defines antinominalism. The nominalist would say that the comparing power is just a tool for knowing, but that all that is known are particular objects. The antinominalist, on the other hand, wants to say that the tool either is part of or mirrors part of what is known. These latter possibilities define the two directions in which antinominalist positions can go. The antinominalist admits that there is an object in itself, but then he asks, "is that object in itself just the comparing power, just the tool, or is that comparing power a reflection of some other object in general, whatever it may be?" According to the first position, conceptualism, universals such as object in itself are in the mind, and they are elements of knowledge. According to the second position, realism, they are held to be elements of knowledge, but they are thought to exist outside the mind, although not necessarily in the physical world.

I believe that Kant rejects nominalism and realism. Instead, he adopts what I will call the new conceptualism. As the name implies, this is a form of conceptualism, but in many ways it represents a new position in the debate about universals. Furthermore, its potential application to the problem of human action paves the way ultimately for the analogy between ethical and causal community as well as for much that is distinctive in nineteenth-century German philosophy. This new conceptualism, in opposition to nominalism, holds that the comparing power of the mind is an element of knowledge. In opposition to realism, it holds that this mental comparing is not, at least as far as we can know, similar to some nonmental object in itself. In line further with conceptualism, it holds that the knowledge that the comparing power gives is of the comparing power itself.

Yet, this new conceptualism allows Kant to accomplish much that realism does, and that the old conceptualism does not, make possible. First, realism allows the distinction between objective and subjective knowledge to be made in such a way that the former is based on universals which are accessible to all minds. In contrast, subjective knowledge is based on nonuniversal perceptions or data. However, the new conceptualism also allows for the distinction between objective and subjective, founding it on the difference between universals common to all minds and structures that individuals may uniquely have created for themselves. Second, realism allows thought to learn about reality by thinking about itself. As the mind concentrates on its universals, it learns about the external universals which mirror them. But the new conceptualism also allows thought to learn about reality by thinking about itself because for Kant we cannot know without knowing universals. There is one definition of reality in Kant (call it "reality I") where it is limited to what we can know. Thus, we can conclude that since universals are a necessary condition for knowledge and since knowledge is a necessary condition for "reality I," therefore universals are a necessary condition for "reality I."[5] They are not, of course, a sufficient condition, since "reality I" is also made up of raw uncategorized material independent of the mind. It is the notion, however, that universals are a necessary condition for a reality other than mental that is denied by the old conceptualism. For this would give universals causal status, whereas for the old conceptualism they can at the most refer to the meaning that the mind imposes on external reality, and cannot be causal.

For the old conceptualist, if one were looking at a tree, its substance-like properties, i.e., the comparisons that one makes or that can be made between it and other substances, are part of what is known, but these comparisons which make up the universal features of the tree are not necessary in order for the tree to exist. They can never be of causal significance. For (1) their ontological location is unclear; (2) these comparisons and similarities would have to be mental and thus subjective; and (3) if the comparisons and similarities were causal factors in the tree's continued existence, they would interfere with the basic causal significance of the data being compared—something it is hard to believe they could do.

Now Kant's theory cannot handle the first two objections fully, but it allows an answer to the third with the claim that the mind has enough ontological force that its prior comparing can break down the basicness of the particular causes. Thus, the continued existence of this substance, the tree, is as dependent on the mind's comparing power as it is on the externality of the tree. The continued existence of the tree, however, can be analyzed in terms of Newton's laws about matter. In Kant's interpretation of these laws, similarities are as objective as particulars and the objectivity of laws is based on the objectivity of similarities. This account also allows a partial answer to the second objection, that the comparisons are mental and subjective: they are mental but that does not make them subjective.

Had Kant been able to answer the first objection, that the ontological location of universals was unclear, his victory over the old conceptualism would have been more likely. He wanted to hold that "reality I," dependent as it is on universals, is more than just the mind, but he could never show how this was so. For him, universals had to be able to answer causal questions as well as questions about the meaning of the mind. At times he himself did not see how this was possible. This tension between the subjective and objective elements in Kant's philosophy comes out strikingly in a letter to Beck:

One cannot actually say that a representation *befits* another thing but only that . . . a relation to something else . . . *befits* the representation, whereby it becomes *communicable* to other people . . . we can only understand and communicate to others what we ourselves can *make*, granted that the manner in which we intuit something . . . can be assumed to be the same for everybody. . . .

The synthesizing itself is not given; on the contrary, it must be done by us: we must *synthesize* it if we are to represent anything as *synthesized* (even space and time). We are able to communicate with one another because of this synthesis. . . . agreement is applied to something that is valid for everyone, something distinguished from the subject, that is, an

object, since it lies exclusively neither in the representation nor in consciousness but nevertheless is valid *(communicable)* for everyone.

I notice, as I am writing this down, that I do not even entirely understand
myself and I shall wish you luck if you can put this simple, thin thread of
cognitive faculty under a sufficiently bright light. Such overly refined hair-
splitting is no longer for me.[6]

Nominalism, realism, conceptualism, and Kant's new conceptualism can all lead to different ways of understanding action. Nominalism would view the action in its uniqueness, concentrating perhaps on
the peculiarity of the physical movement or of the accompanying
mental perception. The general fact that someone was building
would not be as important as the way he was building or the way
he felt about it. Realism would hold that there was some general
description of the action, a real, but not necessarily mental aspect
of it. This objective characteristic may be, for example, its rightness.
Conceptualism in its ordinary variety would hold that the mind
gives a general description of the action, but would not claim that
that description really applies to the action as it is outside the mind.
The action of building would perhaps be described in terms of the
social conventions of the observer. The theory of action associated
with the new conceptualism must, again, modify the old conceptualism in two ways. First, the general description of the action can
be objective in the sense that it holds for all. Second, the action
must be categorized by the mind, so that the universal category
would be a necessary condition for the reality of action.

This theory of action must hover between the old realism and
the old conceptualism. The action is not simply given its substance
by what is outside of it, as in realism, but neither is it simply categorized in a ghostlike way by the mind, with its reality escaping
that category, as in the old conceptualism. Through his own concepts about action, man creates his action in a way that was not
possible according to earlier theories. Furthermore, this new conceptual theory of action can lead to a causal theory of explaining
actions; the very reality of the action is now bound up with man's
conceptual understanding of it. But the understanding of the reality
of the action certainly implies understanding some of the questions
associated traditionally with causal analysis, such as why the action

occurs. For Kant, as I will argue shortly, the question of why such an action as building occurs could be analyzed in two ways. First, there is the deterministic aspect of it, which involves its dependency on the absolute uniformity of nature as necessitated by the universal categories of the mind. This aspect of the action depends on causal community. Its second aspect, the ethical aspect, its rightness, is dependent, I will argue, on ethical community. It is with this background in mind that the relation between holistic causal community and the concept of universality must be examined.

In a very obvious sense, of course, there is a connection between community and universality. Community and the other categories of relation, namely, substance and cause and effect, are simply examples of universals.[7] As universals, they categorize particular examples of substance, cause and effect, and community. Particular objects are seen, for example, in the light of the category of substance. Furthermore, according to the new conceptualism, this categorization is a necessary condition for the continued existence of substances or objects.

This analysis can now be extended to deal with cause and effect over time and communal causality. They are universals in the same way that substance is, except that they are relations rather than predicates. Just as we use the conceptual power of the mind to categorize objects so also we use it to categorize successive or reciprocal cause and effect relations. Upon seeing that an effect follows a cause, the mind immediately compares this relation with other relations of following. On seeing that two events are simultaneously cause and effect, the mind also immediately compares this simultaneity with other cases. In this analysis, then, the categories, including community, entail universality. However, it seems that it could also be argued that universality entails certain features of causal community.

The basic characteristics of community are reciprocity and simultaneity, but do not all universals, simply as universals, have simultaniety and reciprocity? In the universal categories of the mind, there is simultaneity in that the comparing power of the mind ties all the particular objects together at one time in order to make the concept of object in general. Similarly, it simultaneously ties together all the examples of the relations of successive cause and effect and community. Furthermore, in all of these universals there could also be said to be a kind of reciprocity. Each particular object could be said to be the cause and effect of every other object, each particular cause and effect relation could be said to be the cause and effect of every other cause and effect relation, and each particular simultaneous and reciprocal cause and effect relation could be said to be the cause and effect of every other simultaneous and reciprocal cause and effect relation. Why is this? Because to be an object implies that the particular examples of objects are being compared. Object a depends upon objects b, c, d, just as they depend on a and each other. Similarly, cause and effect relation aBc or community relation aCb depends, respectively, on other cause and effect or community relations bBc, cBd, dBc, and bCc, cCd, dCe, and so forth.

However, some problems arise with this analysis. (1) It gives the category of community a fate similar to that of the person who must pick himself up by his bootstraps. Community entails universality, but universality itself is a kind of disguised community, and indeed entails community. This is not an overwhelming objection since there is no necessity to imagine a time when universality existed without community or vice versa. There are two other possible objections which tend to weaken the claim that universality entails community. (2) The universal categories, insofar as they involve reciprocity, involve a mental reciprocity rather than the Newtonian reciprocity that Kant uses to describe the category of physical community. (3) Kant does not stress that each of the entities that are held together by the Newtonian law of equal action and reaction must be similar. But universals, by definition, can only bring simultaneous reciprocity to similar entities.

Keeping in mind these problems of showing the connection between universality and community in nature, I will now show how universality can be related to Kant's theory of action and ethical community. This will allow me to analyze the connection between universality and ethical community and thus ultimately to further test the original hypothesis about the connection between causal community, universality, and ethical community. We will first see how Kant distinguished between actions that are determined and those that are free. Those that are determined are so because they are structured by the categories of nature such as cause and effect and community. Those that are free are so because they are structured by the ethical categories. But both the freedom and the determinism rest upon Kant's new conceptualism in which universals are necessary conditions for action. I show this first in regard to the determinism.

For Kant, all actions defined as real by his new conceptualism are determined through the categories of cause and effect and community. Kant describes these categories as, respectively, the "relation of the existence of one thing to the existence of another which is necessitated by the former," and the situation where substances which "each have their own separate existence . . . depend upon one another necessarily." The meaning of necessity here is that everything in the ordinary world is completely determined by prior and simultaneous causes, and thus could not have been otherwise. The ordinary world is thus a totally deterministic system. It is "the totality of rules under which all phenomena must come in order to be thought as connected in experience." In this realm, "necessity is the property of the causality of all irrational beings [i.e., beings who are sunk in the ordinary world] by which they are determined in their activity by the influence of alien *(fremder)* causes."[8]

Determinism in the ordinary world of "reality I," then, depends upon temporal and communal causality, which in turn depend upon universals as necessary conditions. Determinism, then, depends upon universals being necessary conditions for action. This determinism of action is made possible by the new conceptualism as found in Kant's holistic account of causality. It is paralleled by a type of freedom of action, made possible by the new conceptualism found in Kant's holistic account of ethical action. Kant's concept of the self arises out of the juncture of the free and determined aspects of action.

Kant argues that it might be possible to lift oneself out of the world of ordinarily deterministic experience, the world of "reality I." He argues that this could be done if the self were to cease acting according to the universality which is characteristic of the way that entities in the ordinary world act, and act instead according to a different universality. This universality would be given to the self by the self rather than be taken from the external world. No longer would the self, for example, be bound solely by such laws as Newton's laws of physics; rather, the self would act according to its own principles. The ethical will, as opposed to "reality I," would give laws for actions, but "the estimation of the will as a universal law for possible actions, has an analogy with the universal connection of the existence of things under universal laws, which is the formal element of nature in general." These self-imposed laws of morals, however, are based on the "relation of rational beings to one another," just as the laws of Newtonian physics are based on the relation of parts between universals such as substance and causality.[9]

Stress on this connection between the ethics and the account of causality now comes to fruition. We see that just as the deterministic world ties things together through reciprocal cause and effect, this reciprocal cause and effect being the result of universals, so too the ethical world ties wills together by relating persons to persons. Thus, a will is created which is analogous to the universal connection of things in nature, a connection of wills which is also dependent on universals. The problem, however, is that we do not yet see how that connection between persons is dependent on universals. In order to develop this connection further, I must backtrack over earlier parts of the argument.

My aim was to show the connection between the holistic ethical and causal categories of community by demonstrating their mutual connection with universality. That connection has been shown in that just as causal community makes possible, through universals, the determinism of action in the nonmoral world, so too ethical community makes possible, through universals, the freedom of action in the moral world. However, to understand how it does this the notion of free ethical action must be developed in regard to several points. First, it has already been argued that Kant's new conceptualism allows each person to see things in similar ways. It must now be shown how this also applies to his ethical theory. Second, it was argued earlier that Kant's new conceptualism gives a definition of "reality I" such that it is dependent on universals. This notion is extended to ethical action, and it must be shown how ethical actions are dependent on universals. However, it has also been suggested that the way in which Kant's new conceptualism shows that "reality I" is dependent on universals is by incorporating into the concept of universals the concepts of simultaneity and reciprocity found in the notion of physical community. Thus, my third task is to develop the notion of universal moral laws making the existence of actions possible through simultaneity and reciprocity.

In what sense are ethical actions similar? It has been noted that for Kant universality lacks subjectivity in that it is the same for all minds. If this principle were applied to action within "reality I," it would suggest that all people could see their action similarly in that the actions are categorized by cause and effect. The same thing would seem to apply to the extraordinary action that results from the universal principles of the will. The universal principles must hold for all who want to transcend reality, and thus all who do so can see their action in the same way. For Kant, the principles that selves must follow in order to be free of the influence of external causes are encapsulated in the universal moral law. It is following the universal moral law that makes actions right.[10] Kant never conceives of the possibility that each self might come up with its own principles for creating freedom and morality. In order to be free, selves must follow the basic universal principles which hold for all.

In what sense are ethical actions simultaneous and in their simultaneity dependent on universals? It could be argued that in the realm of ethics, as in the realm of community in nature, the universality of the mind simultaneously connects actions with each other. It is true that this argument seems at first glance to be false Ethical actions do not have to be performed at the same time. Nevertheless, there is an element of truth in this claim. Ethical actions occur side by side in the sense that they arise out of the same communal setting, at least if we take Kant seriously about how these actions must be at least potentially connected with a legislative body. That communal setting could well include a communal time frame. The community of time here, however, would be somewhat different than the simultaneity of time that Kant talks about in his Newtonian model. It would perhaps be similar to the type of community of time described by contemporary French structuralists such as Lévi-Strauss in their discussion of the synchronic aspects of society, or to Fernand Braudel's concept of la longue durée.[11] Both notions of time stress how continuity in society or history can be associated with a homogeneity of time counterposed to the subjective sense of time that the individual associates with his acts.

Finally, in what sense are ethical actions reciprocal, and in their reciprocity dependent on universals? Ethical actions would be reciprocal if each principle giving rise to them were tested in reciprocal debate with all people as members of a legislative body. But does this actually happen? Sometimes, as noted earlier, Kant seems to suggest that the individual must simply imagine that the universal body is legislating. Sometimes, on the other hand, he suggests that it must actually be legislating. Only if it is actually legislating is there homology between reciprocity in causal community and ethical community.

Interestingly enough, when Kant develops the idea further in *Religion Within the Limits of Reason Alone*, he indicates that there must be an actual universal legislation. Kant talks of the idea of community as it is organized in a church. He speaks of the church's

relation under the principle of freedom; both the internal relation of its members to one another, and the external relation of the church to political power—both relations as in a republic *(Freistaat)* (hence neither a hierarchy nor an illuminatism, which is a kind of democracy through special inspiration, where the inspiration of one man differs from that of another, according to the whim of each).[12]

This passage implies the existence of an actual legislative community, for the passage claims that the members of the church are united with each other in a bond of freedom, defined politically as neither a hierarchy nor a system (illuminatism) where people simply do what they want. This is a concrete example of the kingdom of ends of the third formulation of the categorical imperative where freedom is seen to come with following laws, thus not simply doing what one wants, but laws of one's own making, thus not a hierarchy. This formulation is more concrete than the discussion of the kingdom of ends because there is an actual community, the church, which is making these self-imposed laws. Why the church does this becomes clearer if we examine Kant's raison d'être for the church.

After his analysis of human good and evil in the first two parts, Kant begins the third part by noting that "envy, the lust for power, greed, and the malignant inclinations bound up with these, besiege his nature, contented with itself, as soon as he is among men."[13] Kant argues that man is faced with either a good community or a bad community. He concludes that it is, therefore, a moral imperative to strive for an ethical community, the church, in which the kingdom of ends is interpreted as an actually legislative body. This line of argumentation implies that there is actual reciprocity between the members of the legislative community, thus making the parallel between ethical and causal community stronger than if there were only possible reciprocity.

This reciprocal relation between members of a community is only connected by analogy with the reciprocity of the law of equal action and reaction. It is highly likely that occasionally the analogy appeared to Kant in a somewhat crude way as a means of fulfilling his architectonic and triadic fancy. We know, for example, from the *Opus postumum* that empirical examples of holistic community included such things as rubbing and cohesion.[14] In the *Metaphysical Elements of Justice*, Kant talks about justice in terms of "a general reciprocal use of coercion" and goes on to clearly connect this idea with the Newtonian concept of the equal action and reaction in all community of motion:

The exhibition and description of the concept of justice is not made possible so much by the concept itself as by the general reciprocal and equal use of coercion that comes under a universal law and is consistent with it. In the same way that this dynamic concept (of the equality of action and reaction) still has a ground in a purely formal concept of pure mathematics (for example, of geometry), reason has also taken as much care as possible to provide the understanding with a priori intuitions to aid in the construction of the concept of justice.[15]

There is certainly only a very crude analogy between the reciprocity of rubbing and the reciprocity of justice unless perhaps one defines justice as "you scratch my back, I'll scratch yours."

What we must search for is a more interesting connection between reciprocity in nature and in justice, one that clearly makes universals necessary conditions for action, thus blending causality with universality. Support for such a concept is found in Kant's discussion of the notion of the kingdom of ends, again in relation to the third formulation of the categorical imperative which stresses community of wills in the legislative body. He notes that "if we abstract from the personal differences of rational beings and thus from all content of their private ends, we can think, then of a whole of all ends in a systemic connection." Furthermore, Kant indicates that this abstraction will allow people to act according to the moral law and thus according to "the causality of living beings insofar as they are rational."[16] Since it is this abstraction that allows people to act according to rational causality, however, we can say that universality is a necessary condition for attaining that causality.

This is not surprising since we have already seen that it was universality that made the general category of causal community possible in the first place. It has not, of course, been shown that either Kant's concept of universality in general or his application of it to ethical action is exactly the same as the strictly Newtonian conception of causal community. The main difference is that with the former two cases, reciprocity operates in interaction between exemplars of universals, whereas with the last case it operates in an extremely physical way between elements that are not necessarily similar or universal. Nevertheless, we can now see that in all cases, universality in general, universality as applied to ethical action, and universality as applied specifically to causal community, there is a general holistic definition of reciprocity as interdependence of parts. In the case of causal community, this is elaborated by arguing that each part moves at the same time that another part moves. The motion of one is a necessary and sufficient condition for the motion of the other. In the case of universality in general and ethical community, it can also be said that the activity of one part is a necessary and sufficient condition for the activity of another. However, the activity in both cases is not one of physical motion. Rather, following the new conceptualism, the possibility of the continuation or the stability of the particular action or object depends upon there being a potentially infinite number of similar actions or objects to which they can be compared. Thus, in ethical community the general principles of action made by the community create the

possibility of ethical action on the part of individuals. The Newtonian law of the equality of action and reaction expresses an analogy
with this insight into action that arises out of Kant's new conceptualism.

Kant's economic theory of property enters into his holistic conception of ethical community and self. However, it appears as only
one way of interpreting ethical community. Indeed, it represents
the alienated community, although Kant never explicitly draws this
conclusion. In the chapter on Hegel, it is argued that the Hegelian
theory of economy and self attempts to resolve the problem of the
alienated community in Kant's economics, just as Marx again
attempts to resolve this resolution of divided community offered by
Hegel. However, alongside this difference between the *penseurs
maîtres* there is a greater continuity. Each comes to analyze the
division or lack of division in selves by analyzing the common
actions they perform. So far, we have only seen how in Kant this is
achieved by contrasting the universality of freedom with that of
determinism. Yet, it turns out that the universality of freedom is,
as Hegel noted, not concrete enough to carry out this burden. The
problem is that even if the self follows the moral law that law must
be about something. The young Hegel thought that content must
not be simply neutral and opposed to the form of morality.[17] In
that case life would escape ethics. Rather, there must be some inner
connection between the moral law and concrete economic practices.

In the *Metaphysical Elements of Justice*, actions that reflect the
practices of a specific society are referred to much more often than
in the more abstract *Foundations of the Metaphysics of Morals*.
Thus, it is less prone to the Hegelian criticism. Indeed, there is one
specific social institution, property, that forms the basis of much of
the discussion in the *Elements*. Furthermore, the discussion of
property in the *Elements* is intimately linked with the discussion of
cheating within the buying and selling on the market in the *Foundations*. To cheat someone on the market certainly means to cheat
them out of what they own; it means to cheat them of their property.
Thus, the definition of cheating on the market presupposes the
definition of property.

Kant's doctrine of property in the *Elements* first considers the
physical relation of people to objects; then examines the relation of

all wills to all objects; and finally emphasizes that not only must each person respect the right of every other person to own private property, but also that the state must defend this right.[18]

The first half of the *Elements* is devoted to private law, and the second half to public law. The transition from the one to the other occurs when property becomes accepted by the state. The section on private law begins with discussion of the individual simply interacting with external objects. This is the first stage of the discussion. However, the individuals who relate to these external objects recognize the similarities between their claims and those of others, and can thus compel others to enter into a legal system where all claims are protected. This is the second stage of the discussion. Finally, the third stage considers what happens when people actually enter into the state and use it to protect property: "the mode of having something external as one's own property in a state of nature is physical possession, [the first stage] which carries with it the juridicial presumption [the second stage] that, through the union of the will of everyone in public legislation, this possession will be made into *de jure* possession, [the third stage]."[19]

As we have seen, two general types of analyses of property were available to Kant and other seventeenth- and eighteenth-century philosophers. The first was that each individual supplied his own unique criterion for what makes something his property. This analysis underlies the first part of Kant's discussion. The second was that a number of people must agree on the same criteria in order for there to be property. This analysis underlies the second and third parts of Kant's discussion.

Kant must move away from the individualistic stage in order to come up with a universal moral law about property. On the first, individualistic account, property expresses a relation between the individual and an object. This relation is not social, involving the attitudes of others, but rather is physical. It would be difficult to state in general what physical relation between the individual and the object would suffice to allow him to claim the object as his, because sometimes he may be able to state this when (a) he holds the object in his hand, sometimes when he is (b) five feet from it, sometimes when he is (c) ten feet from it. Sometimes people will not take the object when *(a)* holds, sometimes when *(b)* holds, and sometimes when *(c)* holds. Furthermore, it is not just a question of not being able to state general criteria, for the individualistic theory holds that general criteria should be avoided.

Now suppose someone describes his action as, "I chased someone off some land that I held by putting five armed guards around it." The question of whether this could be stated as a universal moral law depends upon which aspect of it is stressed. Suppose the stress is on the protective aspect of the action. It would be very difficult to know whether or not a given protective action could be made into a universal moral law, unless the connection was known between x's criterion for holding land and the criterion that others used. For example, there would have to be some connection between the specific criterion of five armed guards guarding the property and what in general would allow someone to hold some property.[20]

The paradox is that any attempt to state a general moral theory about individual property faces the task of stating a general justification for that which was defined to be in its essence particular. The particular nature of property even seems to be suggested by the etymology of the word. In German, *Eigentum* (property) is connected with the adjective *eigentlich*, which often connotes what is characteristic or peculiar to something or somebody; and in *French*, *propriété* (property) is connected etymologically with the adjective *propre* which often has the same connotation. But how could a general moral law be based on the peculiar or the particular?

The solution offered in the second part of Kant's theory of property arises out of its connection to the peculiarity of the self and its will and desire. Yet, each self, although peculiar, can be said to share the capacity to be peculiar, and thus to own property, with other selves. This shared capacity is supposedly universal, thus creating a connection between the general justification of property and the particular nature of property. By making property more generally justified, Kant can supposedly fit it in more easily with the universal moral law.[21]

So, for Kant, there can be a possible universal moral law based on the similar acts of will involved in property as opposed to the particularistic criteria that those acts of will come up with. The peculiarity of property involves the private use of objects, and the generality of property involves the fact that all people must be able

to have private use of objects. His justification for this double movement is that otherwise "freedom would be robbing itself of the use of
its will in relation to an object of the same will inasmuch as it would
be placing usable objects outside of all possibility of being used."[22]
But Kant's argument, that if we did not have use of private property
then objects would be useless, is unfinished. "Why would objects be
useless?" Is it because objects require one-to-one relations with
individuals? Is it because of some natural fact about the scarcity of
human goods? Is it because psychologically people would not be
able to produce if they did not have private property? Or is it because in the society in which Kant was living the domination of
one man by another expressed itself by creating the necessity for
everybody to at least have the right to own private property? This
second part of the theory falters because Kant never shows that it is
of the essence of the human will to own private property.

The third part of Kant's theory of property involves not only the
peculiarity of private control and the similarity of the wills that
seek private control, but also the state's acceptance of everybody's
right to their peculiar control. The problem with Kant's state theory
of property is that, on the one hand, it seems to arise out of the
individualistic theory and the notion of the will associated with it.
On the other hand, it also seems to arise out of Kant's theory of
right action, especially the third formulation of that theory which
says that right action necessitates acting according to laws which
are potentially legislated by all people. These two possible origins
of the theory push it in two conflicting directions.[23]

This third stage of the theory emphasizes that each person must
respect the right of every other person to own private property.
Unlike the second stage, however, this respect for other people's
rights to private property then becomes incorporated in a system of
property laws upheld by the state. Obligation in regards to property
"comes from a universal rule of the external juridical relationship
[that is, the civil society]."[24] For Kant, obligation is commitment to
perform right actions. His theory of right action now becomes
connected, therefore, with his theory of property. Thus, Kant, in
his account of property, is first concerned with an individualistic
side, then a side based on the similarities in the acts of individual
wills appropriating property, and then a side in which it is recog-

nized that there must be social acceptance of private property. It has been argued here that, if Kant's theory of property had stopped with individualism, then Kant could not have come up with a universal moral law based on property-holding actions because all he could deal with was particulars. In contrast, stress on the similarities between acts of will could give rise to a general moral law. But the similarities themselves are not demonstrated to exist as part of the basic human will. Does the third stage of the theory solve these problems through its invocation of the state?

If one accepts the state definition of property, then the universal moral law seems to be workable, for it would be based on the actual common actions of ethical selves. But Kant should not be able to accept the state definition without asking further questions about it. He must show that state promulgation of property is consistent with the third formulation of the categorical imperative: acting according to laws that a universal legislative body could have made. The categorical imperative, if logically extended, would probably lead to an entirely different view of the social nature of property than Kant's state theory. It would be a social theory based on the universal structures that make the self free, whereas the state theory of property that Kant adopts is based, ultimately, on the individualistic stage of property. Kant tries to graft together the two thrusts of his ethics, but his attempt can only be judged a failure.

The state theory stresses that there is private property, but that it is subjected to social limitations. Furthermore, these limitations are codified in the laws that the legislative body makes. The legislative body makes laws which presuppose certain regularities in action and which simply modify or solidify those regularities. Yet, it is not at all obvious that the third formulation justifies such a move. Indeed, it would seem more likely that it would justify the opposite move: namely, that the legislative body would not only modify the existing private property in a social direction, but also directly create the institution of property. Furthermore, since that creation would arise from the universals that make the self free and true, property itself would have to be like the self that acts according to those universals. Property would have to be social rather than individual with social limitations. The basic characterization that Kant gives of the laws made by the legislative body is that they allow the self to be free, following neither the laws of the world nor individual desires. Desires must be unified through the common social structures that each self follows.

We can add that only if the individual follows these structures will he fail to be alienated. Otherwise, according to Kant's own account, he is following "alien" *(fremder)* desires which do not allow him to be his own *(eigentlich)* self: According to our account of alienation, the laws of his social action would not be seen to clearly derive from him and thus could be said to both belong and not belong to him.[25] If Kant could show that the necessity of each will being able to possess individual property really derives from the universal structures that allow the self to be free, then private property could be shown to be consistent with the creation of the autonomous self. But how could he show that these structures would manifest themselves in the need for all wills to appropriate private property, given that the structures are common and private property strives to be unique? It has been demonstrated that he never shows this. Furthermore, it seems as though the most obvious reason why Kant accepts these laws is that they seem so natural to him that he does not feel they need a complete justification. But the freedom of the self requires complete justification of the laws according to which it acts.

There are at least three different viewpoints with which Kant responds to this problem of whether the free self would simply create universal structures that would allow it to act, or whether it would reform or modify preexisting laws.

For the most part, Kant does not assume that there would be total reconstruction of the laws according to the universals that make men free, although the ideal of the free self seems to call for such a view. There is, however, one passage in *Religion Within the Limits of Reason Alone* suggesting that Kant did have this idea in mind. In describing the realm of autonomy as exemplified by the ideal church and its members, Kant talks about the nature of this church as *"purity,* union under no motivating forces other than *moral* ones."[26] The implication is that in such a church there is no motivation whatsoever arising from property norms, nor even such things as the desire to get food. Here the law is purely moral. It creates actions rather than regulating actions which arise out of the natural desires for such things as food or shelter, or out of such historically changing elements as property practices. Here the action simply is its domination by the universal moral law. This is Kant's first viewpoint.

Basically, however, Kant did not seem to follow this view. This is reasonable since in the extreme form in which it is presented, it involves leaving the material world behind. The second and third viewpoints represent two different attitudes, one toward the political realm and one toward the economic realm. Kant was able to use the theory of the legislative body making laws as an attack on political despotism. He seemed to recognize that in that arena it was not enough simply for the legislative body to amend laws made by a dictator, but rather it must make its own laws. This is the second viewpoint.

Kant seemed to think that economic phenomena, such as property, provided raw material for action, but insofar as property was connected with the laws of the state, then the raw material for action must be subjected to the legislative process. The legislative process, however, can no more get rid of the raw material than the engineer can proceed with his blueprint and get rid of nature. This is the third viewpoint.

Thus, political laws which are not connected with economic phenomena are simply created. Those which relate to economic phenomena are not simply created, but rather regulate the pre-existing economic phenomena. In the latter case, Kant apparently thought that one could begin with an action which is seen as an exemplification of a certain common type and then raise the question of whether the self's autonomy was preserved in the action. The answer is positive if all members of the legislative body that make up the community could wish that this law be enacted and followed. Yet, it seems that insofar as the action already exemplifies a pattern, then the autonomy is already lost if it cannot be shown that the first pattern is consistent with the universal structures common to all moral selves. Thus, Kant takes examples of market exchange and then asks whether market exchange itself is right or wrong according to the legislative body principle. He never shows that the patterns of market exchange in general are consistent with the universal nonalienated self. He is content to accept these actions as given.

Kant has the following problem which simply illustrates the general problem of relating a theory of alienation of the self to a weakly sketched account of common economic actions. Kant certainly holds that right actions must be consistent with structures common to all free selves. He asks whether specific property-holding actions are consistent with the moral structures, but he does not show that property-holding actions in general are consistent with these structures. Thus, he utilizes an element which he is not sure is external to the self, or arising from isolated desires, or arising from the common structures of the free self, in order to help see whether or not his action is consistent with the common structures. If he is not sure that private property in general is consistent with these common structures, how can he be sure that actions associated with private property are consistent with them?

Of course, Kant could argue that it is not the exchange element of the action that is important but its relation to the universal moral law. If Kant says that the fact that an action is an exchange action is simply a convention, something which has no bearing on the action itself, then how can he use his knowledge that it has this pattern to help him relate the action to the universal moral law? According to this view, actions that are described as exchange actions, or actions which violate contracts, or actions of stealing, would be actions in which all these descriptions could be peeled away with nothing left but the raw data of the action. It would then be theoretically possible to have knowledge of pure action without descriptions based on social regularities. If this were the case, however, then it is difficult to see how enough resemblances between actions could be discovered so that they could be related to the universal moral law. On the other hand, if there is no raw action which is left over when all the descriptions, such as breaking a contract or selling in the market, have been peeled away, and if some of these patterns are necessary parts of the action, then even though Kant would be able to make the comparison required, nevertheless the question of whether these actions are right (i.e., whether they followed the laws made by the legislative body) is not answered. These social patterns are not themselves shown to be consistent with such laws; rather, they are simply derived from the already existing state and economy.

Kant must not only solve the problem of what allows one to come up with a universal moral law. He must also solve it in such a way that it helps him deal with the problem of knowing whether an action follows rules made by the legislative body. The attempt to resolve the one problem leads him into difficulties with the other. This means that as Kant makes property-holding actions more capable of being dealt with in a universal moral law, then when he opposes a social theory of property to an individualistic one, we must ask whether social property, as recognized by the state, is consistent with the laws made by the universal legislative body.

The dilemma can be stated in the following way. Either property-holding actions and other economic actions are ladders to universal moral laws or they are not. If they are real ladders, then they are still left standing. Then it must be shown that they are consistent with the laws made by the legislative body. Kant does not do this. If they are not real ladders, then Kant cannot climb them. Then it will be impossible to get to universal moral laws. Thus, Kant's account of the common moral self fails, partially because it does not adequately grapple with the problem of the common nature of property actions.

CHAPTER FIVE

Hegel

Kant's problem of relating self to society also occupied Hegel when he first began to criticize Kant's critical philosophy. Indeed, Lukács has analyzed how Hegel's famous account of subject-object identity arises out of his moral critique of Kant as well as out of his purely ontological concerns.[1] Furthermore, in Hegel, as in Kant, economics plays a role that mediates between a moral theory of the self and a general ontological theory of universals. Hegel's critique of Kant can be understood as a tripartite confrontation with Kant's theory of universals, his concept of the moral self, and his account of society, including its economic structure. As we have seen, Kant oscillates between anchoring the self in the common actions of society and not doing so. In contrast, Hegel insists that the self be anchored in the common actions of society. However, he also thinks that society cannot simply be accepted as it appears. It either has to be changed to the kind of rational society that could be derived from the self's imperatives, or it has to be shown that despite appearances it is the kind of society that could be derived from these imperatives.[2]

In so anchoring the self to society, Hegel deals with common economic actions. Furthermore, in a parallel development Hegel argues that universals not only structure the form of reality, but also enter into its content, thus enabling him to develop the connection between holism and universals.

It should be noted, however, that his critique of Kant, especially as it appears in his early writings, is too severe in that it treats Kant as though his writings suggest no dilemma concerning the relation of the self to social forms. Up to now, much of the work on Hegelian economics has concentrated on this early critique. In contrast, I am going to discuss Hegel's account of economy and self in the later *Philosophy of Right*, where this unfair critique of Kant is not stressed as much.[3] *The Philosophy of Right* is emphasized partially because of its special connection with Marx's account of economy and self. I begin by examining the economic and political content of *The Philosophy of Right* and then turn to a discussion of the methodological issues that arise as Hegel attempts to unify ideas from the mercantilist and Smithian traditions.

Hegel, like Kant and Marx, reveals much about his work through its architectonic structure, hidden and yet potentially obvious in the table of contents.

PHILOSOPHY OF RIGHT

First Part: Abstract Right
> Property (Topic 1)
> Contract (Topic 2)
> Wrong (Topic 3)

Second Part: Morality
> Purpose and Responsibility (Topic 1)
> Intention and Welfare (Topic 2)
> Good and Conscience (Topic 3)

Third Part: Ethical Life
> The Family (Topic 1)
> Civil Society (Topic 2)
> The State (Topic 3)[4]

Three basic topics are treated within the first part, Abstract Right: property, contract, and wrong. In property *(Eigentum)*, Hegel considers what happens when an individual owns something. In his discussion of the first aspect of property, possession *(Besitz)*, Hegel concentrates on the physical relation between the will and the thing possessed. Possession means that the person involved can grasp the material thing physically or mark it in some way. Hegel's view of possession is very close to the physiocratic conception of possession and to the Kantian individualistic stage of property. Hegel's discussion of the use and alienation of the thing, the second aspect of property, does not advance him far beyond possession. With use, emphasis is not on the physical act which makes something one's possession, but on what the possessor does with what is his. "Alienation" (*Entausserung*) of property, the third aspect, does not yet refer to the divided self. Hegel is using it in the same way it was used by British political economists, for whom it referred to the buying or selling of a good.[5]

The second topic, contract, progresses logically from the notion of the buying and selling of goods. In contract, certain general rules are set up which allow people to buy or sell. In this social context, property becomes less like physical possession. Wrong, the third topic, deals with ethical judgments which come to be made on the basis of the general rules for buying and selling.

"Abstract right," then, deals with such heterogeneous topics as physically grasping or marking an object, using it, selling it, following rules in buying and selling objects, and the generation of moral attitudes and judgments on the basis of these activities.

"Morality," the second major part of *The Philosophy of Right*, is in turn generated by the setting up of these moral attitudes and judgments. The basic problem is to find some harmonious basis for moral systems. Here the self becomes confused and feels divided when it is not sure that inner moral judgments are compatible with the judgments of its action that are made by the world. Such judgments look not only at its intention, but also at the external circumstances that help bring about the action.

"Ethical life," the third part, is divided into three topics, all of which are concerned with social institutions: the family, civil society, and the state. The family treats of marriage, family capital, the education of children, and dissolution of the family. For us, family capital, dealing with economics, is of particular importance. Hegel talks of how people have common activities. Marriage is a bond between two people, and this bond is further manifested in the wealth that the family has, "the family capital." However, this common wealth eventually becomes dissolved and instead of family wealth as the basis for the unity of society people now oppose each other on the market, each with his own personal wealth. Thus, the dissolution of the family represents a move to the new kind of wealth which is discussed in civil society.

The three aspects of civil society are the system of needs, the administration of justice, and the police and the corporations. The system of needs deals with what Adam Smith called the market, and Hegel's discussion follows the one that Smith gave of the way that individual actions, such as the hunting of deer, the growing of a certain crop, or the making of a certain manufactured good, relate to other such individual activities through the medium of the market. Of course, contract also deals with the actual moment of buying and selling on the market, when two people sign a contract to give up something for something else. Thus, that section also deals with Adam Smith's market. The system of needs, however, deals not only with the actual moment of buying and selling, but also with the original activity, production, that gave rise to the buying and selling. It also treats of the satisfaction of needs that results after the buying and selling is over. Hegel's understanding that he is working within the tradition of Smith and the liberal British political economists is explicit: "Its [political economy's] development affords the interesting spectacle (as in Smith, Say, and Ricardo) of thought working upon the endless mass of details which confront it at the outset and extracting therefrom the simple principles of the thing."

Hegel stresses aspects of this political economy which have particular relevance for the relation between the individual and the whole. He notes that political economy deals with certain universal needs, such as food, drink, and clothing. As such it is "the science which starts from this view of needs and labor but then has the task of explaining mass-relationships and mass-movements in their complexity and their qualitative and quantitative character. This is one of the sciences which has arisen out of the modern world." The object of this science is "The infinitely complex, criss-cross, movements of reciprocal production and exchange, and the equally infinite multiplicity of means therein employed."[6] What interests Hegel, then, is not just that there is a market action, but how it relates to other market actions; not whether a desire is satisfied, but how that satisfaction of a desire relates to the satisfaction of other desires—in short, how political economy relates the particular to the universal, the individual to the whole.

The second aspect of civil society, the administration of justice, is concerned with various aspects of the law, the most important for us being the law's relation to property. The first concept of property is the individualistic one, close to possession, depicting property as a relation between the will and an object. The second involves the general rules for buying and selling which were discussed in relation to contract. In the third, discussed in the administration of justice, property is analyzed as a system of accepted rules which are incorporated into the legal code.

The third aspect of civil society includes the police and the corporation. "Police" here is used in the eighteenth- and nineteenth-century sense. The police not only have the familiar task of keeping the security, but also the economic one of regulating prices.[7]

Hegel's concept of the corporation is also quite different from the modern one. As an economic unit, it is larger than the individual producer and seller on the market. However, it is not just economic. It could, for example, also be a religious organization with some relation to the production and distribution of wealth.[8] The corporations' first task, among many others, is to provide security for their members. A second job is to provide information to their members concerning their purpose as a corporation as well as more general knowledge. Their educational function is seen by Hegel to accomplish the ethical task of breaking down the isolation of the individual as he appears on the Smithian market: "We saw earlier that in fending for himself a member of civil society is also working for others. But this unconscious compulsion (bewustlose Notwendigkeit) is not enough; it is in the corporation that it first changes into a known and thoughtful ethical mode of life."[9] Third, the corporation provides job security for its members. A fourth task of the corporation is to give evidence that a person has a certain skill so that it can be recognized on the market. Finally, the members of the corporation also do public work for the state.[10]

This last activity is crucial to an understanding of the economic and philosophical importance of the corporations. These institutions consciously create common elements in economic actions. As such, they do not fit in with Smith's notion of the market, that the common elements of action in the market should for the most part not be consciously created. For Smith, each individual does what he wants to do without thinking about the public good; from this welter of individual activity, the public good is served, although not consciously. Hegel's corporations inject a conscious interest in the public good into the activity of individuals on the market. That conscious interest is connected with the fact that the corporations do public work for the state and are connected with the state in other ways as well. Here Hegel supplements Smith's interest in regularities that are not planned, with a more mercantilist stress on the conscious control of the economy by the state. The connection between corporations and the state emerges clearly in Hegel's idea that the state helps to appoint the representative of the corporations. Hegel also refers to the corporations as one of the ethical roots of the state. Furthermore, Hegel's concept of corporations generally follows the Italo-Romanic school of law, which stressed that the corporations were based on the state, rather than the Germanic school, which tended to hold that the state was based on the corporation.[11]

The state is the third institution making up the ethical life. There are close connections between the three political classes of the state and Hegel's three economic classes: the agricultural, the business, and the class of civil servants. The sovereign is a political institution closely connected with the agricultural class.[12] The executive branch is also connected with the economic class of civil servants, for the executive is simply a set of people which includes the civil servants as a subset. Furthermore, the executive uses the police and the administrators of justice, both of whom are subordinated to the class of civil servants.[13] Both the agricultural and business economic classes are connected with the legislature. This connection between business and the legislature is strengthened by the corporations which are closely related to both.

In the legislative branch of the state, there are two estates or classes *(Stände)*. Hegel also uses the term *Stände* to describe the economic classes. One of the political estates represents the agricultural economic class, and the other the business class. This is not a matter of direct suffrage; rather, the corporations choose the agricultural and business representatives which then become part of the political system of classes.[14] Hegel defends this general connection between political and economic power when he argues against the idea that the "classes *(Stände)* of civil society and the estates *(Stände)* which are the 'classes' given a political significance, stand wide apart from each other. But the German language, by calling them both *Stände* has still maintained the unity which in any case they actually possessed in former times. The estates, as an element in political life . . . retain . . . the class distinctions already present in . . . civil life."[15]

The structure of *The Philosophy of Right*, then, attempts to relate the relatively unpolitical economics of classical British political economists, described in the contract and civil society sections, to an account of the state, described particularly in the corporation and state sections, that places Hegel closer to the mercantilism tradition. Furthermore, the common actions of contract and civil society are related to those of the state. However, there are other topics in *The Philosophy of Right* such as property, the family, and morality. Are the common actions of these stages also related to those of contract, civil society, and the state?

To answer this question, a distinction must be made between several different kinds of analysis that are operating in *The Philosophy of Right*. It is between those sections which analyze a society (1) as it exists, (2) as it did exist, (3) as it might come to exist, (4) as it should exist, and (5) as it could have existed. I will call (1) the synchronic analysis, (2) the historical analysis, (3) the futuristic analysis, (4) the moral analysis and (5) the possibility analysis. Like so many of the great political writings of the seventeenth to nineteenth centuries, *The Philosophy of Right* is presented with enough abstractness that it can be seen as dealing with all five elements. Nevertheless, there is a fairly clear sense in which a great part of the book is meant to analyze a society, akin to Hegel's own, or at least to his contemporary Europe. It is very important to distinguish this synchronic analysis from the other four. The synchronic analysis concerns itself with all of the interlocking features of a given society at a given time. It is distinguished from diachronic analysis, which discusses the movement of a society from the past to the present and toward the future.[16] Hegel gives a diachronic analysis, for example, when he combines (1), (2), and (3). When the analyses offered in (2) through (5) are eliminated, a core remains which presents the synchronic analysis: (1) contract, (2) civil society, and (3) the state. The others can be eliminated from the synchronic stage.

Property, for example, as treated in the first part, is an example of a possible institution. Its characteristic is that no one recognizes anyone else's criterion for property. However, in his discussion of civil society and the state, Hegel notes that property in fact must come to be defined by the state and by its role in social production, and that there must be common rules for its acceptance. Thus, property as physical possession is not part of the synchronic pattern of *The Philosophy of Right.* "Wrong" and "Morality," in turn, are examples of moral analysis. "Wrong" deals with the ethical judgments that are made on the basis of property. The basic characteristic of those moral judgments is that they cannot be enforced in the existing society. This fact gives rise to the discussion of morality where Hegel reflects upon the alienation that results when the moral judgments made by the individual cannot be translated into action. Thus, the sections on property and wrong present both an analysis of a possible world and a moral analysis based on it. The possible world is the world where no one respects anyone else's property, and the moral analysis is an analysis of alienation. This society is not an existing society, for Hegel argues ultimately that the state provides a means for securing common acceptance of property claims and thus avoids the alienation based on conflicting claims. The sections on wrong and morality deal with the individual's sense of being wronged by a hostile world. This sense of wrong is tempered by the imagined existence of a world where property claims are accepted by everyone. Thus, the individual in the worlds of wrong and morality wants to act according to the view that property is accepted by all. Nevertheless, he is faced with a world where there are conflicting claims on property and thus where there is no common recognition. For Hegel, this common recognition has to be actually grounded on the state and in civil society.

The section on the family represents a composite of a historical and futuristic analysis; these two aspects are not carefully distinguished by Hegel himself. How is the analysis of the family concerned with the past? For Hegel, the family is an institution which, among other things, allows for the creation of common rules about property ownership. There is no quarreling about ownership of the type that led to the alienation discussed in the section on morality, since common rules of ownership exist and reflect the interest of the whole family. Furthermore, they are not just economic rules, but are closely connected with the rules guiding more personal emotions, such as those of marriage.

The most striking characterization of the family is in terms of what it is not. Hegel talks of how the disintegration of the family leads to the creation of civil society and thus implies that the family was not part of civil society.[17] For Hegel, however, civil society is market society. Therefore, it can be inferred that the situation where the family creates property rules predates market society. This is borne out by Hegel's characterization of the family as being outside market relations. There is clearly a sense, then, in which Hegel recognizes that the family he describes is an institution of the past. Later on, Ferdinand Tönnies, in *Community and Society*, was to follow Hegel's implicit distinction between a society based on the economic life of the family and a society based on the market.[18] For Tönnies the earlier type of society was clearly dead. Hegel's analysis about the connection of the family economy to the market economy and his predictions for the future seem to reflect, instead, a belief that although the actual family economy is dead, its spirit continues to guide future developments. Thus, he presents an implicit diachronic theory suggesting that the growth of market society can be explained simply by the breakup of the family. He gives no account, however, of why the market society became dominant at a certain time; here he is again quite close to Smith.

In one curious passage, Hegel suggests that a society based on the economic life of the family will be resurrected in the future. This proposition, too, becomes intermingled with a causal theory of diachronic change. Hegel suggests that it is the mechanism of the market itself which results in the reestablishment of the economic system of the family. This curious idea appears in the context of a discussion of the acquisition of colonies. Of this activity Hegel says, "This far flung connecting link [Hegel is speaking of sea trade routes] affords the means for the colonizing activity—sporadic or systematic—to which the mature civil society is driven and by which it supplies to a part of its population a return to life on the family basis in a new land."[19] The confusion, as well as the unconscious humor, of this account of imperialism arises from the fact that the remembered institution of the family is seen to be the original cause of the market and of the imperialism to which it gives rise. That imperialism is seen in turn to be the cause of the restoration of the remembered institution of the family. This passage shows once again that the society based on family economy is not part of the synchronic analysis. The difference between the synchronic and nonsynchronic stage of *The Philosophy of Right* is displayed in the following chart. It must be remembered, however, that even contract, civil society, and the state contain some nonsynchronic elements.

Structure of PHILOSOPHY OF RIGHT	Synchronic Structure of PHILOSOPHY OF RIGHT
A. Abstract Right	
1. property	
2. contract	1. contract
3. wrong	
B. Morality	
C. Ethical LIfe	
1. family	
2. civil society	2. civil society
3. the state	3. the state

In order to understand the ramifications of this synchronic analysis, some general aspects of Hegel's epistemology and ontology must be examined. The three major themes are (1) subject-object identity, (2) three kinds of universals, and (3) Being, Essence, and the Notion.

In characterizing Hegelian epistemology and ontology, I am guided by the consideration that modern scholarship has many more sources for reconstructing Hegel's thought than, for example, Marx had. In particular, modern scholars have at their disposal Hegel's early theological writings as well as the early Jena writings, both of which have many interesting economic insights. On the basis of these writings, scholars have been able to give an account of such themes as subject-object identity which do not involve a total ontological view of the nature of all reality, or put the study of nature on the same level as the study of the human activity. Thus, for Emil Fackenheim, Hegel's ontology and epistemology are seen to provide a basis for an account of religious faith and of the nature of the self. Similarly, Lukács' *The Young Hegel* gives an account of the relation of Hegel's ontology to economic activity. Although Lukács displays his accommodation to the Russian philosophy of the day, by arguing that Hegel's ontology applies equally well to reality as a whole, he gives his most convincing arguments when showing precisely how it applies to society and the self.[20] The aim of the present exposition of Hegel's epistemology and ontology is to place his economic account of alienation and common actions in the context of earlier and later ones. Because of the parallels between *The Wealth of Nations, The Philosophy of Right*, and Marx's economics, *The Philosophy of Right* is most crucial for this task. This task, however, also involves understanding something about Hegel's two logics.[21]

According to subject-object identity, being is thought-like, although not necessarily the same as thought. For Hegel, thought is essentially of the universal. Furthermore, the universal helps explain the particular. Thus, the closer we get to subject-object identity, the more the universal aspect of the action helps explain the particular action.[22]

One way of interpreting subject-object identity is to assert that there is immediate and complete identity between thought and being; another, more reasonable, interpretation is that identity is only partial or is in the process of being achieved. Partial subject-object identity or subject-object identity in the process of being achieved appears in Hegel as stress on the common elements of action, coupled with stress on the tension between the common and the particular elements. The more complete the identity of subject and object, the more harmony exists between the particular and common elements.[23]

Whereas subject-object identity is a general account of reality and of how to explain it, the three universals and the Being, Essence, Notion trichotomy present particular perspectives on that general account. Furthermore, there is usually a one-to-one correspondence between the first universal as an explanatory tool and Being; the second universal and Essence; and the third universal and the Notion. This correspondence is worked out in a number of concrete examples in the two Logics, though the examples are so different that it is difficult to see one unified theory. In *The Philosophy of Right*, however, the examples are much more similar; thus, the theory emerges more clearly. Here the oppositions are used to explain concrete economic and political institutions and, in the course of doing so, they elucidate the relation of self-order to the various common economic actions found at different synchronic stages.

The three types of universals are: first, that in which the individuals who participate in the universal are not transformed by it and where the universal is not explanatory; second, that in which the universal is explanatory and the individual elements are transformed, but where this transformation involves opposition between the activity of the universal and the activity of the particular elements; third, a universal which is explanatory, in which the individual elements are transformed by their participation in the universal, and where there is no opposition between that transformation and their own activity.

Hegel refers to the first as the universality of conception, whose peculiarity is the "individualism or isolation of its contents." Each particular, Hegel says, is "unrelated," "isolated," "strung together," "only contiguous." It is also characterized as a universal where there is no necessary connection between the isolated ideas.[24] Hegel also discusses this universal in the context of the social contract theory of the state, where he notes that it is an example of atomism where "the will of individuals as such is the creative principle of the state."[25] All these characterizations back up the central definition of the first universal: that the particular elements are not transformed and that the universal itself is not explanatory of the particular. This universal appears in Hegel's discussion of contract.

Contract, as opposed to mere physical control, involves common rules for property actions. Within them people do not relate to each other only as unique individuals but as people playing common roles: "A person by distinguishing himself from himself relates himself to another person, and it is only as owners that these two persons really exist for each other. . . . This is contract." These rules define common actions, and thus Hegel thinks of the actors as participating in the universal: "Value is the universal in which the subjects of the contract participate as equals." Of this universality he says, "In the bare relation of *immediate* persons to one another, their wills while implicitly *(an sich)* identical, and in contract posited by them as common, are yet particular. Because they are *immediate* persons, it is a matter of chance whether or not their particular wills actually correspond to the implicit will, although it is only through the former that the latter has its real existence."[26] This description gives all the essential aspects of the first universal, for all the explanatory force is given to the particular and not to the common element, and there is no indication that the person is transformed by something outside him. The relation between Smith and Hegel clarifies obscurities in this passage. Hegel is simply referring to the moment of buying and selling on the market, the basic focus of the first five chapters of the first book of *The Wealth of Nations.* The two ideas, that it is chance that leads people to the market and that they see themselves primarily in terms of the abstract roles of the market, are reminiscent of Smith. The first reflects his belief that there should not be conscious planning on the market; the second reflects his deemphasis on noneconomic factors affecting the economic life.

Hegel describes the second universal as "the abstract universality which stands outside and over against the individual, the abstract identity of the understanding *(Verstand)."* Furthermore, "It is obvious at the outset that by existing only in this universal they [the individual elements] do not lie any longer part from one another, but rather are in themselves self-cancelling sides, and what is established is only their transition into one another."[27] The second passage establishes that in the second universal, the individual elements are transformed: they "do not lie any longer apart from one another." But the first establishes that there is some tension between their transformation within the second universal and their individual mode of existence; for the universal "stands over against the individual." That this tension is the result of the activity of the universal, an activity which is still opposed to that of the individual elements, emerges clearly in Hegel's discussion of civil society. For Hegel, understanding *(Verstand)* is a lower form of knowledge than reason *(Vernunft)*. Civil society is "the state based on need, the state as the understanding *(Verstand)* envisages it."[28] Thus, unity is achieved between the particulars, but the second universal which imposes this unity does so by compulsion. The second universal does transform individuals, but there is some tension between its activity and the activity of individuals; for the "unity is present here," but "not as freedom."[29]

The third universal is "concrete in character and so explicitly *(für sich)* universal. . . . This is the universal which overlaps its objects, penetrates its particular determination through and through and therein remains identical with itself."[30] It is this last definition of universality which connects the theme of the three kinds of universals most closely to subject-object identity, which involves anchoring the particular to the universal. The three universals can now be seen as stages in the achievement of that anchoring. The third universal is the last stage and, thus, fittingly describes a situation where the power of the universal over the particular is complete in the sense that it does not involve resistance from the particular. Several aspects of Hegel's description of the third universal make this point quite clear. The universal "penetrates" and "overlaps" its objects, thereby suggesting its transformational force upon particulars. Finally, it is maintained that a situation of identity has been achieved and that the particulars have been penetrated "through and through." Thus, there is identity between thought and being and no longer any tension between the activity of the universal and that of the particulars.

The third universal is operating in the state. Hegel talks, for example, of how the state is associated with rationality, and of how "rationality *(Vernünftigkeit)* consists in the thorough going unity of the universal and the single."[31] Again, the criticism that Hegel levels against Rousseau is that he sees the individual as the only cause of the state; Hegel takes this to be the main distinction between Rousseau's general *(gemeinschaftliche)* will and his own universal *(allgemeine)* will.[32] In contrast, in the Hegelian state, the universal not only helps cause the individual, but does so in harmony with individual activity:

> personal individuality and its particular interests not only achieve their complete development and gain explicit recognition for their right (as they do in the sphere of the family and civil society) but, for one thing, they also pass over of their own accord into the interest of the universal, and, for another thing, they know and will the universal. . . . The result is that the universal does not prevail or achieve completion except . . . with particular interests and through the cooperation of particular knowing and willing.[33]

In the state, then, the universal relations into which people enter are harmonious, whereas in civil society they are disharmonious.

The three universals, then, play explanatory roles in those sections of *The Philosophy of Right* which present a synchronic analysis. The first universal is associated with the realm of contract, the second with civil society, and the third with the state.

The concepts of Being, Essence, and the Notion are connected with the three universals. They have been interpreted in many ways in Hegelian scholarship, and it is not my purpose to give an account of them which will hold good for all of Hegel's writings. What is of interest here is their relation to the three universals and ultimately to the economic and political content of *The Philosophy of Right*. A very common way for Hegel to speak of the Being, Essence, Notion trichotomy is to associate Being with what is immediate and seems unified; Essence with what is divided; and the Notion with the overcoming of that division.[34]

This conception appears in *The Philosophy of Right* when Hegel discusses three stages of the will culminating in ethical life. In the three stages, the will is:

> A   Immediate; its concept therefore is abstract, namely personality, and its embodiment is an immediate external thing—the sphere of abstract or formal right.
> B   Reflected from its external embodiment into itself. The universal here is characterized as something inward, the good, and also as something outward, a world presented to the will . . . the sphere of morality.
> C   The unity and truth of both these abstract moments—the Idea of the good not only apprehended in thought but so realized . . . in the will re-

flected into itself and in the external world . . . universal existence—ethical life.

Ethical life also goes through a similar three stages; "But on the same principle the ethical substance is:
(a) natural mind, the family
(b) in its division and appearance, civil society
(c) the state as freedom."[35]
The economic and political content of *The Philosophy of Right* makes more precise the notion of the move from Being, to Essence, to the Notion as the move from immediacy, to division, to overcoming of division. Basically, at the first stage, even though thought does not appear to be in opposition to being, it actually is; at the second stage, this opposition is more apparent; at the third stage, the opposition between thought and being is overcome. Furthermore, the movement from Being, to Essence, to the Notion can be connected with the movement from the first through the third universal, thus to the synchronic analysis of society: contract, civil society, and the state. However, it is also worked out in a number of other ways. Whenever the theme of the move from Being, to Essence, to the Notion appears, it involves the theme of alienation. This is because at the Being and Essence stages, there is conflict between the thought and the being of the self. In many of these progressions from Being, to Essence, to the Notion, the theme of alienation is not clearly connected with the theme of common economic actions, although it is so in the progression from contract through civil society to the state: thus in the synchronic analysis.

In the passages above, the sphere of property ownership and abstract right is characterized as immediate; it represents the stage of Being. In contrast, the realm of morality represents the "Idea in its division." This makes sense on the basis of our original description of the content of *The Philosophy of Right*. There, property ownership was seen first to be an unproblematic relation between the self and the physical good. The self just appropriated the good; it didn't worry about distinguishing between property and theft, or about making moral judgments based on what it did. In the sphere of morality, however, the self felt uneasy about the relation between itself and the world, and began to reflect on the connections between

its actions and the actions of others, and on the possible moral judgments about its actions. Property and morality, then, correspond
to Being and Essence in the following respect. With the first, property
stage, corresponding to Being, the self that owns property has not
really conquered all the problems of its relation to the external
world, but it feels that there are no problems. It does not feel division
or tension between itself and the world. In the world of morality,
however, corresponding to Essence, the self definitely feels alienated
from the world. There it wants to act as though its claims to property
are accepted by all. Nevertheless, it is faced with a world where
there is no common recognition. There is a division or tension
between its motive for action and the way others see its action. The
Notion, on the other hand, is identified with the end of alienation
and of division. It involves "the Idea of the good not only apprehended in thought, but—in the external world." There is harmony
between the thought of the action and the action itself; subject-
object identity is completed. Furthermore, this identification of
being and thought occurs within the realm of ethical life, i.e., with
the social institutions of the family, civil society, and the state.

Nevertheless, the above progression from Being, through Essence,
to the Notion is not unproblematic. It involves mixing up the various
types of analysis found in *The Philosophy of Right.* Thus, the first,
property stage, with its apparent harmony, involves a possible
world. Morality involves the world as it should exist, and civil
society the world as it does exist. A further complication is that the
progression from Being, to Essence, to the Notion actually appears
a number of times in *The Philosophy of Right.* For example, Hegel
goes from the Being, Essence, Notion triad in (1) abstract right,
(2) morality, and (3) ethical life, to its replaying within ethical life,
where the family represents Being, civil society represents Essence,
and the state represents the Notion. Once again, Being, the family,
represents seeming lack of alienation; Essence, civil society, represents alienation; and the Notion, the state, represents the overcoming of alienation. Finally, a third way of seeing the Being, Essence,
Notion triad is through the synchronic sections where it is tied most
closely to the method of the progressive explanation through the
three universals.

Structure of PHILOSOPHY OF RIGHT	Being, Essence, and Notion in PHILOSOPHY OF RIGHT As a Whole	Being, Essence, and Notion in Ethical Life	Being, Essence, and Notion in the Synchronic Stages
A. abstract right	1. Being		
1. property			
2. contract			1. Being
3. wrong			
B. morality	2. Essence		
C. ethical life	3. Notion		
1. family		1. Being	
2. civil society		2. Essence	2. Essence
3. the state		3. Notion	3. Notion

It is the synchronic manifestation of the Being, Essence, Notion trichotomy, in contract, civil society and the state, which is most important to us. A question arises, however. What is the difference between Hegel's use of classical British political economy in the first two synchronic stages (contract and civil society) and his use of mercantilist themes in the third synchronic stage (the state)? Hegel's mercantilist discussion of the state is meant to be more explanatory than his more Smithian account of contract and civil society. The third universal involves more identity between thought and being than the first and second. Any explanation in terms of Smith should ultimately be undercut by an explanation in terms of mercantilism. Indeed, the use of the Smithian theory should not be so much to describe reality as to describe our misperception of reality. It might seem that the discussion of civil society and its universality is explanatory. In reality, however, what happens in civil society and in contract are explained not by classical British political economy, but by the more mercantilist theories about the state and its universality. There are, however, two interpretations of how mercantilist explanations undercut Smithian explanations.

If subject-object identity is interpreted as the claim that there is immediate and complete identity between thought and being, then the explanations in terms of civil society and contract are totally illusory. Both the seeming lack of alienation in contract and the seeming presence of alienation in civil society would be also illusory. After all, the alienation of civil society is deduced from economic explanations peculiar to classical British political economy: explanations which are undercut by the mercantilist theory. Only the nonalienated condition represented by the state would not be illusory. This interpretation is consistent with the synchronic analysis. It would not be claimed that the realm of contract and the realm of civil society do not exist with, but simply that they must be explained by, their role in the state.

If the opposite reading of subject-object identity is utilized, namely, that identity is only partial or is achieved only after a long process, then it could be held that the first and second universals corresponding to Being and Essence as represented in contract and civil society are not simply illusory. They do have explanatory power, which, it is true, is undercut by the explanatory power of the universal rules of the state. On this account the alienation of civil society is not totally overcome.

We have already seen how Hegel's final attitude toward subject-object oscillates somewhat. It seems that sometimes he wants to say there is immediate and complete identity rather than partial identity or progression to identity, but then he can't really show what he wants to show. His problem is to relate the three institutions and the universals that characterize them. Together these three institutions make up a whole, but the parts of that whole are not simply particular elements. Rather, they are also themselves the universal or common actions of the given institution. The whole of modern society is made up not just of particular actions, but also of actions which follow the common rules of contract, or of civil society, or of the state. Hegel's method shows how the common actions in the realm of contract are related to the common actions in the state. If Hegel uses subject-object identity to assert that there is immediate and complete identity between thought and being, then he must say that the common actions of the state explain the presence of common actions in civil society and contract. If they seem to be explained by their own rules, then that is completely illusory. But can Hegel succeed in showing that this is the case? If he can, then he can also hold that the alienation found in civil society is completely illusory. Otherwise he cannot. Close analysis of what he says about universals in civil society and the state suggests that he does not succeed in showing that the common actions of civil society are completely explained by the common actions of the state. He does succeed, however, in showing that the common actions in the realm of contract are completely explained by the common actions in civil society.

The connection between civil society and the contract is different from the connection between the state and civil society. Hegel is able to show that contract entails civil society and that civil society entails contract. However, he is not able to show that state entails civil society, although he is able to show that civil society entails the state.

The difference between Hegel's analysis of the relation of contract to civil society and the relation of civil society to the state is that contract simply is the civil society looked at from a limited point of view. But civil society is not simply the state looked at from a limited point of view. The whole section on contract simply describes the market as it exists from the point of view of the individual who buys and sells. He sees no connection between his buying and selling and the social distribution of goods, but that does not mean that the connection is not there. For Hegel, the universal used to explain contract is not meant to explain reality fully, but rather it shows a tendency on the part of individuals who do not understand the whole to think about reality in a certain way. Hegel did not think that the atomistic society of people who only meet on the market, Adam Smith's society of petty commodity producers, could account for the tendency of men to perform as many common actions as they did. Thus, the realm of contract, analogous to Smith's petty commodity production, is shown by Hegel to be explained only in civil society, where the total social distribution of goods is analyzed along with the class divisions that accompany that social distribution. For Hegel, the difference between contract and civil society is the difference between a limited aspect of a whole and the whole itself. Thus, the analysis that he gives of contract does not conflict with the analysis that he gives of civil society. It is true that in the one case individuals are the sole cause of their action, and in the other case, the whole of society and the common elements of action help explain individual action. There is no contradiction, however, between the mode of explanation appropriate for contract and that appropriate for civil society, for the one explains an illusion and the other a reality. This methodology separates Hegel from Smith because for Smith there is a contradiction between the individualism of petty commodity production, which he conceives of as a reality, and the analysis that he gives of developed capitalism.

An analysis must now be given of how the explanation of contract in terms of civil society is different from the explanation of civil society in terms of the state. The first issue is property. In the realm of contract, property is still seen to arise out of the individual's physical relation to material goods. However, in civil society, property must be defined by the courts, and in the section on the state, Hegel shows that the courts of civil society serve the end of the state. Thus, contract is first explained by the courts of civil society, but those courts are in turn explained by their role in the state.

The principle of rightness passes over in civil society into law. My individual right, whose embodiment has hitherto been immediate and abstract, now similarly becomes embodied in the existent will and knowledge of everyone, in the sense that it becomes recognized. Hence property acquisitions and transfers must now be undertaken and concluded only in the form which that embodiment gives to them. In civil society property (Eigentum) rests on contract and on the formalities which make ownership capable of proof and valid in law.[36]

The fact that contract is now seen as a necessary condition for property belies the contention, found in the property section, that property is simply an expression of the relation of the will to the external world. Property now entails contract. Furthermore, contract is now seen to entail the realm of law as found in the courts of civil society. The courts, however, are ultimately part of the executive branch of the state. Thus, contract entails not only civil society, but also the state. Moreover, civil society as a whole entails contract. Civil society involves market exchange, which involves the contracts that people make who buy and sell on the market. Civil society entails contract because contract stands to civil society as the part stands to the whole.

The relationship of civil society to the state is much different. The courts of civil society entail the state. Furthermore, it can be shown that other aspects of civil society entail the state. In spite of Hegel's efforts, however, he never does show that the state entails civil society.

In showing the relation between civil society and the state, Hegel presents a picture much different from Adam Smith's, who preferred to abstract from the state. Even differences between Smith's and Hegel's accounts, which do not seem to involve the state directly, nevertheless often involve it indirectly. One of the primary ways in which Hegel differs from Smith is that he is more insistent in claiming that it is not just particular elements (individuals on the market) versus laws of the market which are the objects of study in economics. Rather, different individuals are grouped together into economic classes or corporations, and these groups are also part of the object of political economy. The market is the competition not of individuals but of groups. This is true of each of the three classes and also of the corporations. Hegel's greater stress on group rather than individual competition is linked with his concept that classes are both political and economic. The business classes and the class of civil servants are dependent upon the state.[37] The class of civil servants is simply part of the executive branch of the state, and the members of the business class are represented in the state by the corporations to which they belong. The members of the corporations, furthermore, are themselves partially appointed by the state. Thus, since for Hegel civil society is defined as the competition of groups and since those groups are partially created by the state, it therefore follows that the competition which is found in civil society is dependent upon the state.

This account of state intervention in the groups that make up the market shows how for Hegel the more Smithian theory is undercut by the more mercantilist theory. It also shows how explanation in terms of the second universal is undercut by explanation in terms of the third universal. For civil society, taken by itself, deals with individuals striving for ends which they do not see as being naturally consistent with the ends of all. Indeed, insofar as the ends of all are accomplished, this seems to be something which does not happen because of their particular motive, but rather because of external elements that they do not control. Hegel describes this situation both in concrete economic terms and in terms of the second universal. The economic content goes back to Smith with his theory that individuals strive on their own to accomplish things, and that then the good of all is attained by a causal process other than their own—what Smith calls the "invisible hand." The individual buys and sells for his own interest on the market. The invisible hand, acting through the law of supply and demand, brings it about that he may be forced to move into a different area of work. Finally, the invisible hand brings it about that the good of all is somehow accomplished. For Hegel, as we have seen, political economy describes this process. It is

the science which starts from this view of needs and labor but then has the task of explaining mass-relationships and mass-movements in their complexity and their qualitative and quantitative character. This is one of the sciences which have arisen out of conditions of the modern world. Its development affords the interesting spectacle (as in Smith, Say, and Ricardo) of thought working upon the endless mass of details which confronts it at the outset and extracting therefrom the simple principles of the thing, the understanding (Verstand) effective in the thing and directing it. It is to find reconciliation here to discover in the sphere of needs this show of rationality (Scheinen der Vernünftigkeit) lying in the thing and effective there; but if we look at it from the opposite point of view, this is the field in which the understanding (Verstand) with its subjective aims and moral fancies vents its discontent and moral frustration.[38]

The "understanding effective in the thing" is simply the activity of the second universal which brings it about that things work out for the good of all. Here Hegel's philosophical interpretation of Smith does not change the basic content of Smith's theory. The basic content does become changed, however, when Hegel holds that it is only an illusion to think of the efficacy of the second universal as opposed in some way to the causal force of individuals. For to think this leads to the moral fancy venting its discontent and frustration, a process which was described in the sections on wrong and morality as leading to alienation. Now Hegel wants to say that this alienation is only an illusion. However, in spite of Hegel's claim to have shown the illusoriness of this alienation, his own analysis of alienation definitely represents an advance over previous theories.

Alienation follows from the presence of the second universal because that element of action which arises from the individual as unique cause is in tension with that aspect of his action which is brought about by the relation of his action to other common actions. The economic content of this theory is that the individual's action of producing a good or of selling on the market is explained both by his unique desire and by its relation to the whole of society's actions. Unlike the whole of property-holding actions, the whole of actions producing for the market cannot be explained by the conscious following of a code written down on paper. Furthermore, the absence of such a code makes the common elements in these actions and their relation to the whole much more difficult to see. This helps explain why there is tension between the common and individual aspects of the action. Another reason for this tension is that the individual does not control the common aspect of his action which relates him to the whole in the way that he controls the unique aspect. When Hegel argues that we see the illusoriness of alienation in civil society when the role of the state is understood, he stresses how the state intervention in the economy increases control and consciousness of both common actions and the individual's relation to the whole.

Hegel now proceeds to show that civil society is actually dependent on the state. Thus, explanation in terms of the second universal is undercut by explanation in terms of the third universal. This undercutting involves Hegel's own account of the alienation of civil society being overthrown. Where Smith had thought that the market either arose from individuals or from the invisible hand, Hegel now argues that it is planned by the state. This intervention of the state in the market prevents the alienation that Hegel associates with the Smithian market. The state does not represent the invisible hand, some holistic causal force which is independent of individuals; rather, it represents the conscious activity of individuals as a group in planning economic activity.

This intervention of the state appears in a number of other ways, all of them designed to show the illusoriness of the alienation which appears to exist in the market: the opposition between the individual as cause of his action and the economy as a whole as cause of his action. One example is the way that the state helps to create the groups that compete in the market. A second example is the activity of the corporations themselves. As we have seen, they consciously strive for job security for their members. They help educate their members and they give them the knowledge of their role in the economic life. In Hegel's description of the corporations, it is very clear that he is opposing the alienation of the Smithian market to the lack of alienation in his own state-dominated civil society: "We saw earlier that in fending for himself a member of civil society is also working for others. But this unconscious compulsion is not enough. It is in the Corporation that it first changes into a known and thoughtful ethical mode of life." Hegel's conception of the activity of the police again shows how he imagines that the alienation of Smith's market is prevented by state intervention into the market. One task of the police is to regulate prices. Hegel justifies this activity on the basis that the state must put order into particular interests:

The differing interests of producers and consumers may come into collision with each other; and although a fair balance between them on the whole may be brought about automatically, still their adjustment also requires a control which stands above both and is consciously undertaken. The right to the exercise of such control in a single case (e.g., the fixing of prices of the commonest necessities of life) depends on the fact that, by being publicly exposed for sale, goods in absolutely universal daily demand are offered not so much to an individual as such, but rather a universal purchaser, the public.[39]

The notion that goods on the public market are sold to a universal purchaser leads to one final general point about the role of state intervention in the market. For Hegel, the aim of the state is to uphold the common interests of the community. In speaking of the state's relation to the individual, he notes that in it "the individual's destiny is the living of a universal life."[40]

Hegel, then, has succeeded in showing that the market entails the state. The third universal, present in the state, is now shown to be the most explanatory. There is no opposition in the state between the thoughts of people and their deeds, nor is there any opposition between their activity and the activity of the universal. Alienation is ended, or so it seems. But now a skeptical question arises. Alienation will only really be ended if the rules of the state completely explain civil society, if the rules of civil society are shown to be totally illusory. We should, then, be able to understand civil society and contract by understanding the nature of the state. Civil society should not only entail the state; the state should also entail civil society. But never in *The Philosophy of Right* does Hegel show that the state entails civil society or even anything close to that. Indeed, it is apparent that Hegel's method was to take the market as he knew it and then to idealize it in certain ways, so that it could be seen to entail the state. Thus, he looks at the market and notes that there are class divisions. Instead of explaining this fact within market rules, he argues that these classes arise from the state and reflect the harmony found there. But he never shows why the state should take such a long way around to achieve social distribution. Why should it create classes which then compete in the market, which then results in social distribution. Why doesn't the state bring about social distribution of goods directly? Thus, Hegel never shows that the state entails the market. The rules of the capitalist market have an autonomy of their own which cannot be explained away by mercantilism.

The plan of *The Philosophy of Right* shows the connections between various institutions: the contract and the market (the paradigm of the classical British political economists), and the state (the paradigm of the mercantilists). Subject-object identity emerges in *The Philosophy of Right* as, among other things, the theory that the more mercantilist explanation undercuts all others. Hegel's theory attempts to show that the universals of the state are more explanatory than the universals of civil society and contract. However, it fails to show that the universals of civil society and contract are completely explained by the universals of the state. Hegel claims that the state has ended alienation. But the realistic description of alienation found in the realm of essence, the second universal, civil society, suggests that alienation is not overcome in the state, the Notion, the third universal. The state hovers between being the

actuality that overcomes alienation and being the hope that alienation will be overcome.

The plan of Marx's economic writings also shows a connection
between the common actions of various institutions. Marx, however, does not even attempt to show what Hegel failed to show;
that complete subject-object identity holds. Thus, the third universal and the Notion do not operate in Marx's critique of capitalism.
Furthermore, Marx, will bring to fruition the theory of alienation
that Hegel begins to elaborate, but then argues is only an illusion.

Marx

The section on Marx has the following structure: Chapter Six analyzes the structure of Marx's economics, in conjunction with the notion of the progression from the abstract to the concrete. Marx's plan leads him to a holistic analysis of capitalist society, which is seen as being made up of three separate social wholes: the realm of the market and production for value (the paradigm of classical British political economy), the realm of social reproduction (the paradigm of physiocracy), and the realm of political economics (the paradigm of the mercantilists). Chapter Seven concentrates on the ghostly or nonmaterial objectivity of value, showing how it is bound up with holism and ultimately with a concept of how the universal aspect of man's action in capitalist society is set against him and alienated from him. Chapter Eight delineates a concept of political exploitation or alienation more directly bound up with the way the capitalist uses force against the workers in order to keep the realm of value and social production going. Chapter Nine expands the concept of alienation arrived at in the previous chapters and examines how many types of alienation exist in capitalist society as a whole. Chapter Ten analyzes the epistemological and ontological bases of the concept of a social whole.

CHAPTER SIX

The Structure of Marx's Economics: The Abstract and the Concrete

Toward the end of 1857, a significant cluster of events was occurring in the life of Karl Marx. Between 1852 and 1856, he had been forced to abandon his plan for a great synthesis of economics. Bad health and the necessity of earning a living through journalism had not given him time. Now, however, he was trying to achieve his synthesis, spurred on partly by his desire to understand more fully the economic crisis that was enveloping the capitalist world. His excitement is reflected in his letters: "I am working madly through the night on a synthesis of my economic studies, so that I at least have the main principles *(Grundrisse)* clear before the deluge."[1] This renewed work on his economic studies was accompanied by a new interest in applying aspects of Hegel's methodology to economics:

By the way, things are developing nicely. For instance, I have thrown over-board the whole doctrine of profit as it has existed up to now. In the method of treatment the fact that by mere accident I again glanced through Hegel's *Logic* has been of great service to me. . . . If there should ever be time for such work . . . , I would greatly like to make accessible to the ordinary human intelligence, in two or three printer's sheets, what is rational in the method which Hegel discovered but at the same time enveloped in mysticism.[2]

From this time until his death in 1883, Marx produced *The Grundrisse der Kritik der Politischen Ökonomie (Grundrisse), A Contribution to the Critique of Political Economy (Critique),* an "Introduction" which can be seen as a foreword to either the *Critique* or the *Grundrisse*, the three volumes of *The Theories of Surplus Value*, the three volumes of *Capital*, the sixth, unpublished, chapter of *Capital*, the "Critique of the Gotha Program," the "Marginal Notes on Adolph Wagner's *Lehrbuch der Politischen Ökonomie*," plus a number of economic notes and drafts that are just now being published.[3] These works have a unity, centering on such themes as surplus value and labor power, which set them off from Marx's earlier works. They form the basis for my accounts both of Marx's economics and his notion of self and alienation.[4] This chapter is concerned with the overall structure of Marx's post-1856 economics. In the introduction to the *Grundrisse*, Marx presents that structure in relation to the progression from the abstract to the concrete. Understanding the nature of that progression demands textual analysis of Marx's plan for structuring his economics. We can examine that plan in two different stages: first, by comparing one of Marx's *Grundrisse* plans and the structure of *The Philosophy of Right*; second by examining the relation between Marx's *Grundrisse* plan and the plan for *Capital*.

There is strong evidence for a connection between Marx's *Grundrisse* plan for his economics and the synchronic structure of *The Philosophy of Right*. In both cases there are five categories:

Grundrisse	The Philosophy of Right
1. General abstract definitions	1. Contract
2. The categories which make up the inner structure of *bürgerliche* society and on which the fundamental classes rest—capital, wage labor, landed property	2. Civil *(bürgerliche)* Society
	3. The state
	4. The state in relation to foreign states
3. The synthesis *(Zusammenfassung)* of bourgeois society in the form of the state	5. International law[5]
4. International relations of production	
5. The world market	

The most obvious parallels are between the last four categories. Hegel's and Marx's discussions of *bürgerliche* society portray a capitalist economy, particularly in its class basis. Furthermore, as we will see, Marx's concept of the synthesis of *bürgerliche* society in the state parallels Hegel's methodology of relating the explanation of *bürgerliche* society when understood by itself to its explanation when understood in relation to the state. It was suggested earlier that Hegel's state had mercantilistic aspects. That Marx is also considering the mercantilistic aspects of the state is suggested by his stress on the state's relation to national wealth:

> The concept of national wealth creeps into the work of the economists of the 17th century—continuing partly with those of the 18th—in the form of the notion that wealth is created only to enrich the state, and that its power is proportionate only to this wealth. This was the still unconsciously hypocritical form in which wealth and the production of wealth proclaimed themselves as the purpose of modern states and regarded those states henceforth only as means for the production of wealth.

Marx goes on to talk of the "Synthesis of bourgeois society in the form of the state. Viewed in relation to itself. The 'unproductive' classes. Taxes. State debt. Public credit. The colonies. Emigration."[6] Taxes and public debt clearly reflect mercantilist interest in the state as an active economic factor. The unproductive classes were discussed by the Physiocrats in conjunction with the role of the state in the economy. The topics of colonies and emigration reflect the state's role in furthering international economic activity.

The fourth and fifth categories correspond also, except that Hegel describes the political state in regard to other states and then describes world law, whereas Marx first describes international relations of production and then world trade. This correspondence is particularly striking because Marx follows Hegel's curious differentiation between the topic of the one state in relation to all other states and the topic of the relations of all states, without considering the perspective of one particular state. Marx discusses the progress from the "internal structure" of production to "the synthesis of the whole in the state," then to the international relations of production, and finally to the world market.[7] This suggests that Marx is not merely mimicking the formal structure of Hegel's distinctions. Rather, production is seen first in its internal structure, then in its synthesis in the state, then in its external relations, and finally the external relation, the world market itself, is concentrated upon.

The problem of the relation between the first categories, Marx's general abstract definitions, and Hegel's contract, is somewhat more complicated. The general abstract definitions are concepts associated with Smith's petty commodity production, which Marx often calls "simple exchange" or "simple circulation."[8] As with Hegel's discussion of contract and Smith's of petty commodity production, the general abstract definitions give an analysis of the market without class division. For Marx, that means also leaving out the buying and selling of labor power, just as for Hegel it means leaving out corporations and for Smith leaving out the distribution of commodities among the classes. It would be a mistake to imagine Marx's plan in the *Grundrisse* as simply mimicking the structure of Hegel's *Philosophy of Right*. To the themes of petty commodity production, capitalism, and the state, Marx also adds concern with social production and general opposition to any theory which begins with individuals, conceived of as outside of social relations: "Individuals producing in society—hence socially determined individual production—is, of course, the point of departure." Furthermore,

The population is an abstraction if I leave out, for example, the classes of which it is composed. These classes in turn are an empty phrase if I am not familiar with the elements on which they rest, e.g., wage labor, capital, etc. These latter in turn presuppose exchange, division of labor, prices, etc.[9]

Population, of course, was discussed by all economists, but there was a certain group who stressed it: those who emphasized the role of demand in economic theory. Marx thought those who ignored social relations conceived of population as "a chaotic conception of a whole *(Ganzen)*" rather than as a "whole" *(Totalität)* of many determinations and relations."[10] A relation, as we saw in our discussion of Kant, is simply a type of common element or universal. Those who begin with population see individuals without relations as opposed to those who see individuals in their relations within society as a whole.[11] It is important to realize that population, when seen as a "chaotic conception of the whole"—that is, as made up of individuals without relations—becomes a "whole of many determinations and relations" when the individuals are seen in the light of the social relations of (1) petty commodity production, (2) the capitalist market, (3) social production, and (4) the state. Basically, then, Marx's *Grundrisse* plan emphasizes four topics. First, it is concerned with the difference between petty commodity production and capitalism, the latter being bound up with classes, and the former not. This account is connected with the classical British political economists' account of the market. Second, the plan is more concerned with the topic of social production, of individuals producing together, than either Smith or Hegel had been. This is a typical physiocratic theme. Third, it is concerned with the role of the state. This is a typical mercantilist theme. Fourth, it opposes those who begin with common relations between individuals, whether these relations be in the market (as, for example, the classical British political economists), in social production (as, for example, the Physiocrats), or the state (as, for example, the mercantilists), to those economists who begin with individuals seen without common relations and abstracted from the whole of society.

We now must compare Marx's plan as it appeared around the time of the writing of the *Grundrisse* and the *Critique* (1857-1859) and his plan as it appeared around the time he was getting ready to publish *Capital*, volume one (1867). Roman Rosdolsky has presented the following comparison between one of the 1857 plans and one of the later plans.

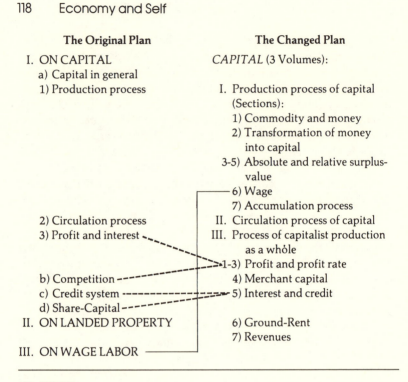

The Original Plan

I. ON CAPITAL
  a) Capital in general
    1) Production process

    2) Circulation process
    3) Profit and interest

  b) Competition
  c) Credit system
  d) Share-Capital
II. ON LANDED PROPERTY

III. ON WAGE LABOR

The Changed Plan

CAPITAL (3 Volumes):

I. Production process of capital
  (Sections):
  1) Commodity and money
  2) Transformation of money
    into capital
  3-5) Absolute and relative surplus-
    value
  6) Wage
  7) Accumulation process
II. Circulation process of capital
III. Process of capitalist production
    as a whole
  1-3) Profit and profit rate
  4) Merchant capital
  5) Interest and credit

  6) Ground-Rent
  7) Revenues

IV. STATE
 V. FOREIGN TRADE
VI. WORLD MARKET[12]

Basically, three separate topics figure in both plans. First, there is the discussion of petty commodity production and the production process of capital which has to do with the creation of new value for the market. This can be seen as simply a part of the proposed discussion of *bürgerliche* society in the *Grundrisse* plan. As a matter of fact, it is the primary topic of the first volume of *Capital* and of the first one hundred or so pages of the chapter on capital in the *Grundrisse*. The second topic is the circulation process of capital which is discussed primarily in the second volume of *Capital* and throughout the second half of the *Grundrisse*. Here the concept of social production is deepened, going beyond the *Grundrisse*'s stress on individuals producing together, to include the whole macro-economic idea of the total production of goods and distribution of labor and goods in the economy. When Marx developed this concept, he was very much taken with Quesnay's *Tableau Économique*— enough so that we can now refer to this aspect of Marx's economics as social reproduction. The third topic is how the value created in production is sold on the market. This includes discussion of competition, share capital, profit and profit rate, credit and interest, and ground-rent and landed property. This topic appears in the third volume of *Capital* and in various sections of the second chapter of the *Grundrisse*.[13]

We can now see more clearly how the plan for *Capital* corresponds to the *Grundrisse* plan:

Grundrisse	Capital
1. Petty commodity production and *bürgerliche* society	1. Petty commodity production and the production process of capital
2. Social production	2. Social reproduction
3. The state	3. ?
4. Population	4. Competition

Two questions arise about the comparison of the two plans. First, does the discussion of competition in *Capital* parallel the discussion of population in the *Grundrisse*? The answer seems to be yes. In both cases, stress is laid on individual variations amidst general tendencies. Concern with population shows how individuals work in unique ways within the general abstract categories; concern with competition shows how the general amount of value produced by labor is divided on a day-to-day basis by individual firms.

The second question is, does the plan for *Capital* include the proposed *Grundrisse* section on the state? The answer is that careful reading of the description of Marx's object of study in the "Preface" to *Capital* suggests that there is room for the state or of the political aspect of economics: "In this work I have to examine the capitalist mode of production and the relations of production and interaction (*Produktions-und Verkehrsverhältnisse*) that correspond to that mode." Moore and Aveling translate this as: "In this work I have to examine the capitalist mode of production and the conditions of production and exchange corresponding to that mode."[14] But *Verkehrs*, which Moore and Aveling translate as "exchange" and I as "interaction," cannot be limited to the realm of exchange, nor did Marx ever do so. It has to do with human interaction in general. The advantage of my translation is that it allows the possibility that, had he finished his work as originally planned, Marx would have included the state, or at least the political aspect of economics.

I offer the following plan as a combination of the terminology of the *Grundrisse* and *Capital* plans:

1. Petty commodity production and the production and distribution of value in capitalism
2. Social reproduction
3. The state or political economics
4. Individual elements seen in relation to general laws or forms

These four categories can be related to Marx's famous method of progressing from the abstract to the concrete. For Marx, the relation of petty commodity production to the capitalist economy is an example of the relation of the abstract to the concrete. I will argue, however, that it is only one example and that there are two other ways of relating the abstract to the concrete. A second is the relation of the general laws of the capitalist market to individual interactions on that market. The third is the relation of the capitalist market, social reproduction, and the state to each other.

Marx's discussion of the abstract and the concrete contains one of his most explicit accounts of his relation to the Hegel. Discussing two paths that economics could take, beginning with abstractions or not, Marx notes that the former is obviously the scientifically correct method, and that both he and Hegel utilize it at the beginning of their work in economics.[15]

Petty commodity production and contract are abstract, as opposed to the capitalist economy and civil society, which are concrete. Petty commodity production and contract, abstract, for example, from classes. In one of the *Grundrisse* plans, Marx declares: "The economic conditions of existence of the three great classes into which bourgeois society is divided are analyzed under the first three headings (capital, landed property, wage labor)."[16] These three classes, as we have seen, are the ones described by Adam Smith in *The Wealth of Nations* from the sixth chapter of the first book to the end. These classes, however, are not discussed in the first five chapters dealing with petty commodity production, just as they are not described in the section on contract in *The Philosophy of Right*. Classes make their appearance in *The Philosophy of Right* only with the discussion of civil society, and in *The Wealth of Nations*, only with capitalism.

Nor does Marx differ from Smith and Hegel in starting right out with a discussion of class society. Of the *Critique* he observes: "The first part of the first book, dealing with Capital, comprises the following chapters: (1) the commodity; (2) money or simple circulation; (3) Capital in general. The present part consists of the first two chapters."[17] Thus, capital is never even reached in the *Critique*. Furthermore, it can be understood in what sense it is not reached if the *Critique* is compared to the *Grundrisse* and to *Capital*. Section (I), part (1) of *Capital* is called "Commodities and Money"; section (2) is called "The Transformation of Money into Capital." It is only in the second section that Marx begins to talk specifically about capitalism. In the *Grundrisse, Capital*, and the *Critique*, there are two sections to be spelled out before capital is introduced: commodities and money. This discussion took Marx so long in the *Critique* that the book never got to capital.[18]

It is the division of the subject in the *Grundrisse* that sheds the most light on the distinction between petty commodity production and capitalism. The *Grundrisse* has two chapters: one on money and one on capital. Discussion of classes originates in the second chapter with the discussion of the buying and selling of labor power. On the other hand, the *Critique* and the first sections of *Capital* and the *Grundrisse* present interconnected definitions of value, money, commodity, exchange, and labor that are appropriate for both petty commodity production and capital and do not entail classes. The *Critique* and the first sections of *Capital* and the *Grundrisse* do not present the buying and selling of labor power which is a class concept and appropriate only for capitalism, not for petty commodity production.[19]

It is the concept of labor power that gives Marx a clue to resolving the problems in Smith's account of the relation between petty commodity production and capitalism and the related problem of inequalities and the labor theory of value.

As noted in the chapter on Smith, the problem in his account of value is that if the value of the good is equal to labor time, then if the worker sells his labor time he should sell it for the value of the good he produced. In capitalism this does not happen.

Since Marx wants to show that the labor theory of value holds in capitalism, he must, therefore, get around this objection to it. He does so by arguing that the worker does not exchange his labor time, but his labor power. Labor power is the ability to create labor time. The worker sells his ability to create labor time to the capitalist rather than the labor time that he creates. This ability to create labor time is called labor power. It can be looked at from the perspective either of the labor time which is necessary to create it, or of the labor time which it creates. If looked at from the first perspective, what is measured is the value of what is necessary to create labor power; if looked at from the second perspective, the value that labor power creates is measured. It is the first perspective that allows wages to be understood, whereas it is the second that allows surplus value to be understood. Surplus value is measured by labor time that labor power creates minus the labor time necessary to create labor power.

In an illustration of this account in *Wages, Price and Profit*, Marx analyzes a situation where the labor time necessary to create labor power is six hours, but where the worker works for twelve hours.[20] The wage of the worker is determined by the six hours rather than by the twelve hours. The reason is that the wages are determined by the value of the labor power as measured by the labor time necessary to create that labor power; they are not measured by the value of the labor time which that labor power creates. When the labor time or value necessary to create the labor power is subtracted from the labor time that the labor power creates, the result is surplus value. In this case, value worth six hours of labor time goes to pay the wages of the worker. That six hours is subtracted from the whole value created, which is equal to twelve hours of labor time. What remains is the surplus value which goes to the capitalist. In this case, since six subtracted from twelve is six, the surplus value of the capitalist is measured by six hours of labor time.

Thus, Adam Smith's problem of wages is solved. It is not necessary to do as Smith did and develop an account of the distribution of wealth which is inconsistent with the labor theory of value.

When it is seen that the worker exchanges his labor power rather than his labor time, then the logical implication of the labor theory of value is not that he should tend to get the value of the product that he produces as his wage.

Furthermore, it is now possible to state more precisely the relation between petty commodity production and capitalism. Petty commodity production implies a market run according to the labor theory of value in a situation before labor power is introduced as a commodity. Capitalism implies a market run according to the labor theory of value in a situation where labor power is bought and sold on the market and thus has commodity status.

Is petty commodity production, then, a totally illusory realm for Marx? "The predominance of capital," he notes, "is the presupposition of free competition, just as the despotism of the Roman Caesars was the presupposition of free Roman 'private law.' "[21] Yet Marx did not hold that all examples of petty commodity production presupposed capitalism; he was simply critical of the idea that petty commodity production could bring about social reproduction, an idea that Smith sometimes falls into. For Marx, however, petty commodity production is either a onesided way of looking at the capitalist economy, which really brings about social reproduction, or a minor factor in bringing it about in a noncapitalist society.

In either case, one can conceive of the economic relations between the exchangers in all their simplicity, "without connection to more highly developed production relations."[22] For Marx, those more highly developed relations, which include the buying and selling of labor power, are presupposed whenever exchange relations dominate, even though this does not always appear to be the case: "In order for individuals to face each other in circulation, in the simple relations of buying and selling as free private producers, there must exist more complex relations which more or less conflict with their freedom and autonomy."[23]

The question of the existence of market forms before capitalism has been a confusing point in Marxian scholarhip because the first part of *Capital* stresses petty commodity production so much and because some of Marx's own comments on this point are so ambiguous. Marx, for example, has told us that "exchange value leads an antediluvian *(antidiluvianisches)* existence," which is obviously a kind of jest.[24] If Marx means by antediluvian that it preceded the flood, then he is just pulling our leg. If he just means that it is old, then there is a lot he must fill in:

There would still always remain this much, however, namely that the simple categories are the expressions of relations within which the less developed concrete may have already realized itself without having posited the more many-sided connection or relation which is mentally expressed in the more concrete category; while the more developed concrete preserves the same category as a subordinate relation. *Money may have existed and did exist historically, before capital existed, before banks existed, before wage labor existed, etc.* Thus in this respect it may be said that the simpler category can express the dominant relations of a less developed whole, or else those subordinate relations of a more developed whole which already had . . . historic existence before this whole developed in the direction expressed by a more concrete category.[25]

Money, which for Marx is a type of exchange value, is the abstract category here, and capital the concrete category. But what does it mean to say that the abstract categories or petty commodity production can exist within the "less developed concrete," or the "less developed whole," before the concrete category of capital comes to exist? Marx notes that although

the simpler category may have existed historically before the more concrete, it can achieve its full (intensive and extensive) development precisely in a combined form of society. . . .
    . . . . The intimations of higher development among the subordinate animal species . . . can be understood only after the higher development is already known. The bourgeois economy thus supplies the key to the ancient, etc. But not at all in the manner of those economists who smudge over all historical differences and see bourgeois relations in all forms of society. One can understand tribute, tithe, etc., if one is acquainted with ground rent. But one must not identify them.[26]

This commentary shows that it is only in a very limited sense that Marx thought that market forms existed before the buying and selling of labor power. Either they appear to exist as dominant, which is an illusion, or they do exist, but not as dominant, which is no illusion.[27]

I have now used one aspect of the abstract-concrete dichotomy to analyze the relation between petty commodity production and the capitalist economy, which seems to parallel the relation between contract and civil society in *The Philosophy of Right*. Several aspects of Hegel's philosophy must be recalled at this point before I turn to the other two interpretations of the progression from the abstract to the concrete.

For Hegel, the progression from the first to the third universal was in terms of the ability of universals to transform particulars— from no domination in the first to transformation which is in conflict with the particular in the second, to harmonious domination in the third. This meant that explanation in terms of particulars was subordinated to explanation in terms of universals, and that explanations in terms of each universal were subordinated to explanations in terms of the next universal. Subordination of explana- in terms of the first universal to explanation in terms of the second universal was accomplished quite simply. It only meant that the common actions of contract had to be explained by the common actions of civil society. This was the more easily done since it could be shown economically that the full development of contract required the development of capitalism, and that this full development of contract involved the abandonment of the presupposition of isolated individuals contracting with each other. It was not so easy to accomplish the subordination of explanation by the second universal, which had to do with the description of capitalism given by Smith, to explanation in terms of the third universal, which had to do with a more mercantilistic description of capitalism. To do this, he must not simply show that capitalism, as described by the liberal British political economists, entails the state. He must also show that the state entails capitalism. This he does not do; thus, he does not show that explanation in terms of the third universal undercuts explanation in terms of the second universal.

Marx's use and critique of Hegel can be understood against this background. Like Hegel, Marx moves from the abstract to the concrete, interpreted as moving from contract to civil society (Hegel), or from petty commodity production to the capitalist economy (Marx). In both cases, that move involved progression from very general ways of defining common actions to more specific ways of defining common actions. Thus, for Marx, actions connected with exchange value could occur in any market society, but actions involving capitalism could occur only in societies where exchange value measures labor power as well as other commodities. The difference between the two should not overshadow the fundamental similarity that for Marx and Hegel, both the abstract and the concrete as applied, respectively, to contract and civil society or to petty commodity production and the capitalist economy, involve common ways of defining action. It is just that the abstract relations of petty commodity production and contract provide common definitions that have greater generality than the more concrete relations of the capitalist economy and civil society. On this point, then, there is homology between Hegel's method and Marx's method. Marx, it is true, rejects what he conceives to be the Hegelian theory that the forms of society proceed from the mind. As we have seen, however, this dependence of being on thought is not entailed by Hegel's distinction between contract and civil society. Thus, Marx's rejection of the former Hegelian point does not prevent him from utilizing the latter one.[28]

The second mode of moving from the abstract to the concrete is Hegelian in a different way. It is from the general laws of the market to particular variations on these laws.

We have seen that beginning with the whole and the common relations in it is opposed to beginning with nonrelational individuals of the population economists. From this opposition is developed the second interpretation of the progression from the abstract to the concrete. On the first interpretation, there is a progression from a more abstract common definition of action in terms of petty commodity production to a more specific but still common definition in terms of capitalism. On the second interpretation, there is progression from the common elements of a whole to particulars. "Thus, if I were to begin with the population, this would be a chaotic conception of the whole, and I would then, by means of further determinations, move analytically towards ever simpler concepts, from the imagined concrete towards ever thinner abstractions until I had arrived at the simplest determinations. From there the journey would have to be retraced until I had finally arrived at the population again, but this time not as the chaotic conception of a whole, but as a rich totality of many determinations and relations."[29] In terms of economic theory, the result of an analysis that proceeds from discussing the common relations of the whole to discussing the parts is a move from general regularities in market prices to the variation in market prices brought about by the variations in the makeup of individuals or individual firms that compete in the market. This involves a greater attention paid to supply and demand as well as other factors which determine how well individual firms do on the market.

On the first interpretation, the progression is from abstractions to the whole, and on the second, from abstractions to particulars. In neither case, can Marx be said to be emphasizing particulars rather than common elements. In the first case, he stresses moving from very common ways of looking at action to less common ways; in the second case, he stresses moving from common relations to the particulars that enter into them.

Insofar, then, as the second interpretation is connected with Hegel, it is connected to the domination of universals over particulars rather than with the domination of one universal over another. On the first interpretation, the move from the abstract to the concrete is from an illusory realm, petty commodity production, to the reality of the capitalist economy. On the second interpretation, it is from the generality of theory to empirical particularity.

On the third interpretation, the move from the abstract to the concrete is from each element of the capitalist economy considered by itself, value and its relation to the capitalist market, social reproduction, and the political whole, to the whole formed by uniting each part with the other part. This third aspect of the progression from the abstract to the concrete has been obscured because Marx sometimes sounds as though the abstractions are always those of petty commodity production.[30] But the state and the other elements that make up the capitalist economy (value and social reproduction) are all abstractions too. As abstractions, they do not have the illusoriness that surrounds the forms of petty commodity production. They all, however, define actions in terms of common elements, although the abstract concepts of petty commodity production give more general definitions than do the more specific but still common concepts of value, social reproduction, and the state, as they define capitalism as a whole, "a rich totality of many determinations and relations."

In Hegel, the third progression from the abstract to the concrete would be from civil society to the state. Civil society and the state, like value, social production and politics, are social wholes. For Hegel and for Marx, the concept of social whole is bound up with the progression from the abstract to the concrete. That method involves examining particular actions in the perspective of social relations. A social whole is a combination of social relations and the particular actions that occur within those social relations. However, there is a difference and continuity between Marx's and Hegel's use of social wholes in the third progression. For Hegel, civil society is ultimately explained not by its own laws, but by the laws of the state. There is alienation in civil society, but that alienation is shown to be illusory when looked at from the point of view of the capitalist state. For Marx, on the other hand, each social whole, value, social reproduction, and the state, has a certain amount of independence from the other. Marx does not have anything that plays the same role as the state. In Hegel's view, the common rules of the state not only explain the particular actions of those who act within the state, but also show that the rules for action of the marketplace are illusory and must be explained by the rules of the state. Thus, the state is the super totality which supersedes all other possible social wholes. In Marx's economics, none of the three social wholes can totally explain the operations of the other. Rather, (1) certain aspects of each particular action must be understood in relation to the common rule of a given social whole, and (2) each common rule has some connection with every other common rule.[31]

The similarity in their treatment is that the third progression is from one common way of defining action to another equally common way. For Hegel, however, there is no possibility of conflict between these two ways of defining action, since in the end only the definition of action that arises out of the state is true; the others are illusory. For Marx, in contrast, each common way of defining action, value, social reproduction, and the state has a certain amount of truth; this results in a possible conflict between the various ways of giving common definitions to action. The possibility of this conflict also makes alienation possible, arising out of the individual's relation to the whole.

When the move from the abstract to the concrete is from value to social reproduction to the political whole, then the abstract is each considered by itself and the concrete is all considered together. Here the concrete must be the collection of rules which can simultaneously provide common definitions for action. It is a social whole, which includes the social wholes of value, social reproduction, and the state. Within capitalism as a whole, each smaller social whole, with its common way of defining action, is linked with the other two wholes and their way of defining common action.[32] The third move from the abstract to the concrete links the common actions of those who buy and sell labor power, those who work together in social reproduction, and those who participate in the political and state relations that affect the capitalist economy. Civil society and the state, like value, social production and politics, are social wholes. For Hegel and for Marx the concept of social whole is bound up with the progression from the abstract to the concrete. That method involves examining particular actions in the perspective of social relations. A social whole is a combination of social relations and the particular actions that occur within those social relations.

In the chapter on Marx's conception of alienation and the self, I will suggest that Marx's conception of alienation in the *Grundrisse* and *Capital* is linked with the way the social wholes of capitalism are reproduced. Before this can be done, however, more features of the value and political wholes must be examined.

CHAPTER SEVEN

Economic Value and Ontology

We have already encountered the famous labor theory of value in our discussion of Smith. We have also seen how value is one of the social wholes that Marx reaches in his progress from the abstract to the concrete. But what is economic value? Although value is often closely connected with price, in that it is meant to explain why things sell the way they do, in a larger sense value theory supplies the broadest possible framework for an economic theory—what modern philosophers of science have called a paradigm. Ronald Meek has perspicuously captured this broader aspect of value theory as it operates in Marx:

> In Marx's hands, the theory of value is not simply a theory which sets out to explain how prices are determined: it is also a kind of methodological manifesto, embodying Marx's view of the general way in which economics ought to be studied and calling for a restoration of the essential unity between the different social sciences.[1]

Of course, there is a common denominator in all economic value theories or paradigms. They are all concerned with price in some way. However, the classical value theory of Smith, Ricardo, and Marx is concerned with price in a different way from, for example, the subjective value theory of a Jevons.[2]

By relating to price, theories of economic value hook up with theories of value in general, for value in general has to do with what is worthwhile. Price is related to value in general insofar as price is related to what is worthwhile, for what is worthwhile is in some sense desirable. Prices reflect in some way what people find desirable. Thus price and value in general as something worthwhile are connected through the concept of the desirable.

How then is price related to economic value as opposed to value in general? In subjective value theory, the answer is easy. Prices, as we have just seen, can be related, through their desirability, to the worthwhile, thus to value in general. Insofar as economic value theory examines price as something worthwhile, it is a subcategory of general value theory. Subjective value theory has an edge over other economic value theories insofar as it presents a straightforward continuity between the ordinary concept of value and the economic concept. In classical value theory, however, particularly Marx's, the continuity between the concept of value in general and economic value is broken down.

In classical value theory, price continues to be related to the generally valuable. Economic value, however, is now not the same as that part of the generally valuable which has a price. Rather it is, among other things, the essence behind the price. By showing how economic value is the essence of price, Smith, Ricardo, and Marx create a rift (not unbridgeable, but still a rift) between economic value and value in general.

For whereas it is intuitively obvious that what has price is desirable and in that sense worthwhile, it is not so intuitively obvious that the essence behind the price is worthwhile and desirable. It is intuitively obvious that the price is worthwhile because the fact that people are willing to pay a price for something shows that it is desirable. But there is no reason for assuming that because the price is worthwhile and desirable, the essence behind the price is therefore worthwhile and desirable. Smith, Ricardo, and Marx admit that price expresses the desirable and worthwhile, but their economic value theory attempts to get at the essence behind that price, and that essence may or may not be desirable and worthwhile.

However, is not the labor of an economy something which is desirable and worthwhile? Certainly. So insofar as Smith, Ricardo, and Marx say that labor is the value which is the essence of price, don't they in fact wind up with an economic value which is simply an aspect of value in general? The only difference between them and the subjective value theorists would be that for the classical value theorists value is what is ultimately worthwhile and desirable rather than, as is the case with the subjective value theorists, what is immediately worthwhile and desired—i.e., price.

Thus, if value is labor, there is no essential dichotomy between Smith's, Ricardo's, and Marx's concepts of value and that of the subjective value theorists in that both concepts of economic value would *ultimately* exhaust their meaning in the ordinary concept of value as what is worthwhile and in the concept of price. However, the argument holds that there is no essential dichotomy between subjective and classical value theory only if we accept the notion that labor, which is certainly worthwhile and desirable, is economic value and the essence of price. However, I will argue that Marx, contrary to popular opinion, did not accept the notion that value is labor. For Marx, not labor in general, but a special kind of labor, abstract labor, alienated labor, is the essence of value. I will further argue that abstract labor involves a holism of common elements which is necessary to truly differentiate Marx's value theory from theories like subjective value theory. This holism often receives its expression in a doctrine of what Colletti has called "nonmaterial objectivity."[3]

My first task in this chapter, then, is to analyze the concept of the nonmaterial objectivity of value and its relation to the idea that not labor in general but abstract alienated labor is the essence of value. My second task is to show how this nonmaterial objectivity relates to the concepts of holism and common elements of action. My third task is to lead into the discussion of alienation in Chapter Nine.

The best way to understand Marx's concept of nonmaterial objectivity is through the history of the interpretation of his labor theory of value, a history in which the Russian economist I.I. Rubin plays a special role.[4] Rubin's work arises out of a tradition that began with the Neo-Kantian movement in Germany, particularly the writings of Franz Petry and Rudolph Hilferding on the labor theory of value.

Both Rubin, as a Hegelian Marxist, and Hilferding and Petry, as Neo-Kantian Marxists, stressed that Marx in his labor theory of value was not concerned with the same questions as the subjective value theorists. This sharp differentiation between Marx and subjective value theory was first taken up by Hilferding in 1904 in his reply to Böhm-Bawerk's criticism of Marx. Hilferding argued that Marx's labor theory was concerned with social relations whereas subjective value theory was not.[5] A variation on this point was taken up again in 1916 by Petry, who argued that there was a clear distinction between those who were concerned with the material and technical sides of value theory and those concerned with social relations. Petry said that the former were occupied with the quantitative, the latter with the qualitative, value problem.[6] Lukács and Korsch, writing in 1923, also stressed the social side of value; and Paul Sweezy began *The Theory of Capitalist Development* in 1942 by quoting from Hilferding, Petry, and Lukács, and arranging the opening chapters of his book around the distinction between the quantitative and qualitative value problems.[7]

Some theorists, working within the tradition of seeing value as a social form and bound up with social relations, have noted the peculiar way that Marx speaks of the objective nature of value. Lukács talks of how behind the reified commodity form, Marx stresses activity rather than things, so that his basic theme can be characterized as "the retranslation of economic objects from things back into processes, into the changing relations between men." Rancière argues that the objectivity of value "only exists as the expression of a social unity, human labor." Rubin talks of how the labor that creates value "must be understood as a social category in which we cannot find a single atom of matter."[8]

The concept of nonmaterial objectivity in Marx's economics has a complex history. On the one hand, those who have approached Marx's economics from the material, technical side have been blind to it.[9] On the other hand, even some, such as Petry and Hilferding, who have recognized the social basis of Marx's theory have been unable to clearly recognize the concept of nonmaterial objectivity. Others, like Rancière, Lukács, and Colletti, who have seen both the social basis of value and the ontological reality of nonmaterial objectivity, have not given an adequate economic analysis of these concepts. Rubin has supplied an adequate economic analysis of the concepts of social form and nonmaterial objectivity and has sketched their Hegelian basis, but he has tended to remain at the surface of the Hegelian philosophy. Lukács has come closest to giving an adequate ontological analysis, but his account needs to be supplemented by Rubin's economic account; and both need to be complemented by the concept of a holism of common elements.[10]

Before we sketch Lukács' and Rubin's analyses and a possible way of extending and synthesizing them, we must show how both Rubin and Lukács, as Hegelian Marxists, were reacting against a philosophical current which was responsible for both the achievements and the limitations of the Marxist interpretation of Hilferding and Petry; i.e., we must understand the Hegelian reaction against the Neo-Kantianism of late ninteeenth- and early twentieth-century German philosophy. If it was Neo-Kantianism which gave rise to the social reality interpretation of value, it was the Hegelian reaction against Neo-Kantianism that paved the way for understanding value as nonmaterial objectivity.

Lucien Goldmann has given an interesting analysis of the relation between Neo-Kantianism and Hegelianism in this period. Goldmann argues, as I have, that the basic categories of thought and action in Kant are collective in that all men, potentially or actually, share them. All men, for example, think causally. However, in Kant these categories are separated from the world. The man who thinks and acts according to the collective forms of ethics or science wonders whether these forms describe or operate in objective reality. Goldmann argues that Kant wanted to anchor these collective forms in the world, but because he could not fulfill this desire, his was a tragic vision. The tragic vision belongs to all who believe in man's communal nature but can only give a mental or spiritual account of it—where in man's thoughts he is communal but in practice, in the world, he is not. For Goldmann Neo-Kantianism is very different from Kantianism.

For the Neo-Kantians, the collective subject only existed as a series of ultimately subjective mental or social forms. The Neo-Kantian transformaton of philosophy, occurring as a reaction against Hegel in the latter part of the nineteenth century, was most apparent in Marburg, home of Neo-Kantian philosophy of the natural sciences, but it was also found in the *Südwest-deutsche Schule*, which included Freiburg and Heidelberg. However, it was precisely in these latter two universities that a reaction against Neo-Kantianism from within began to emerge in the early twentieth century. In Freiburg this came from Husserl; in Heidelberg the main figure was Emil Lask. Goldmann stresses that both of these thinkers returned to Hegel by attacking the separation of man from the world and deepening the Kantian and Neo-Kantian stress on collective forms by giving them objectivity. Out of this milieu finally came Lukács' *History and Class Consciousness*. This most decisive break with Neo-Kantianism and the German Marxism of the second international ultimately originated in Heidelberg, where Lukács had been Lask's student and where, between 1913 and World War I, he had begun to work his way out of Neo-Kantianism.[11]

The relation between Neo-Kantian and Hegelian approaches to the labor theory of value, a subject which Goldmann does not analyze, is very complicated. For, as we have seen, it was Neo-Kantian interpretations, such as those of Petry and Hilferding, which had argued against the dominance of the technical and material side of value; and Hegelian Marxists like Lukács and Rubin agreed with the Neo-Kantians on this issue. For the Neo-Kantians, however, the nontechnical social side of value too often tended to become like a form of the mind which had no objectivity. As we have seen, Neo-Kantian approaches characteristically conceived of social reality as ultimately subjective. The idea of a social whole which is both external and internal, of the sort that we saw operating in the *Philosophy of Right*, was foreign to Neo-Kantianism. But classical value theory, particularly Marx's, expressed what happened when people were dominated by a whole which was not simply mental but had the objectivity of something external to the mind, i.e., had a nonmaterial objectivity.[12]

We can understand this external aspect of the value whole better by underlining the difference between the mercantilist method of defining common actions in terms of property and the classical British political economists' method of defining them in terms of value. For mercantilism, the similarities between property actions were consciously understood, because they followed a rule which was recorded in lawbooks. Thus, mercantilism reflected the traditional rationalist interest in the conscious activity of individuals. The concept of value, on the other hand, stresses that there are regularities which cannot be reduced to the conscious following of a rule written down on paper. We saw earlier how the concepts of property and value, as they operated for the eighteenth-century economists, worked to explain the process by which certain actions were brought about. The concept of value, however, since it did not heavily stress the individual's conscious understanding of what he was doing, lent itself much more than the concept of property to forming the basis of a theory of alienation. Theorists of alienation hold that actions are brought about because of social structures which the individual neither understands nor controls. This lack of consciousness associated with value-creating actions is recognized by Marx when he talks of how the "whole" of value-creating actions "arises out of the interactions of conscious individuals, but does not lie in their consciousness and as a whole is not controlled by them."[13] Other passages also emphasize this lack of consciousness and control:

In order for men to relate their products as commodities, they are forced to equate their different types of labor as abstract human labor. They do not know that they are doing this, but they do it insofar as they reduce the material thing to the abstraction value. This is a natural and hence un-conscious instinctive operation of their brains, which necessarily grows out of the particular mode of production and of the relations in which it sets them.[14]

It was Lukács' merit to have shown that there was an opposition between the active creation of the value whole and the reified existence of the value whole as it interacted back on the people who actively created it. But Lukács left his analysis too general. He Hegelianized Marx without showing in detail how Hegelian categories operated in Marx's economics. Because of this failure, he was never able to decisively defeat either positivistic or Neo-Kantian approaches to the labor theory of value.[15] Before we supplement Lukács' philosophical Hegelianism with Rubin's economic Hegelianism, we must look at some of Marx's own comments on the social nature of value and its nonmaterial objectivity.

Marx commonly talks about the "natural form" of the commodity. The natural form is just the commodity's physical properties, which have a use value. Of the commodity as use value, Marx stresses that it is "an external object," and that it is conditioned by its "physical properties." Value or exchange value, as opposed to this, "cannot be a geometrical, physical, chemical or any other natural property of commodities," and "has a purely social reality." In another context, Marx talks of value as a "characteristic which belongs in an objective *(sachliche)* way to the thing itself, although this objectivity does not appear in its natural form."[16]

What is the basis of the opposition between social and physical objectivity of value? A basic philosophical presupposition of Marx's account of the physicality of commodities is that they are external to the mind and cannot be understood simply through an analysis of action. They have a certain independence from action even though action may transform them. Marx wants his own analysis of the importance of action in economics to avoid two dangers: that of mistaking actions for something material and that of mistaking something material for actions. The first mistake is "material fetishism . . . where not only the difference between man and animal disappears but even the difference between a living organism and an inanimate object." The second mistake is made by thinkers like Hodgskin in whose economics the "whole objective world, the 'world of commodities', vanishes . . . as a mere aspect, as the merely passing activity, constantly performed anew, of socially producing men."[17]

Marx condemns Hodgskin for underplaying the natural physicalness of objects. Yet this very nonphysicality of Hodgskin's system is what makes it so important for Marx's theory of value, which in many ways is much more based on social action than on physical objects.[18] Marx was on the side of Hodgskin when he warned against the attempt to give a physical interpretation of the objectivity associated with value and the abstract labor that creates it:

How much some economists have been tricked by the fetishism that clings to the commodity world, or by the objective appearance of the societal determination of labor *(gegenständlichen schein der gesellschaftlichen Arbeitsbestimmungen)*, is shown, among other things, by the boring, absurd quarrel over the role of nature in the creation of exchange value. Since exchange value is a specific social means of expressing the labor which has been put into a thing, it can no more contain natural material than the rate of exchange can.[19]

It is not, however, just commodities that have nonmaterial objectivity. It is also the abstract labor that produces them. Marx thought that one of the three most important discoveries of *Capital* was that the distinction between value and use value must be complemented by a similar distinction between the abstract labor which produces value and the concrete labor which produces use value. Labor is abstract because it has a common or universal element that creates value. It is "labor in this general form," labor "as such" *(überhaupt)*, labor which is "simply labor" *(Arbeit schlecthin)*, which has "abstract universality" *(abstrakten Allgemeinheit)*, and which has "indifference toward the specificity of labor." *(Glechgültigkeit gegen die bestimmte Arbeit)*.[20]

The abstract labor that produces commodities, like the commodities themselves, has a peculiar type of objectivity. On the one hand, the abstractness of labor "is not merely a mental product." On the other hand, it is not something natural either, for Marx complains of Boisguilbert, who confused the "labor which is objectified" with the "immediate natural activity of individuals."[21]

All this is not to say that abstract labor does not need the physical side of commodities. Labor itself does not have value. It must be congealed in a commodity to have value: "human labor—power in its fluid state, or human labor creates value, but is not itself value. It becomes value only in its coagulated state, in objective form."[22] Without commodities with their physical forms, there could be no abstract labor. However, it is equally the case that without abstract labor there could be no commodities. Abstract labor and commodities go together and both have nonmaterial objectivity. That both labor and commodities have nonmaterial objectivity is stated strikingly by Marx when he notes that in socialism as opposed to capitalism "just as little does the labor which has been transformed into a product, appear as the value of that product, as an objective *(sachliche)* quality possessed by it."[23] This passage affirms that the objectivity associated with value is possessed both by the commodity and by abstract labor. For it is the labor which appears as the value, the *sachliche* property, and similarly it is the commodity which has this value, this same *sachliche* property. For the phrase "the labor which has been turned into the product" we could substitute the phrase "the product which has been transformed from labor." The point is that when one is talking about the x that is represented by value, then one can substitute the phrase which has labor for the subject for the phrase which has the product for the subject, suggesting an interchangability, if not an identity, between value and abstract labor.

The linguistic form that Marx uses to express the relationship between labor, on the one hand, and the value of commodities, on the other, also suggests identity between the two. For he commonly talks of how labor is representative *(dargestellte)* in the value of commodities. If Marx had simply been talking straightforwardly about one entity, labor, which produces another, the value of commodities, it would have been easier to talk of labor creating value. However, the very term "represent" suggests that value is simply a manifestation of labor. Rancière has argued that the concept of representation, *Darstellung,* suggests that commodities are not treated "simply as things" but rather are analyzed in terms of the labor represented in them.[24] Because the commodity is not simply a thing, it cannot be referred to by simply pointing at it. It is *sinnlich-übersinnlich* (perceptible-imperceptible). It includes not only the physical properties of the good, but also the abstract labor connected with the good. Unfortunately, the very fact that Marx uses the term "commodity," with its connotation of materiality and thinghood, tends to suggest that, like other economists who had used the term, he is dealing simply with a physical thing which happens to be sold on the market. Yet, all of Marx's warnings should militate against such a confusion on the part of the reader.[25]

Since the whole concept of the mysterious objectivity of value and abstract labor has been so much ignored and misunderstood, it is worthwhile to look in more detail at the language that Marx uses to express the objectivity of value.

In the *Critique,* Marx refers to value as a "crystalization" *(Kristallisationen)* and "materialization" *(Materiature)* of societal labor, as "objectified labor" *(vergegenständlichte Arbeit),* as "congealed labor time" *(festgeronnener Arbeitzeit),* and as "objectified universal labor time" *(vergegenständlichte allgemeine Arbeitzeit).*[26]

In *Capital,* values are "objective" *(sachliche)* expressions of the human labor spent in production. Commodities are "societal things" *(gesellschaftliche Dinge),* and the value of a commodity "is simply an objective reflex of expended labor, but this is not reflected in its body."[27]

Similar language appears in the *Grundrisse*. "Each commodity . . . is the objectification *(Vergegenständlichung)* of a specific amount of labor time." Money (which for Marx is a type of value) "presupposes the objectification *(Versachlichung)* of the societal bond"; "individuals' own exchange and production stands over against them as an independent, objective *(sachliches)* relationship." The development of exchange value is identified with "the exchangeability of all products, relations, against a third, objective *(sachliches)* thing."[28]

One path toward unraveling the mystery of what Marx means by the objectivity associated with the value of commodities and abstract labor is philological. In German the adjective *sachliche* has a very different meaning from simply material. In general, it has the connotation of factuality or objectivity. Thus, the phenomenological motto *zu den Sachen Selbst* (to the facts themselves) does not refer to material objects but to the aim of achieving objectivity. When Marx says that the objective property *(sachliche Eigenschaft)* of commodities disappears in socialism, he cannot mean that the material properties of the commodity will disappear. Given these linguistic points about how the term *sachliche* is used in general and by Marx in particular, we must now ask: What is the economic basis for Marx's concept of the nonmaterial objectivity associated with both the commodity and the abstract labor that produces it? The key to answering this question lies in showing the closest possible relation if not identity between the value of the commodity and the abstract labor that produces that value. Showing this will ultimately have the additional advantage of allowing us to show that value is not itself something that is generally valuable in the noneconomic sense (as value is for the subjective value theorists), but rather something that is alienating.

The economic analysis of the relation between the value of the commodity and abstract labor has been best accomplished by Rubin. Rubin also sketches an ontological basis for his theory of economic value. However, as we will see, his ontological account often fails to get beyond the periphery of the Hegelian basis of Marxist economics, concentrating on such concepts as for n and content which, although important in Marx and Hegel, are not as central as the concept of holism out of which they arise. After we have seen how Rubin lays the basis for the economic analysis of nonmaterial objectivity, by showing the close connection between value and abstract labor, we will relate his account to a holism of common elements, which we will see as forming the ultimate ontological basis both for Marx's theory of the nonmaterial objectivity of value and abstract labor and for his account of alienation.

Rubin's first argument is that critics have neglected an important way of talking about the labor theory of value, namely in terms of the question of why labor becomes value or takes the form of value. Rubin, more clearly than other interpreters of Marx, has stressed the opposition between the form and content of value. For Rubin the concept of the form of value or the social form of value is very much bound up with the stress that critics like Hilferding and Petry had put on social relations as opposed to individual desires and technology. However, unlike Hilferding and Petry, Rubin stresses the Hegelian rather than the Kantian basis of the form/content opposition.

One cannot forget that, on the question of the relation between content and form, Marx took the standpoint of Hegel, and not of Kant. Kant treated form as something external in relation to the content, and as something which adheres to the content from the outside. From the standpoint of Hegel's philosophy, the content is not in itself something to which form adheres from the outside. Rather, through its development, the content itself gives birth to the form which was already latent in the content.[29]

Rubin's point is that for Hegel (and for Marx) the form, as for example the form of value, is a definite modification of the content. Marx himself stresses the importance of form: "It is scarcely astonishing," Marx observes, "that economists, completely under the influence of the interest in content, have overlooked the formal aspect of the relative expression of value, given that before Hegel even professional logicians overlooked the formal aspect of their models for judgements and conclusions."[30]

Rubin gives economic content to the form/content opposition. In analyzing Marx's statement that not only the magnitude but also the form of value must be analyzed, Rubin notes that "from value seen as a quantitatively determined magnitude, we must pass to value which we treat as a qualitatively determined social form. In other words, from the theory of the magnitude of value, we must pass to the theory of the form of value *(Wertform).*"[31]

Rubin argues that for Marx the form of value is tied with the market, but the content is not. It is remarkable that Rubin's discovery of this point should have remained so unrecognized and so unduplicated, since Marx has repeated the same point in so many places. For example, Marx utilizes the distinction between the form and content of value in a critique of the German economist Rodbertus:

> If he had searched further for the concept of value he . . . would have discovered that the value of a commodity only expresses in historically developed form what has existed in all other societal formations albeit in another form, namely the societal character of labor insofar as it exists as the expenditure of societal labor power. If the value of a commodity is only a determinate historical form of something that exists in all societal formations, then too, however, this is also true of the social use value as it characterizes the use value of the commodity. Herr Rodbertus has gotten the measure of the quantity of value from Ricardo. However, even as little as Ricardo has he searched for or conceived of the substance of value, for example the societal character of the labor process in primitive communities as the common organism of interconnected labor powers and therefore of labor, i.e., the expenditure of these powers.[32]

A similar distinction between the form and content of value is made in a letter to Kugelmann where Marx notes that there are two aspects of the labor theory of value: the part which deals with a natural law (Marx uses the language of the Physiocrats here) and the part which deals with a particular form of that natural law. The natural law is the necessity of every society to distribute labor in such a way as to reproduce a certain level of economic wealth—i.e., what we have called the content of value. The particular form of the natural law, the form of value, is the production and distribution of value for the market which is one way, but not the only way, of accomplishing social reproduction. The natural law cannot be abolished, but the way in which the natural law is manifested, its form, can be changed: "Natural laws cannot generally be abolished *(aufgehoben)*. What can be changed in historically different circumstances is only the form in which these laws assert themselves," a form which Marx goes on to identify with exchange value.[33]

The distinction between what is accomplished through value relations and the value relations themselves is referred to again in a discussion of a precursor of physiocracy, Boisguilbert. Marx contrasts his positive contribution, which was to talk about the reproduction of the total social wealth through the distribution of labor, with his negative contribution, which was to identify this distribution with the form that it takes in capitalist society: "Boisguilbert, indeed, sees only the material *(stoffliche)* content of wealth, its use value, enjoyment of it, and regards the form of labor, the production of use values as commodities and the exchange of commodities, as the naturally appropriate *(naturgemasse)* social form in which individual labor attains this object."[34]

Value in terms of its general form, then, must be understood as the way in which the natural activities of producing together and of distributing labor and goods are achieved. What is achieved is the content of value, which was discussed primarily by the Physiocrats under the rubric of social reproduction. The way of achieving social reproduction is the form of this content and is similar to the realm of value and the market discussed by Smith and Ricardo.[35]

I have said that Rubin has stressed how critics have neglected to approach Marx's concept of value in terms of why labor takes on the form of value. The next stage in his argument is to stress the difference between this dialectical method of approaching value and the more conventional analytic method. Whereas the dialectical method is to begin with labor and then ask why it expresses itself in value, the analytic method is to begin with value and then, by asking what is the substance of value, move to labor. Now both ways of formulating the theory of value lead to a stress on labor. Furthermore, both say something true about value. The dialectical method is concerned with the way that labor becomes value, whereas the analytic method implies that the substance of value is labor. Their starting points are different. One begins with value, the other with labor. Their end points differ as well. With the dialectical method, labor is analyzed in terms of a social form rather than seen as labor in general. In contrast, with the analytical method, since one starts out with value, and then moves to labor, labor is not defined in terms of a social form, but simply as labor in general, labor which is the same for all historical epochs independent of their social forms. Rubin argues that the difference between the method of beginning with value and the method of beginning with labor reflects itself in the characterization of the labor which is the substance of value.[36]

In the literature at least two different kinds of labor have been seen as the substance of value: social labor and abstract labor. Let us consider social labor first. For Rubin labor "is social if it is examined as part of the total mass of homogeneous social labor or, as Marx frequently said, if it is seen in terms of its 'relation to the total labor of society'."[37] Social labor is what we have called the content of value, the natural interconnectedness of labor in social reproduction. It is the same for all societies and is seen as the substance of value by those who begin with value, move to labor, and ignore labor's social form.

What, then, is meant by abstract labor? Abstract labor is not social labor in general, but that social labor which produces the value of commodities. Abstract labor is seen as the substance of value by those who begin with labor and then ask why it takes on a given social form. Marx has clearly illuminated the opposition between social labor and abstract labor. "Labour which manifests itself in exchange-value appears to be the labour of an isolated individual. It becomes social labour by assuming the form of its direct opposite, of abstract universal labour."[38]

In summary, Rubin argues that if one approaches Marx's theory from the standpoint of value and then asks what the substance of value is, then one is inclined to say that it is social labor. However, if one begins from another perspective, i.e., with labor and asks why it takes on the social form of value, then one is inclined to say that the substance of value is abstract labor. It is not intuitively obvious why social labor in general should take on the commodity form of value. One can only arrive at the concept of abstract labor by asking what happens to action in a market society. At the time that Rubin was writing, there was a debate going on in Russia about the existence of value under socialism. Some had held that there would be value in socialism, some that there would not be. Rubin notes that he takes a middle road in these debates. From the perspective of the analytical method, the labor that produces value is an eternal necessity. From the dialectical perspective, the labor that produces value is bound up with market society.[39]

The distinction between the form and content of value has the advantage of allowing us to distinguish between action in a market economy, which has both the form and content of value, and action in a nonmarket economy, which has only the content of value. Often in precapitalist economic formations, for example, social reproduction occurs without the market. Goods are directly distributed through the conscious plan of society rather than through the market.

Activity, regardless of its individual manifestation, and the product of activity, regardless of its particular make-up, are always *exchange value*, and exchange value is a generality, in which all individuality and peculiarity are negated and extinguished. This indeed is a condition very different from that in which the individual or the individual member of a family or clan (later, community) directly and naturally reproduces himself, or in which his productive activity and his share in production are bound to a specific form of labour and of product, which determines his relation to others in just that specific way.[40]

Communal production without the market is also characteristic of socialism and communism. "Within the cooperative society based on common ownership of the means of production, individual labor no longer exists in an indirect fashion," as in capitalism, "but directly as a component part of the total labor."[41] Marx's account of the difference between market and nonmarket society was bound to remain obscure until the publication of the *Grundrisse*, where Marx elaborates on the distinction between belonging directly and indirectly to the total labor of society. Individual labor belongs indirectly to the total social labor when its role there is not determined until the good is sold on the market. It exists directly when its role in society's labor is seen without the good being sold on the market.

The labour of the individual looked at in the act of production itself, is the money with which he directly buys the product, the object of his particular activity; but it is a *particular* money, which buys precisely only this *specific* product. In order to be universal money directly, it would have to be not a particular, but universal *(allgemeine)* labor from the outset; i.e. it would have to be posited from the outset as a link in universal production. . . . But on this presupposition it would not be exchange which gave labor its universal character; but rather its presupposed communal character would determine the distribution of products. . . . On the basis of exchange values, labor is posited as universal only through exchange. But on this foundation it would be posited as such before exchange. . . . In the first case the social character of production is posited only *post festum* with the elevation of products to exchange values and the exchange of these exchange values. In the second case the social character of production is presupposed, and participation in the world of products, in consumption, is not mediated by the exchange of mutually independent labors or products of labor.[42]

Thus, in the nonmarket system labor becomes common or universal, in the sense that it serves the interests of society as a whole, through the direct conscious control of the participants. In the system of production and distribution for the market, however, people must sell the good that they have created before it can be distributed; thus the labor that produced that good is not seen to be common until that sale is made. In the first case the commonness is apprehended immediately. In the second case it only becomes apprehended later. As we will see, the first type of commonness is in harmony with individuals, the second opposed and alien to them.

Why is social labor, connected with the content of value, in harmony with individuals, and abstract labor, associated with the form of value, not in harmony with them? The three characteristics of social labor are (1) that physiologically most labor is expenditure of muscle and brains, (2) that the quantity of labor is always of importance to societies, and (3) "as soon as men start to work for each other in any way, their labor also assumes a social form."[43] These three characteristics are either physical or social without being abstract and possessing nonmaterial objectivity. Like use value, concrete labor has a naturalness, a sensuality, opposed to the nonmaterial objectivity of the labor which produces for the market. In contrast, when abstract labor produces for exchange, "the product of particular labor must prove itself as objectification of universal societal labor by taking the form of a thing, money, something which is presupposed exclusively as the immediate objectification of universal labor." When universal labor must be objectified in this way, it must exist to the individual exchangers as "an independent subject opposing them, as something which is at the same time an independent external, chancelike objective element *(Sachliches)* which opposes them."[44]

We now begin to see more clearly the importance of Marx's utilizing the Hegelian as opposed to the Kantian conception of form. Only the Hegelian conception allows the form to really transform the content. Abstract labor, which opposes individuals, is labor which has had its natural qualities transformed by the social form into which it has entered. As we will see, to fully understand the difference between social and abstract labor, we must supplement the concept of the form and content of value with the concept of a holism of common elements.

We have now analyzed and extended Rubin's program of showing the importance of beginning with labor and then asking why labor takes the form of value. An effect of Rubin's argument is to show the close connection, if not identity, between value and abstract labor. This point emerges more clearly with Rubin's analysis of the relation between the equalization of labor and commodities and the concepts of actual and potential exchange.

What is the equalization of commodities and abstract labor? We arrive at the necessity of its concept by again contrasting the way labor is distributed in a market and a nonmarket society. "In an organized economy," Rubin notes, "the relations among people are relatively simple and transparent."[45] Such a community must examine where to put labor and equalizes labor in the sense that it sees each part of labor as comparable with every other part. Now this same process of distribution of labor is accomplished in a market, but there the equalization of labor is dependent upon the equalization of commodities on the market, i.e. the process by which commodities are compared. Marx describes this process in the following way:

Men do not therefore bring the products of their labour into relation with each other as values because they see these objects merely as the objective *(sachliche)* integuments of homogeneous human labour. The reverse is true: by equating their different products to each other in exchange as values, they equate their different kinds of labour as human labour. They do this without being aware of it.

We can see from the key word *sachliche* that Marx is talking about the nonmaterial objectivity associated with abstract labor. Rubin is quite clear on this pont too, as he draws the conclusion that "there is nothing more erroneous than to interpret these words as meaning that the equality of things as values represents nothing more than an expression of physiological equality of various forms of human labor."[46] The equalization both of labor and of commodities involves the ghostly objectivity of the abstract labor that produces value. Equalization has nothing to do with the physical nature of the commodity, but rather with the social form in which objects become commodities. The simultaneous equalization of the value of commodities and the abstract labor that produces them again show the close relation if not the identity between value and abstract labor. When equalization is related to the concept of actual and potential exchange, the near identity of abstract labor and value is established even more strongly.

A commodity has value before it is actually compared on the market with other commodities. It then has the potential for exchange. A commodity has exchange value when it is actually being compared on the market with other commodities. It then has the actuality of exchange.[47]

Rubin connects the concepts of equalization and actual versus potential exchange. He argues that for Marx, value, what we have called potential exchange, can only be equalized if the labor that produces it is oriented toward actual exchange. Rubin's critics have seen in this point a backsliding toward nonclassical economy, toward the notion that value arises out of exchange rather than being created in production. Rubin, however, argues that value is only created in a production which is oriented to exchange.

In the second edition of *Capital* we find the well-known sentence: "The equalization of the most different kinds of labor can be the result only of an abstraction from their inequalities, or of reducing them to their common denominator, viz., expenditure of human labor-power or human labor in the abstract." In the French edition Marx, at the end of this sentence, replaced the period with a comma and added: "and only exchange brings about this reduction, opposing the products of different forms of labor with each other on the basis of equality."[48]

Rubin draws the interesting conclusion from Marx's doctrine of the equalization of labor that it shows, on the one hand, that value has to be based on labor expended in production relations and, on the other hand, that labor itself already bears the form of exchange if it is labor that is oriented toward exchange. Value, then, is not based totally on production relations thought of as independent of exchange (the interpretation of those in Russia who held that value continued to exist in socialist society; the position that Smith and Ricardo sometimes seemed to hold, and that one might deduce from that aspect of the labor theory of value which begins with value and then asks what is the labor that produces value). Neither is value based totally on exchange itself (the position held by Bailey and the vulgar economists in criticizing Ricardo and by Böhm Bawerk and the subjective value theorists in criticizing Marx). Value and the abstract labor that produce it are based on production for exchange and cannot be separated from either producton or exchange.

How does the close connecting of value and actual exchange help build the concept of the identity or near identity of the nonmaterial objectivity of value and of labor? Stress on exchange value continues Marx's emphasis on nonmaterial objectivity. This is made clear when Marx says the commodity "is the abstract objectified reflex of the expended labor. However, it does not reflect this in its physical nature. It manifests itself, receives perceptible expression through its value relation to the coat."[49] Marx is here elaborating his notion that the value of a given commodity will eventually be compared to the value of another commodity, i.e., will eventually appear as exchange value. But if the value of a commodity is not expressed until there is an actual comparison between it and other commodities, then the objectivity of value and of the labor that creates value is not so expressed either. Yet, Marx holds that all commodities, whether they are actually being compared to other commodities or not, have the objective quality of value. Thus, the objective quality of value is not identical with its expression, i.e., with the comparison of physical goods. This shows conclusively that the objectivity of value cannot be identified with the physical nature of the commodity. For that physical nature remains the same whether or not the commodity is actually being compared with other commodities. The value, however, is expressed only when there is such comparison, although it exists even without the comparison.

Rubin's arguments for the close connection between value and actual exchange help establish the near identity of abstract labor and value in a second way also. Although value has to be traced back to labor, and the equalization of commodities has to be traced back to labor, they can only be traced back to a labor which is oriented toward producing for exchange. The value gets its meaning from the labor, but the labor in turn gets its meaning from the value. This point is connected with Rubin's stress on form. For if one begins with value and asks what is its substance, then value gets its meaning from labor, but labor does not get its meaning from value. If, however, one begins with labor and asks why it takes on the social form of value, then labor is defined in terms of value. Rubin's emphasis on actual exchange thus sharpens his stress on the way the social form of value modifies the natural characteristic of labor and turns it into something abstract characterized by a ghostly objectivity. Rubin's problem is that he does not characterize that objectivity adequately—a task I will argue, which can only be accomplished through a holism of common elements.

Nevertheless, Rubin's concept of equalization does lead him to the fringes of the concept of holism. Individuals in all societies are faced with the necessity of distributing a total amount of labor and of commodities. However, that totality is present in a different way in commodity and noncommodity societies. Rubin observes of this contrast that

In a society with an organized economy, the labor of an individual in its concrete form is directly organized and directed by a social organ. It appears as part of total social labor, as social labor. In a commodity economy the labor of an autonomous commodity producer, which is based on the rights of private property, originally appeared as private labor. The labor of the commodity producer displays its social character, not as concrete labor expended in the process of production, but only as labor which has to be equalized with all other forms of labor through the process of exchange.[50]

The peculiar way in which the social whole of the market faces the individual producer and exchanger is never correctly grasped by subjective value theory, because subjective value theory never grasps the whole. Rubin notes that subjective value theorists gave a practical standard for measuring the value of commodities, whereas Marx's value theory gave a causal analysis of how commodities are measured.[51] Rubin does not note, however, how this difference reflects the difference between individualism and holism. Classical value theory gives an analysis of how social groups unknowingly relate to the whole social process of measuring value. Subjective value theory measures the particular relations that an individual has to a commodity, and the calculations and measurements that he knowingly makes of that commodity. Classical value theory, like mercantilism, analyzes the cause of men's actions arising out of the social whole. Unlike mercantilism, it is primarily concerned with a social whole which has escaped from man and cannot be captured by the laws and conscious rules of the politics. Nevertheless, by analyzing the social whole, classical value theory concerned itself with some of the same phenomena that mercantilism analyzed. The realm of value is thus not limited in classical political economy, particularly Marx's, to the realm of what is worthwhile or desirable. Indeed, for Marx the total amount of commodities and the total amount of abstract labor is not desirable in itself but only because it is a way (an extremely roundabout way) of bringing about social reproduction.

The identification or near identification of the *sachliche* character of abstract labor and the *sachliche* character of commodities leads to an interesting asymmetry in Marxist economics, which forces him to reveal with particular clarity the holistic ontological basis of his economics. In particular, there is a passage, from the little-known appendix to the first edition of *Capital*, adduced by Rubin, Colletti, and Rancière as evidence for the mysterious nature of value and abstract labor, which I will argue shows the holism of common elements which Marx is led to by his concept of non-material objectivity. The asymmetry is between the use value/value dichotomy and the concrete labor/labor dichotomy. The first chapter of *Capital*, volume one, tells us that commodities have both use values and values and also that the labor that produces commodities is concrete when looked at as producing use values, and abstract when looked at as producing values.[52] We can see how an action can have both a concrete and an abstract sense. It is concrete insofar as it is physical labor which produces a physical good. It is abstract insofar as it participates in the social rules and forms of a society that produces values and exchange values. It is also easy to see how commodities have use values, for commodities are at least physical goods which have physical properties that people can use. As soon as it is said, however, that commodities have values, problems arise. Values are produced by actions, i.e., abstract labor. In so far, then, as commodities have the abstract characteristic value doesn't this quality derive from the abstract characteristic of actions? There seems to be symmetry between the use value and the value of commodities, and the concrete labor and the abstract labor that produces commodities. Actually, however, there isn't. Concrete labor, abstract labor, and values are defined in terms of action. Only use value is defined apart from action.

The priority of action emerges with particular clarity in Marx's discussion of the objections that Samuel Bailey had made to classical economic theory. Marx is replying to an objection that Bailey had made against Ricardo—that Ricardo's theory of value has no scientific worth since it attempts to explain price, which is observable, with value, which is unobservable. Thus, for Bailey as opposed to the classical British political economists, there is no such thing as a theory of value which accounts for general regularities in prices. There is only price as found in day-to-day market transactions.

Marx replies that the value of a commodity only *appears* when the commodity is related to another commodity on the actual market, i.e., exchange value, that this is the only way that value can be *expressed*. He argues, however, that value is not simply value's expression, since value is created in production before any actual market trading occurs.[53] Bailey denies this notion that there can be value without any actual trading. He remarks that a thing can be no more full of value without relation to another thing than a thing can have distance without relation to another thing, to which Marx replies: "Is social labor, to which the value of a commodity is related, not another thing?"[54]

The query, "is social labor . . . not another thing," reflects Marx's notion that the whole of social labor has a substantiality, making it as real as a thing, although of course different from a thing in many respects. Bailey overlooked these points and thus denied the status of reality to social labor. In elaborating on his methodological opposition to Bailey, Marx notes that if

a thing is distant from another, the distance is in fact a relation between the one thing and the other; but at the same time the distance is something different from this relation between the two things. It is a dimension of the space, it is a certain length which may as well express the distance of two other things besides those compared. But this is not all. If we speak of the distance as a relation between two things, we suppose something "intrinsic" some "property" of the things themselves, which enables them to be distant from each other. What is the distance between the syllable A and a table? The question would be nonsensical. In speaking of the distance of two things we speak of their distance in space. Thus we suppose both of them to be contained in the space. Thus we equalize them as being both existences of the space, and only after having them equalized *sub specie spatii* we distinguish them as different points of space. To belong to space is their unity.[55]

Several aspects of this argument must be separated. At first, Marx sounds as though he is just reiterating as arguments for value, the arguments that Kant addressed against the account of space given by the British empiricists. The parallel is very close. The empiricists had thought that space was simply the abstraction from the sum total of particular spatial relations. Against them Kant had argued that there must be space as a whole before there could be any particular spatial relations. Similarly, Marx argues that value is not simply an abstraction from all the particular acts of exchange on the market. Rather, the existence of value as a whole is a presupposition for those particular acts of exchange. This analogy with Kant cannot be pushed too far. Unlike Kant, Marx is not describing a relationship such as space which has always existed, for it is only with capitalist society that the value relationship comes to be dominant. It is true that, like Kant's analysis of space, Marx's analysis of value depends upon finding the common substance of what is being analyzed. For Marx, it is a historically specific common substance that he finds: abstract universal labor. It is Marx's discovery of abstract labor that allows him to answer the question that he poses, "what is this unity of objects exchanged against each other?"[56] This unity is supplied by abstract homogeneous labor, and the thousands of actual exchanges are only expressions of the same value.[57]

There is, however, a problem with Marx's Kantian characterization of value, suggesting an ultimate priority in Marx's account, of the commodity's connection with action over the commodity's connection with physical goods.[58] For Kant, space was one homogeneous whole. For Marx, the social whole of value, which includes the abstract labor that produces value, is not so clearly one homogeneous whole. What is the extent of the abstract labor whole? How many actions does it include? And what is its relation to the total amount of commodities? How many commodities does that include? Perhaps the value whole cannot be separated from the total amount of commodities. If the social whole of value includes both commodities and action, is it as homogeneous as Kant's space? Some light is shed upon these questions as Marx continues to argue against Bailey's empiricist position that there is no value, no general regulator of price, but only particular prices on the marketplace:

the value of a pound of coffee is only relatively expressed in tea; to express it absolutely—even in a relative way, that is to say, not in regard to the time of labor, but to other commodities—it ought to be expressed in an infinite series of equations *with all other commodities*. This would be an *absolute* expression of its relative value; its absolute expression would be its expression in *time of labor* and by this absolute expression it would be expressed as something relative, but in the absolute relation by which it *is* value.[59]

Thus, there is a distinction between (1) the relative expression of value, (2) the absolute expression of the relative value, and (3) the absolute expression of the absolute relation by which it is value. (1) is exchange value, when one commodity is actually related to another commodity on the market. (2) is the exchange value that would be found if commodity were to be related to all other commodities on the market. (3) is value as produced by abstract labor in production. (1) and (2), however, are thought of as relative. The first is relative because it is a relation between only two commodities, each of which could be related to any other commodity. Thus, exchange value does not capture all the possibilities inherent in value itself. The second, on the other hand, seems to capture all the possibilities that are present in the total amount of commodities. Why, then, is it thought of as relative in relation to the third? The fact that the second is relative to the third suggests an asymmetry between the total amount of commodities and the whole of abstract labor, which includes all of the abstract labor that has been used to create all the commodities that could possibly be sold in the market.

The schema can be summed up as follows. (1) One commodity is compared to another in the marketplace. This actual comparison of two commodities on the market is relative to (2), the total amount of commodities and their comparison on the marketplace. Thus, the fact that two commodities can be compared on the market must be understood in the light of the fact that all of the commodities can potentially be so compared. Just as (1) is relative to (2), the latter, in turn, is relative to (3) all of value and the labor that produces it. That (2) is relative to (3) is due to the fact that insofar as commodities have a value, it is because abstract labor is embodied in them. It is the abstract labor rather than the physical qualities of the good that measures the value. Thus, measurement of physical goods is subordinate in Marxian economics to measurement of action.

These points can be connected with Marx's analogy between space and value. It is clear that the spatial analogy is less appropriate as applied to the total amount of commodities when compared on the market than as applied to the whole of abstract labor. This further strengthens the priority that the theory of abstract labor has as an explanatory tool over the theory of the total amount of commodities as an explanatory tool; this shows the priority of action over material objects in Marx's economics. In building up his definitions of space and value, Marx implies that he is operating with a conception of possibility. He develops the notion that the value of any commodity can be expressed in an infinite series of equations with other commodities. In spatial relations, any object can potentially be related to any other object in space. Marx shows, further, that he is concerned with the problem of possibility when he asks about commodities, "What is, therefore, their identity which enables them to be exchanged in certain proportions for one another. As what do they become exchangeable?"[60]

How close is the connection between the possibility of exchange and the possibility of objects being in a spatial relation? In Kant, spatial relations are made possible by the existence of space as a whole. All things are always in space and thus are always related to one another. The possibility of spatial relations is the basis for all particular relations. Value relations seem different. A given segment of abstract labor is always connected to the whole of abstract labor, and thus the possibility of exchange is always present in that respect. But all commodities are not always being compared with each other. The total amount of commodities, then, is considerably different from the total amount of things in spatial relations. The spatial relations are always there, but there are times when the total amount of commodities is not being compared on the market, and (conceivably) even times when no commodities are being compared on the market. On the other hand, the relations between the segments of abstract labor are always present in the same way that relations between things in space are always present.

Thus, commodities, as opposed to the whole of abstract labor and the whole of objects in space, are not always actually related to each other, though always potentially. Marx notes that during the time that they are only potentially related to other commodities, they appear only as use values. Thus, sometimes commodities only appear as half of themselves, as use values, and sometimes they take on their full role as commodities, that is, as combinations of use values and values. Actions that create commodities, however, always have both a concrete and an abstract side.

In a little-known text, the appendix to the first German edition of *Capital*, Marx further deepens this asymmetry between the two aspects of the commodity, use value and value, and the two aspects of the action that creates commodities, abstract labor and concrete labor:

Within the value relationship . . . the abstract universal is not reckoned as a property of the concrete sensuously real, but on the contrary the sensuously concrete is reckoned as the form of appearance of the abstract universal. The labor of the tailor which, for example, is contained in the equivalent coat, does not possess the universal property of being human labor. Rather, the opposite is the case. It is its essence to be human labor. To be the work of the tailor is only its apparent form. . . . This quid pro quo is unavoidable, because the labor which is represented in the product is only the creator of value in so far as it is undifferentiated human labor. Thus, the labor which is objectified in one product is completely undifferentiated from the labor which is objectified in the value of a different sort of product. This reversal, whereby the sensuously concrete is reckoned as only the form of appearance of the abstract universal, as opposed to the case where the abstract universal is a property of the concrete, characterizes the value expression. At the same time it makes its understanding difficult. If I say Roman law and German law are both systems of law, that is self-evident. In contrast, if I say, the law, this abstraction, actualizes itself in Roman law and German law, these concrete systems of law, this connection becomes mystical.[61]

Here universal labor is not taken to be simply a fiction, abstracted from many particular elements, any more than the abstract forms which Marx recommends that economists begin with are simply abstractions from particulars. When labor creates value, it does this not because of its particularity but because of its relation to the universal: "the labor which is represented in the product is only the creator of value, insofar as it is undifferentiated human labor." Yet, what Marx claims about the relationship of concrete action to universal action he does not claim about the relationship of use value to value, even though he had meant the use value/value dichotomy to parallel the concrete labor/abstract labor dichotomy.[62] This is a very significant asymmetry, since, in general, there is a clear parallel between the opposition concrete labor/abstract labor as applied to action and the opposition use value/exchange value as applied to commodities. That the parallel breaks down here once again confirms the difference between the roles that the total amount of commodities and the whole of abstract labor play in Marx's explanatory scheme.

Marx's language in this passage clearly suggests that he has a different attitude toward universals or common elements in material objects and human society. In society, the common element is dominant: the concrete labor is an appearance of the abstract labor. With material objects this is not the case: the concrete use value is not an appearance of the value. Furthermore, Marx recognizes that the ontological domination of the universal is particularly strong in economics as opposed to law, thus confirming our argument that nonmaterial objectivity is associated with the new economic paradigms of the market which tended to denigrate the mercantilist stress on law.

This opposition between the particular and the universal forms the basis for several other discussions in the *Grundrisse*. Among the three discoveries that Marx considered the great accomplishments of *Capital* is "the general form of surplus value." Its discovery meant that Marx did not have to look simply at "fragments of surplus value."[63] This concept of surplus value in general leads to the concept of "Capital in general (allgemeine)" which, "as distinct from the particular capitals does indeed appear . . . only as an abstraction. . . . (2) however, capital in general, as distinct from the particular real capitals, is itself a real existence."[64] Is the common property simply abstracted from the particular elements, or does it have a reality of its own? Marx opts for the latter view here and in the following:

Nothing is more erroneous than the manner in which economists as well as socialists regard society in relation to economic conditions. Proudhon, for example, replies to Bastiat by saying: "For society the difference between capital and product does not exist. This difference is entirely subjective and related to individuals." Thus he calls subjective precisely what is social and he calls society a subjective abstraction. . . . Society does not consist of individuals, but expresses the sum of interrelations, the relations within which these individuals stand. As if someone were to say: Seen from the perspective of society there are no slaves and no citizens: both are human beings. Rather they are that outside of society. To be a slave, to be a citizen, are social characteristics, relations between human beings A and B. Human being A, as such is not a slave. He is a slave in and through society. What Mr. Proudhon here says about capital and product means, for him, that from the viewpoint of society there is no difference between capitalist and workers; a difference which exists precisely only from the standpoint of society.[65]

Although Marx says, "Society does not consist of individuals," this statement cannot mean that there are no individuals. For he indicates that individuals can be looked at from a nonsocial perspective: "they are that (human beings) out side of society." Marx is not dissolving the individual into his common or universal relations with others. He is simply affirming that he does have such common relations and that they cannot be reduced to the individuals who participate in those relations. The common property is not simply abstracted from the particular elements, for if it were, then one could not hold that "Society does not consist of individuals," and deny that the relations between individuals are subjective. Marx could be implying, however, that relations are not subjective because the mental apprehension of the universal is not unique for each individual. Each individual apprehends the same universal and that implies that the universal as mentally apprehended cannot be abstracted from particular mental apprehensions. On this account, universals may be mental themselves, but they are not abstracted from particular mental apprehensions. On the other hand, Marx could be implying that universals are not subjective for another reason: that they are not totally mental, but characterize the world independent of the mind and are not abstracted from particular occurrences in the world.

However, there is at least one reason for not interpreting Marx as holding that mental universality is involved. This is that the universality he talks of does something which a mental universal probably could not do, namely, it renders man's social action independent of him: "Men are henceforth related to each other in their social process of production in a purely atomistic way. Their own relations of production therefore assume an objective structure (sachliche Gestalt) which is independent of their control and their conscious individual action."[66] In such a situation the worker "relates to his own combination and cooperation with other workers as alien."[67]

Having reached the connection between the value whole and alienation, we must now turn to the political whole, and then return to a more general analysis of how alienation occurs as social reproduction and the value and political wholes work together.

CHAPTER EIGHT

Marx's Political Economics

I have been arguing that Marx's economics connects two earlier theories of the capitalist economy: (1) physiocracy, concentrating on social reproduction, and (2) classical British political economy, concentrating on the production and distribution of value for the market. As we saw earlier, the plan of the economics was ultimately to connect all three of the major pre-Marxist theories of capitalist economics, including something like the mercantilist theory of the state and politics. It was to link the realm of value, social reproduction, and the political whole.

In capitalism, the political whole aids in achieving social reproduction and the continuance of the value whole. There is an aspect of politics bound up with rights and expectations, and common to all societies where social reproduction occurs. Economic societies are often also bound up with a more limited aspect of politics, what Lenin called "special bodies of armed men."[1]

All societies must achieve social reproduction, which includes the division of labor. This must be done by making sure that certain people have the expectation and the obligation to perform work in some areas, others in other areas, and that all people have a right to expect others to do their share.[2] Some societies utilize special bodies of armed men which are the ultimate backup group for preventing people from not following the division of labor.

This last point, however, introduces a second meaning for the division of labor, which should be distinguished from the characterization given to it earlier as the distribution of labor achieved in social reproduction. This second meaning has to do with the way in which not laboring activities, but men, are put in a certain strategic relationship to each other in terms of their consumption of goods, and a certain geographical relationship to each other in order to consume and labor in a certain way. This is the division of labor as division of men.

When a group of people controls the division of labor as division of men for another group, then both groups can be called classes. In capitalism, the class which controls the division of labor is identical to those who buy labor power. The class whose division of labor is controlled is identical to those who sell labor power. The given division of labor is one that follows the aims and needs of those who buy labor power.[3] If the people who sell labor power rebel at this, then the armed bodies of men will try to make sure that the status quo is continued anyway.

Marx's economics describes the relation between the three social wholes of value, social reproduction, and political economics. It expresses the alienated form that actions must take in order to distribute the labor of a given society in the proper proportion (the physiocratic paradigm) through the mechanism of producing value for the market (the paradigm of the classical British political economists). This alienation will exist as long as the state (the mercantilist paradigm) and its special bodies of armed men make sure that the division of labor as division of men characteristic of capitalism continues to exist. This division of men is necessary for value relations, and the bodies of armed men ultimately keep it going.

It is the *Grundrisse* which sheds the most light on Marx's analysis of politics in its relation to economics. It is different from *Capital* because it represents Marx's freely flowing discussion of capitalism as a whole, including its political aspects. What follows states the case for the view that Marx's economic plan must deal with the political whole as well as with social reproduction and the value whole. Evidence is presented for the view, and yet the picture is not complete. Marx never fully integrated his political theory with his economic theory.

Several important pieces of evidence have already been presented. It has been shown that Marx planned to give an account of the state in relation to the market. The basic objects of his study were

(1) capital, (2) landed property, (3) wage labor, (4) the state, (5) foreign trade, and (6) the world market. Marx says of this plan that the "economic conditions of existence of the three great classes into which modern bourgeois society is divided are analyzed under the first three headings; the interconnection of the other three headings is self-evident."[4] Marx could have saved us some scholarly headaches if he had pointed out the obvious here, but this passage certainly suggests that whereas the first three categories deal with the economic existence of three great classes, the fourth would deal with their more political existence. This would imply analysis of something like their control, through the state, of laws that state the expectations, rights, and obligations associated with the division of labor, as well as with their use of the special bodies of armed men which back up those laws.

Such an analysis is consistent with the relation of the economic to the political that Marx had stated in a letter to Weydemeyer. Marx noted that the French historians had discovered the concept of class long before him, but that his accomplishment was to connect their political definition of class with the economic definition that he found implicit in the liberal British political economists. Thus, Marx showed "that the existence of classes is only bound up with particular historical phases in the development of production."[5]

Furthermore, Marx's definition of the subject of *Capital* indicates that there was room for just such an account of the interrelation between the political and the economic: "the capitalist mode of production and the relations of production and interaction corresponding to that mode."[6] That "interaction" *(Verkehrs)* could certainly include the relations between those who use the state to control both the laws defining the division of labor and the armed bodies of men in that state, and those who are controlled by those laws and by those armed bodies of men.

In addition, a constant principle of Marx's post-1856 political writings is that the working class must utilize political action as well as economic action. They must fight against (1) the laws defining the division of labor, and (2) the armed bodies of men that uphold those laws. The first is shown by Marx's insistence on the importance of gaining the legal enactment of a limitation on the working day, and the second by his defense of armed revolution as in the Paris commune.[7] The general principle that the working class must fight politically as well as economically is stated throughout Marx's later political career in such places as the debates with the anarchists in the First International, where he notes that the working class must struggle against the capitalists and against their "class power as organized in the state."[8]

The *Grundrisse* elaborates this intertwining of politics and economics in a number of ways. First, it gives an account of property, showing that it involves the domination of one class by another. Second, it describes how the direct despotism of precapitalist class societies, when armed bodies of men imposed their will on those whose labor must be distributed, is also found in capitalism, although usually in a different form. Third, it sees the division of labor as involving the domination of one class by another. Fourth, it presents an analysis of how the commodity labor power becomes introduced. This explains the genesis of capitalist market relations and is a diachronic account. Fifth, a sketch is given of why it is that in capitalism social reproduction is accomplished only through the reproduction of the capitalist market totality. This is a synchronic account. The first two points will be discussed together.

Marx introduces the first point, that property involves the domination of one class by another, in *Capital*, Volume 1, when he has finished the general discussion of commodities and is turning to their exchange. The general discussion of commodities is concerned primarily with the value of those commodities as measured by the labor expended in production. Thus, it only deals with the market very abstractly, with the value produced for the market but not with the actual mechanism of buying and selling on the market. Therefore, the movement from commodities to exchange of commodities involves a move from the abstract to the concrete in the sense that the progression is from the general laws of buying and selling on the market, to the specific variations on those laws found in the day-to-day world of the market:

Commodities cannot themselves go to market and perform exchanges in their own right. We must, therefore, have recourse to their guardians, who are the possessors of commodities. Commodities are things, and therefore lack the power to resist man. If they are unwilling, he can use force; in other words he can take possession of them. In order that these objects may enter into relation with each other as commodities, their guardians must place themselves in relation to one another as persons whose will resides in these objects, and must behave in such a way that each does not appropriate the commodity of the other, and alienate his own, except through an act to which both parties consent. The guardians must therefore recognize each other as owners of private property. This juridical relation, whose form is the contract, whether as part of a developed legal system or not, is a relation between two wills which mirrors the economic relation.[9]

This implies that in order for there to be market exchange, there must be a system of expectations and rights that allows people to define something as their own. Indeed, previously we had argued that this is simply a logical necessity for market exchange. This passage, however, can easily be misinterpreted. Marx says that the juridical relation that defines these property rights is a reflex of the economic content. Does this mean that the political has no part in Marx's theory of economics? Rather, we must distinguish between (1) the creation of a system of rights, expectations, and obligations, and armed bodies of men to defend that system, and (2) the expression of these rights and obligations in law and the justification of these armed bodies of men through the law. The former would be a relation of interaction or production, whereas the latter would be the legal expression of that relation. This usage follows Marx's own distinction between the relations of production and their legal expression when he speaks of "The relations of production or, what is a juridical expression of them, property relations."[10]

But the realm of political economics cannot be reduced to its legal expression. If it could be, and if the legal were a reflex of the economic, then Marx would not be concerned with organizing the working class to take political power. If the political was just a reflex of the economic, then the taking of the economic power, the reflex, would not at all be followed by the taking of economic power. It seems, however, that the political is not just the legal. Therefore, it is not just a reflex of the economic. Far from it being a reflex of the eocnomic, the economic could not exist without the political.[11]

In the *Grundrisse*, Marx suggests that the property ownership necessary for commodities to exchange on the market entails the domination of one class by another. He distinguishes between property as defined by law and the production of material existence upon which that property is based:

Property, in so far as it is only the conscious relation—and posited in regard to the individual by the community, and proclaimed and guaranteed as law—to the conditions of production as *his own*, so that the producer's being appears also in the objective conditions *belonging to him*—is only realized by production itself. The real appropriation takes place not in the mental but in the real, active relation to these conditions—in their real positing as the conditions of his subjective activity.[12]

Here it is implied that the person's relation to thought (the legal relation) is not as significant as the person's relation to material production. Yet, we know that for Marx the economic involves not only material production, but also the production of social relations. Thus, he talks of how the production process of material life in general takes place within the context of "producing and reproducing these production relations themselves."[13] But this implies that the legal relation may express not only the relation of the individual to material production, but also his relation to the political violence which ensures that classes continue their special relation to material production.

This connection between force and property is elaborated further when Marx notes that the type of personal service characteristic of precapitalist societies

forms at bottom merely the mode of existence of the landowner, who no longer labors himself, but whose property includes the laborers themselves as serfs, etc. among the conditions of production. What we have here as an essential relation of appropriation is the relationship of domination. Appropriation can create no such relation to animals, the soil, etc., even though the animal serves its master. The appropriation of another's will is presupposed in the relationship of domination. Beings without will, like animals, may indeed render services, but their owner is not thereby lord and master. However, what we see here is, how the relations of domination and servitude also enter into the formula of the appropriation of the instruments of production; and they constitute a necessary ferment of the development and decay of all primitive relations of property and production. At the same time they express their limitations. To be sure they are also reproduced in capital, though in an indirect, (mediated) form, and hence they also constitute a ferment in its dissolution, and are the emblems of its limitations.[14]

This makes it clear that both in capitalist and in precapitalist societies the realm of material production is associated with the domination of one class by another.

It remains now to show that the domination found in the political whole can be expressed in legal relations, but is not itself any more reducible to legal relations than is the individual's relation to material production. Marx certainly thinks that in capitalist society this political power was often expressed in legal relations:

the lords of the land and the lords of capital will always use their political privileges for the defense and perpetuation of their economical monopolies. So far from promoting they will continue to lay every possible impediment in the way of the emancipation of labor. Remember the sneer with which, last session, Lord Palmerston put down the advocates of the Irish Tenants' Right Bill. The House of Commons, cried he, is a house of landed proprietors.[15]

Thus, Marx recognizes that in capitalism the control over the division of labor was accomplished partly through laws and legal relations. Furthermore, he was aware of this fact as it applied generally to capitalist and precapitalist economic formations and that this control of the division of labor has a certain independence of legal relations and laws. It can be accomplished without law by using force, in which case that force itself might be said to be the "law."

Every form of production creates its own legal relations, form of governments, etc. . . . . All the bourgeois economists are aware of is that production can be carried on better under the modern police than, e.g. on the principle that might makes right. They forget only that this principle is also a legal relation, and that the right of the stronger prevails also in their "constitutional republics" as well, only in another form.[16]

The despotism of precapitalist societies, then, when armed bodies of men imposed their will on those whose labor had to be distributed, is carried over into capitalism. Both the modern police and the system characterized by the principle "might makes right" certainly involve armed bodies of men, and according to our analysis, those armed bodies of men enforce a system of rights, expectations, and obligations. This enforcement is simply done differently in capitalist and precapitalist societies. In precapitalist societies, people were dependent upon others and were forced to do their bidding. In capitalist societies, on the other hand, people are dependent on abstractions, on objective *(sachliche)* powers: "These objective *(sachliche)* states of dependence, as opposed to the personal states of dependence. . . . are also characterized by the fact that the individuals are now controlled only by abstractions whereas earlier they were dependent on one another."[17]

This concept of objective *(sachliche)* power supplements the concept of nonmaterial objectivity possessed by the abstract labor that produces for the market. Complete analysis of this objectivity must include an account of the relation between social reproduction and the political and value wholes. It is only with the relation between all three that we see alienation as a whole.

Marx contrasts the two types of domination found in precapitalist and capitalist societies in remarks that presage Tönnies' distinction between the personal *Gemeinschaft* and the impersonal *Gesellschaft:*

The dissolution of all products and activities into exchange values presupposes the dissolution of all fixed personal (historic) relations of dependence in production as well as the all-sided dependence of the producers on one another. . . . The reciprocal and all-sided dependence of individuals who are indifferent to one another forms their social connection. This social bond is expressed in exchange value, by means of which alone each individual's activity or his product becomes an activity and a product for him. . . . In exchange value the social connection between persons is transformed into a social relation between things; personal capacity into objective *(sachliche)* wealth. . . . Rob the thing of this social power and you must give it to persons to exercise over persons. Relations of personal dependence (entirely spontaneous at the outset) are the first social forms in which human productive capacity develops only to a slight extent and at isolated points. Personal independence founded on objective *(sachlicher)* dependence is the second great form in which a system of general social metabolism, of universal relations, of all-round needs and universal capacities is formed for the first time.[18]

We have now seen how social reproduction implies a system of rights, expectations, and obligations. This system includes rights to use goods, expectations about which goods one can use, and obligations to allow others to use certain goods. These three elements help define property relations as relations which may or may not be expressed in law. Property relations are also connected with expectations about where one's labor and the labor of others will go, obligations to distribute one's labor in a specific way, and the right to have others do likewise. This system of rights, obligations, and expectations can be backed up by special bodies of armed men, who are controlled by some classes and who control others. These elements of the political whole may or may not involve a legal code.

In capitalist society, domination by bodies of armed men is expressed partially through the value whole. The domination cannot succeed unless it keeps the market going. We have also seen that the political whole is more often expressed in capitalism through legal relations than it is in precapitalist societies.

What is the connection between the growing importance of the market and the growing importance of legal relations? They are clearly connected in that the political whole is expressed through the market and legal relations. But why does this happen? Since Marx does not give a clear answer, the following is an attempt to supply one.

As the market comes to dominate society, people come to think that its continued existence involves no domination by armed bodies of men. This is the consciousness associated with petty commodity production. Thus, it comes to be held that the laws that govern the market also involve no domination by special bodies of armed men. Unfortunately, *Capital* itself, because of the formal method it follows of going progressively from one whole to another, in some respects backs up this illusion. That is why Marx's discussion, in the *Grundrisse*, of property relations backed up by force, is of particular importance. Furthermore, once it is understood, the relationship of the division of labor to armed bodies of men, the introduction of the commodity labor power into the market, and the reason for the continued entrance of the commodity labor power into the market, all become clearer.

Marx discusses three laws of property. The first two, connected with petty commodity production, suggest that associated with the realm of the market, when it is thought to be free of armed bodies of men, there is thought to be a realm of property law that allows those market goods to be exchanged and that is also free of armed bodies of men. Marx discusses these laws using the same methodology found in his discussion of the relation of petty commodity production to capitalism. We have already seen how he talks as though there is a fully developed exchange system without capitalism and then shows that such a system entails capitalism. So, too, he talks as though there really are only these two laws of property, and then shows that a third law holds, one that controverts both of the first two. The first two do not show the connection of property with armed bodies of men and coercive violence in general, whereas the third does.

The first law spells out the individual's right to appropriate what he has worked for; the second, his right to sell what he has appropriated on the market: "First law: appropriation through one's own labor. Second law: alienation *(Veräusserung)* or transformation of the product into societal form."[19] However, at the very end of the chapter on petty commodity production in the *Grundrisse*, Marx states unequivocally that the existence of these two laws of property is illusory (just as we have seen the realm of petty commodity production to be illusory). Another law of property comes to characterize capitalism, a law that entails coercion and alienation:

As we have seen, in simple circulation as such the action of the individuals on one another is, in its content, only a reciprocal, self-interested satisfaction of their needs; in its form [it is] exchange among equals (equivalents). Property, too, is still posited here only as the appropriation of the product of labor by labor and of the product of alien labor by one's own labor, insofar as the product of one's labor is bought by alien labor. Property in alien labor is mediated by the equivalent of one's own labor. This form of property—quite like freedom and equality—is posited in this simple relation. In the further development of exchange value this will be transformed, and it will ultimately be shown that private property in the product of one's own labor is identical with the separation of labor and property so that labor will create alien property and property will command alien labor.[20]

The first two laws of property are connected with the freedom and equality supposedly associated with petty commodity production. Individuals labor by themselves, and each owns his own property. Capitalism, however, implies the existence of a different kind of property. One group of people owns property and the other group does not: the third law. Of course, Marx is not denying that most people own their own toothbrushes. He is referring to the fact that the seller of labor power has nothing to sell but his labor power, whereas the buyer of labor power owns the means of production that will allow him to put the labor power to use:

The exchange of equivalents, which seems to presuppose ownership of the products of one's own labor—hence seems to posit as identical: appropriation through labor, the real economic process of making something one's own, and ownership of objectified (vergegenständlichte) labor . . . turns into, reveals itself through a necessary dialectic as absolute divorce of labor and property, and appropriation of alien (fremde) labor without exchange, without equivalent.[21]

The concept of the division of labor as division of men spelled out in the Grundrisse simply follows the third law of property.[22] The relevant passages oscillate between a synchronic analysis of the division of labor in capitalism and a diachronic discussion of the role of force in the division of labor. The former concentrates on why labor power was introduced as a commodity in the market, and the latter on why labor power continues to be bought and sold on the market. The innovative aspect of the Grundrisse discussion is its stress on the fact that although the manufacturing capitalist eventually presents isolated workers with a factory and, thus, provides a way of dividing labor, nevertheless he begins by simply taking over the division of labor that already exists: "The development proper to manufacture is the division of labor. But this presupposes the (preliminary) gathering-together of many workers under a single command."[23] Marx observes that sometimes this gathering-together had already been accomplished by feudal relations, which, as we have seen, depended upon armed bodies of men:

Certain branches of industry, e.g. mining, already presuppose cooperation from the beginning. Thus, so long as capital does not exist, this labor takes place as forced labor (serf or slave labor) under an overseer. Likewise road building, etc. In order to take over these works, capital does not create, but rather takes over the accumulation and concentration of workers.[24]

Indeed, the growth of capitalism presupposes the capitalist finding as many free productive elements as possible: "The societal powers, the division of labor, do not cost the capitalist anything."[25]

By showing how the capitalist brings the laborer into the capitalist market, Marx is also filling in a lacuna that we have already seen to exist in Smith's economic writings. As we saw earlier, Smith's discussion in *The Wealth of Nations* oscillates between a time when everybody owned their own means of production and did not have to work for anybody else, and another time when suddenly there were capitalists employing people who do not own their means of production. Marx is supplying a historical analysis of that transition. In *The Wealth of Nations* itself, there was little suggestion that political violence could have been responsible for the transition, at least in the published version. Marx's suggestion that the capitalist takes over the system of forced labor that existed under feudalism fills this lacuna and adds to his discussion in the chapter on primitive accumulation in *Capital* of the role of the state in the creation of a market in labor power.

It is interesting to note that in *Capital*, Marx's method prevents him from giving a synchronic account of the role of politics in economics. The section on primitive accumulation, however, is a purely diachronic account of how the people who want to buy labor power use their control of the law and also of armed bodies of men to force people off the land and into the cities where they become the modern proletariat with nothing to sell but their labor power.[26]

The diachronic account of the growth of the division of labor explains, then, how labor power was introduced into the market through direct force and law. In contrast, the synchronic account of the division of labor explains why labor power continues to be introduced into the market. It does this in terms of force and law, too, but it also emphasizes alienation and a complex causal analysis of the violence that is used to force people to continue the existing division of labor.

The diachronic and synchronic accounts are intertwined in the following:

If capitalist leadership is thus twofold in content, owing to the twofold nature of the process of production which has to be directed—on the one hand a social labor process for the creation of a product, and on the other the process for creating new value for capital—in form it is purely despotic.[27]

Earlier we saw Marx distinguishing between the content of value (social reproduction) and the form of value (the value whole). Here he refers to both as parts of the dual aspect of the content. "The social labor process for the creation of a product" is simply social reproduction, whereas the "process of creating new value for capital" is the goal of the production and distribution of value. This content, then, is what is accomplished by the capitalist leadership. The form, however, refers to the way in which the capitalist leadership brings about this process, and is said to be despotic.

This process of despotism is described using the concept of alienation and certain elements from Hegelian philosophy:

The association of the workers, as it appears in the factory, is therefore not posited by them but by capital. Their combination is not their being, but the being of capital. . . . He [the worker] relates to his own combination and cooperation with other workers as alien, as modes of capital's effectiveness.[28]

Hegelian categories are also used to describe the difference between when the capitalist simply takes over the existing division of labor and when he determines the nature of the continued division of labor. In both cases, the capitalist is a unifying force bringing about common actions. In the first, however, the particular workers have a great deal of control over those actions, whereas in the second the common nature of their actions is determined solely by the capitalist, by something outside of them. In the first, the forces represented by capitalism have only begun to dominate the particular workers, but in the second case that domination has proceeded much farther:

The point of unity of all these scattered workers lies only in their mutual relation with capital, which accumulates the product of their production in its hands, and likewise, the surplus values which they created above and beyond their own revenue. The coordination of their work exists only *in itself (an sich)* insofar as each of them works for capital. . . . Their unification by capital is thus merely *formal* and concerns only the product of labor and not labor itself.[29]

Here, although the capitalist has become the dominant buyer and seller, he does not yet determine exactly where each buyer and seller will go in the given division of labor. The modern factory situation has not yet been created. In the second situation, however, there is

suspension of the independent fragmentation of these many workers, so that the individual capital no longer appears toward them merely as a social collective power in the act of exchange, uniting many exchanges, but rather gathers them together in one spot under its command, into one manufactory and no longer leaves them in the mode of production found already in existence, establishing its power on that basis, but rather creates a mode of production corresponding to itself, as its basis. It posits the concentration of the workers in production, a unification which will initially occur only in a common location, under overseers, regimentation, greater discipline, regularity and the posited dependence in production itself on capital.[30]

Here both a diachronic and synchronic account is being presented. The capitalist has gradually become the source of the common actions of the workers; this is the diachronic account. Marx also analyzes what happens when this is achieved. This is the synchronic account which tries to explain why the worker remains a worker and why the capitalist remains a čapitalist; why labor power continues to be bought and sold on the market. With the synchronic account, Marx is addressing himself to a question that we raised earlier about Smith: "Why does social reproduction have to be achieved through the production of value for the market?"

Political economy has indeed analyzed value and its magnitude, however incompletely, and has uncovered the content concealed within these forms. But it has never once asked the question why this content has assumed that particular form, that is to say, why labor is expressed in value, and why the measurement of labor by its duration is expressed in the magnitude of the value of the product. These formulas, which bear the unmistakable stamp of belonging to a social formation in which the process of production has mastery over man, instead of the opposite, appear to the political economists' bourgeois consciousness to be as much a self-evident and nature-imposed necessity as productive labour itself.[31]

Once again, social reproduction is the content and value the form. The question is why is social reproduction brought about by value in capitalist society? Marx does not answer this question at this point in *Capital* because his method prevents it. The account of the division of labor in the *Grundrisse*, however, suggests that, as opposed to the account given in classical political economy, social reproduction is brought about by the value whole, partly because of the force used by the buyers of labor power and their special bodies of armed men to make sure that labor power continues to be sold on the labor market.[32]

CHAPTER NINE

Self and Alienation

Roman Rosdolsky once wrote an essay called "The Esoteric and the Exoteric Marx," a dichotomy which can serve as an introduction to this chapter.[1] Throughout this work, I have been arguing that analysis of the common actions of economic society is a key to understanding alienation. Marxist economics analyzes, among other things, the common actions of economic society and should then help us better understand Marx's theory of alienation. However, the basis of Marx's post-1856 account of alienation is not fully explained and certainly lacks the detailed description that is given of, say, surplus value. Can we say, then, that the economic structure represents the exoteric Marx and the theory of alienation the esoteric Marx?

The answer to this question must be located in the unfinished nature of Marx's post-1856 writings. Of the many thousands of pages represented by the *Grundrisse*, the three volumes of *Capital*, the *Theories of Surplus Value*, and *A Contribution to the Critique of Political Economy*, only about a thousand were actually published by him: the first volume of *Capital* and the *Critique*. Furthermore, Marx never wrote his analysis of the Hegelian method that he had talked about.[2]

It is in these unpublished writings that we find the more interesting characterizations of alienation, even though the concept and often the word is found in all of Marx's post-1856 writings, published and unpublished.[3] It seems that one feature of Marx's work led to this difference between the published and unpublished writings: its systematic nature. Marx wanted to approach things using a step-by-step method. This is why, in the *Critique* for example, he never even got to a discussion of capitalism. He only made a few steps. Indeed, the steps were never completed in any of the published writings; nor were they in the unpublished writings, but at least there he felt freer to inject insights from a proposed later section into an earlier section. Nevertheless, even with this difference between the published and unpublished writings, it is still true that the economic structure is more carefully explained in Marx's corpus than is alienation. In that sense, the economics is more exoteric, and alienation more esoteric.

Nevertheless, we have shown how many of the economic themes center on social wholes and common actions, concepts which also allow Marx to construct an account of alienation in which common actions are imposed on people and thus could be said to both belong and not belong to them. Thus, the concepts of social wholes and common actions create a bridge between what at first appears to be an esoteric theory of the self and a more exoteric theory of the economy.[4]

I now have two tasks which take up this and the following chapter: first, to show in more detail how the social theory of alienation implied by the holistic economics operates; second, to show how the holistic concept of common actions, by demonstrating how community is divided from man, provides an ontological basis for both the economic structure and the theory of alienation.[5]

In order to talk about alienation we must determine to what extent any of the social wholes are necessary and to what extent they imply each other. Are any of the three social wholes necessary? It is clear that Marx thought that only social reproduction was so. Indeed, he refers to the necessity of achieving social reproduction as a natural law. Thus, he even follows the terminology of the Physiocrats on this issue, who also thought that social reproduction was necessary. "That this necessity of the distribution of social labor in definite proportions cannot possibly be done away with by a particular form of social production but can only change the mode of its appearance, is self-evident. Natural laws *(Naturgesetze)* can not generally be abolished."[6] No society, Marx continues to argue, could endure for very long without this kind of distribution of labor. This reasoning seems sound in relation to almost all known societies, where economic individuals are not self-sufficient. The fact that they are not self-sufficient means that they have to rely on the labor of others, and thus labor must be distributed in a proportion which allows those needs to be met. It therefore seems reasonable to say that social reproduction is necessary if individuals in society are not totally independent economically, and this is a true description of most known societies. Indeed, it is hard to see how individuals could survive without some form of the division of labor.

Further, since social reproduction entails some system of expectations, rights, and obligations concerning the societal distribution of labor, it follows that some such system is necessary in a society where social reproduction is necessary.

Social reproduction has to exist in a context of expectations, rights, and obligations which give specific shape to the division of labor, which is one aspect of political economics. Social reproduction includes the division of labor in certain proportions around the economy, but it does not entail any specific distribution. Rights, obligations, and expectations must specify that distribution of labor. Thus, a society has the necessity of achieving social reproduction, but it will want to do this by making sure that at a given time certain people have the expectation and the obligation to perform work in some areas, others in other areas, and that all groups have the right to expect others to do their share. This system of rights, obligations, and expectations, however, does not have to be implemented through special bodies of armed men, the other aspect of political economics.

Social reproduction does not have to exist in the context of any particular set of rights, obligations, and expectations. Thus, before capitalism, it existed within tribal and feudal relations. With capitalism, it exists within the context of the capitalist market totality and the political totality. Marx thought that after capitalism it would exist within the context of socialist relations.

In summary, Marx clearly thought that social reproduction was necessary and that the value whole and one aspect of political economics, special bodies of armed men, were not necessary. It also appears that the second aspect of political economics, rights, expectations, and obligations, is necessary, but this is less clear in Marx.[7]

Following the above analysis, social reproduction would not imply the value whole, nor would it imply special bodies of armed men. Rather, it would imply rights, expectations, and obligations. Similarly, the rights, expectations, and obligations of politics would imply social reproduction but not the realm of value. Special bodies of armed men would also imply social reproduction, but not value. Political power must always include the power over the distribution of labor throughout the economy, but this does not have to be accomplished through the market.[8] Value, however, is dependent on the political whole in both aspects, rights, expectations, obligations, and armed bodies of men. The capitalist market could not keep going for long without the distribution of labor in certain proportions throughout the economy. Furthermore, the capitalist class could not continue for long to have a ready supply of labor power if it also did not control a state which could potentially use physical force to cause the sellers of labor power to continue selling it at a price that allows the capitalist class to make a profit.[9]

This analysis of the relationship between the three totalities involves certain diachronic aspects. It could not be established that social reproduction did not necessitate the market, if it were not possible to compare historical situations where social reproduction utilized the market with other situations where it did not. Similarly, it could not be established that the political whole necessitates social reproduction but not the value whole, if different historical situations could not be compared.

Thus, the diachronic and synchronic elements play different roles in the theory of alienation. Alienation occurs within synchronically connected social wholes. From the synchronic perspective, each social whole seems to necessitate each other. But a diachronic perspective reveals that this is not the case. Thus, the synchronic relation between the three social wholes allows us to describe the alienated actions, whereas the diachronic comparison allows us to show that some of the connections between the synchronically related wholes are not necessary connections.

It is important to remember that the three social wholes are co-existent. Logically, it is true there could be a type of alienation associated with each whole, as well as with each possible combination of them. Indeed, there is alienation connected with (I) petty commodity production and the realm of value in capitalism, and (II) the political whole. The other two types of alienation that Marx concentrates on are (III) the relation between social reproduction and value, and (IV) the relation between value and politics. However, it must be remembered that these forms of alienation are simply abstracted from the total alienation connected with the simultaneous reproduction of all of the three social wholes. Total alienation is connected with the third move from the abstract to the concrete: the progression from three common ways of defining action, value, social production, and politics, which are abstract until they are combined in the concrete social whole of capitalism. In that concrete social whole, common modes of defining action are synchronically connected. The main link between the concept of the synchronically connected social wholes and alienation is what Marx calls the reproduction of relations. Marx says at the beginning of *Capital*, "In this work I have to examine the capitalist mode of production and the relations of production and interaction corresponding to that mode." At the end, he says:

We have seen that the capitalist process of production is a historically determined form of the social process of production in general. The latter is as much a production process of material conditions of human life as a process taking place under specific historical and economic production relations, producing and reproducing these production relations themselves.

By the reproduction of capitalist society, Marx seems to mean that common actions in social wholes are repeated and this involves reproducing and continuing the existence of the whole as a stable entity.[10]

I turn now to an analysis of each type of social alienation as it is found in (I) petty commodity production and the realm of value in capitalism, (II) the political whole, (III) the relation between social reproduction and value, and (IV) the relation between value and politics. In several of these specific types of alienation, we will see concretely how the concept of the reproduction of relations is connected with the concept of nonmaterial objectivity.

I. Alienation in petty commodity production and the realm of value in capitalism

The first chapter of the *Grundrisse* is supposedly limited to petty commodity production, but actually gives a description of a highly developed capitalist system. It also includes a discussion of the political and social differences between this and precapitalist systems. A basic theme is the contrast between these earlier societies, which had depended on personal relations, and capitalist society which depends on more impersonal relations.[11]

Thus, the first chapter of the *Grundrisse* deals with petty commodity production, but the account of alienation given goes outside of the step-by-step, abstract to concrete method. It deals not only with an economy but also with a whole society, including political institutions, dominated by market relations. We saw earlier, however, that market relations cannot dominate until there is capitalism. It is in the first section of the second chapter of *Grundrisse* that Marx gives a more deliberate contrast between the somewhat illusory realm of petty commodity production and capitalism. It is here that Marx most carefully follows the Hegelian method of describing a given institution from within and then going on to a description of a second institution which actually is entailed by the first—even though within the imaginary consciousness of someone in the first institution it does not seem to be so entailed. This is the Hegelian and Marxist method of simultaneously utilizing and ridiculing the Smithian illusion of the realm of freedom and equality of petty commodity production. Their method allows them to describe this realm from the inside and then go on to show its illusoriness.

This method also allows a clear account of the difference between alienation in petty commodity production and in the capitalist market. Marx argues that there would be alienation in petty commodity production, although of a somewhat illusory nature, arising out of division between the self and the self's identification with objects. In contrast, alienation in the capitalist realm of producing value for the market arises because the common actions of the working class are brought about by an external source. In petty commodity production, the individual subjectively identifies with the commodity that he is buying or selling on the market. This identification is in conflict with other strivings toward self-identification, and the result is a breakdown of the self into conflicting aspects. In the capitalist market, self-identity is broken down because the individual's activity actually does become bound up with the external structures that help cause it. He may not even think about this situation, but it still happens. This, in turn, once again results in the self, or rather the self's activity, becoming divided into conflicting aspects. Furthermore, Marx discusses these two types of alienation in the context of, respectively, the first and second Hegelian universals.

Marx begins his discussion of alienation in petty commodity production by giving a limited definition of the economic life in terms of its form. This social form defines the common actions of individuals who participate in exchange. From the standpoint of the form, the content of the act of exchange is not seen to be part of the social or economic relation in which the individuals participate. The content of each act of exchange is unique in this sense: it is constituted by the specific desires or needs that brought the individuals to participate in the act of exchange and by the specific nature of the goods exchanged. Both the desires or needs and the goods are connected with the realm of use value rather than exchange value, which is, rather, part of the social form.

Within this abstract social form, each subject in the process of exchange objectifies or reifies himself for the other, yet is indifferent toward the other. This paradox can be explained on the basis of the concept of universality that Marx is operating with. The two exchangers are indifferent to each other because they are participating in a type of universal form in which the individuals are not transformed by their relationship. This, then, is Hegel's first definition of universality, and he uses it in *The Philosophy of Right* to describe the formal structure of the property contract. Marx's point, then, is that the individuals perform similar actions, but that this similarity seems then only to make them blandly equal, blandly alike, and finally, blandly indifferent to each other. For Marx, the indifference that the subjects of exchange have toward each other is connected with their formal equality. This again follows Hegel's use of the first universal; for the formal equality must be seen as arising out of the formal commonness of the actions involved. The result is that this equality, which is the equality of indifference, causes the individuals to objectify or reify themselves and also to think of themselves as autonomous or as capable of completely causing their own actions.[12] The reification and the sense of equality and autonomy are connected.

The individuals reify or objectify themselves, or turn themselves into things, in that they, as subjects of the process of exchange, come to have the same qualities as the money or exchange value which is exchanged: "the equivalents are the objectification of each subject for the other."[13] The process of reification is then connected with a sense of equality because the individuals who objectify themselves in exchange value see themselves as sharing the equality of the equal amounts of exchange value traded on the market. The realm of exchange also brings about consciousness of autonomy. Each individual "has a reflection of himself in the act of exchange as its exclusive, controlling and determining subject."[14] Thus, each individual sees his participation in the process of exchange as self-caused. Why is this? Marx does not draw out his chain of reasoning explicitly here, but the answer must be that because of the universal in which the individual is participating, which is formal and excludes the content of the act, he comes to see himself as determined not by the connections between the common actions that occur on the market, but rather by his own desire and need for use value. He is even indifferent to the other participants in the process of which his act is a part.

Both reification and consciousness of freedom and equality are generated by the particular form of universality that the individual participates in within the process of exchange. The account of alienation and reification displayed here concentrates on the tendency of the individual to identify with economic value. This form of self-identification, however, is in conflict with other possible methods of self-identification such as with the reciprocal nature of the meeting of needs as manifested in the economic act, i.e., what Marx calls "the common interest" or what we have called social reproduction.[15]

But this identification in terms of social needs involves the content of the economic act and thus would be excluded from the mode of consciousness associated with petty commodity production. In another context, Marx steps outside of this mode of consciousness and comments on this paradox of an extreme emphasis on individuality coexisting with a highly develped communal interest:

Only in the eighteenth century, in "civil society," do the various forms of social connectedness confront the individual as a mere means toward his private purposes, as external necessity. But the epoch which produces this standpoint, that of the isolated individual, is also precisely that of the hitherto most developed social (from this standpoint universal) relations.[16]

The universality associated with petty commodity production is itself transformed through capitalist social relations into another kind of universality similar to Hegel's second universal. Here it is not as easy for the social relations to hide behind an emphasis on individuality. In describing this transformation in the *Grundrisse*, Marx gives an important epistemological interpretation which does not appear either in the *Critique* or *Capital*.

One of the reasons given earlier for the reification in petty commodity production is that, if seen from the point of view of the form of exchange and if the economic life is defined in terms of that form, then the use value of the commodity is not part of that form, not part of the economic life. This is what causes the apparent equality of the exchangers as well as the indifference that they have for each other. However, in the exchange between the laborer and the capitalist, the use value of the laborer's commodity, i.e., the use value of his labor power, does enter into the economic process in precisely the way in which Marx said that ordinary use values do not. The use value of labor power is to create more value than is necessary to create it: it is to create surplus value. Thus, when the exchange is between capitalist and laborer, a strong reason has disappeared for thinking that there will be the indifference, the seeming equality, the reification and the artificial autonomy associated with the realm of simple exchange.

Apropos the distinction between use value in petty commodity production and in capitalism, Marx notes that when a commodity is exchanged, its use, "its consumption, falls entirely outside of circulation" and "has nothing to do with the form of the relationship. It lies outside of circulation itself and is a purely material interest and only expresses a relation of individual (a) in his naturalness to an object of his isolated need."[17] How the commodity is used is "a question which lies outside of the economic relationship." In capitalism, however, the use value of labor power "appears as a special economic relationship." The relationship between the capitalist and the laborer is so different from the relation between other exchanges that it is only by misuse that it is called exchange and "is directly opposed to exchange, essentially another category."[18]

A reason for not calling the buying and selling of labor power exchange is the fact that within exchange there is indifference to the nature of the use values exchanged, whereas "the relationship in which the laborer stands to the capitalist is as use value in specific form, a form differentiated from exchange value and in opposition to value as such."[19] From this, Marx concludes precisely that the relationship between the capitalist and the laborer cannot be one of equality. However, it would be easy to deduce that the equality of the exchangers, which seemed to hold under simple exchange, could no longer hold under capitalism, since the exclusion of the use value of the commodity from the universal form of exchange was one of the preconditions for that equality. Furthermore, it can also be deduced that the reasons that had been given earlier for the reification of individuals and the creation of consciousness of autonomy are no longer as strong, since these phenomena had occurred as a result of the indifference and formal equality associated with the realm of petty commodity production. That indifference and formal equality had been generated by the fact that the use value of the commodity did not enter the economic process.

Why did Marx hold that the use value of labor power entered the economic relation between the exchangers in a way that the use value of ordinary commodities did not? Inasmuch as Marx is not entirely explicit on this point the following is an attempt to expand his line of reasoning. The use value of labor power has a peculiar relationship to the world of exchange which the use values of other commodities do not have. The reason is simply that the use value of labor power is to recreate the world of exchange itself by creating new exchange values—and, of course, for Marx it is the only commodity that has this capability. Its use is to create a measuring system, exchange value, which cannot turn back on itself and measure what created it.

I have talked about how a certain kind of consciousness becomes associated with petty commodity production. How true is this consciousness? There are two ways of answering this question. One is to ask whether anything like the realm of petty commodity production, or the Hegelian realm of contract, actually existed. The other is to leave aside that question and ask whether, if it had existed, the consciousness associated with it would be false. Another question that arises is whether the consciousness, true or false, associated with petty commodity production could also be found under capitalism.

As we have seen, the answer to the first quesiton is that for Marx petty commodity production was never a dominant economic form in any country or geographical region. As for the second question, Marx does not really give an answer to it. However, it is possible to deduce an answer from the analysis that he did give. It is fairly apparent that, if, as a matter of fact, the common actions of others do not help bring about one's actions, then there is autonomy in the sense that the lack of autonomy and the alienation connected with the second universal are not present. However, the autonomy that the exchanger in simple exchange thinks he has goes beyond this limited sense. One reason why he thinks that he has autonomy in exchange is that the causal importance of the need for use values is eliminated from his understanding of the act of exchange. This is false consciousness. Thus, there is a sense in which his consciousness of autonomy is true and a sense in which it is false. Furthermore, insofar as this autonomy arises from the individual's identification with exchange value, and specifically with the money or the commodity that passes hands, then that autonomy is based on reification. Identification with exchange value or money or the commodity represents only one possible mode of self-understanding, and thus to make that the only mode is certainly to have false consciousness. Therefore, autonomy based on reification, and reification itself, represent false consciousness. Still, there is a sense in which reification also represents true consciousness. Identification with exchange value is made possible by the formal equality represented by exchange value. Since people are equal as exchangers, it is a natural move, although not the only move, to identify with the source of that equality; the source of that equality is in the long run exchange value, money, and commodities. Thus, there is an element of true consciousness in reification, but when reification becomes the exclusive mode of self-identification, then it represents false consciousness. The first universal may actually explain reality in the realm of petty commodity production, but it would be a mistake to go from that and assume that it explains the whole of reality.

I have been arguing that both reification and the sense of autonomy may represent a mixture of true consciousness and of false consciousness. The feeling of autonomy is true in the limited sense that, with the first universal, common elements of action do not help explain particular actions. The sense of reification is true in the sense that, with the first universal, there are good reasons for identifying with exchange value. Both of these elements of true consciousness are related to the sense of equality: the first because it arises out of the formal universality of actions, a universality which does not explain the particular and thus where the particular seems to have autonomy; the second because money represents the realm of formal equality in which there is abstraction from differences in content. But to what degree is the consciousness of equality true?

There are strong reasons for holding that the sense of equality represents true consciousness. People definitely are equal within the social relation of petty commodity production, even though that equality only touches upon a small portion of their relationships to others. It does not touch, for example, upon the way in which each person serves another's need. It does not touch upon class relationships, for class relationships do not exist in a market society without the buying and selling of labor power. Thus, the truth of the consciousness of equality in petty commodity production does not mean that that same consciousness would be true in capitalism.

The last question is whether the consciousness, false or true, appropriate to petty commodity production could also be found under capitalism. Can the workers, who under capitalism are forced to act because of common elements of action, nevertheless think of themselves as equal, reified, and autonomous in the way characteristic of petty commodity production? The answer is that they can. After Marx has established that within capitalist social relations the laborer no longer has good reasons for thinking himself a partner in petty commodity production, he concludes that "this appearance exists like an illusion on the side of the worker." Furthermore,

production based on exchange value and community based on exchange value appear to posit property deriving solely from labor and private ownership of the product of one's own labor as conditions. Actually, however, they both presuppose universal labor as the condition of wealth and produce the separation of that labor from its objective conditions. The exchange of equivalents occurs, but it is merely the surface layer of a production which rests on the appropriation of alien labor without exchange but under the appearance of exchange.[20]

For Marx, the exchange of equivalents is the "surface layer" of a system which appropriates alien labor. The surface layer is the buying and selling of commodities at a price based on labor time. Beneath that surface layer the labor of others is appropriated through the buying and selling of labor power at the value necessary to create it rather than at the value that it creates. For Smith, there is a contradiction between the surface and the deeper structure that underlies the surface. Analysis of the surface buying and selling of commodities leads to the conclusion that if labor time is sold, it must be worth the commodity it produces. But the deeper structure shows that the worker gets less than this. For Marx, the surface is connected with false consciousness; when one penetrates to the deeper structure, that false consciousness is eliminated.

That understanding should move from the surface of things to a deeper underlying structure is often stated as a general methodological principle by Marx: "All science would be superfluous if the outward appearance and the essence of things directly coincided." "A scientific analysis of competition is possible only if we can grasp the inner nature of capital, just as the apparent motions of the heavenly bodies are intelligible only to someone who is acquainted with their real motions." For Marx, economy which stresses demand rather than labor, vulgar economy, "relies . . . on the mere semblance as opposed to the law which regulates and determines the phenomena."[21]

By beginning with the surface, where there is no consideration of the buying and selling of labor power, and then moving to consideration of a deeper structure where there is such consideration, Marx is able to explain a potential mode of false consciousness of the working class. The situation of the working class is described more accurately in the chapter on capital in the *Grundrisse* and the section on the buying and selling of labor power in *Capital* than in the opening sections of the *Grundrisse* and *Capital*. These sections, abstracting as they do from the buying and selling of labor power, explain how it is possible for the members of the working class to make the same abstraction: "the exchange of equivalents occurs, but it is merely the surface layer of a production which rests on the appropriation of the labor of others without exchange, but under the appearance of exchange."[22]

Thus, although a relation is set up, within the production process of capitalism and between the capitalist and the laborer, that is completely different from the relationship between exchangers in petty commodity production, nevertheless the laborer can come to regard himself precisely as an exchanger in the midst of petty commodity production. He is suffering from a double illusion. His most basic form of alienation is created through his relation to the capitalist. But it is possible for the worker under petty commodity production to forget about this alienation and to think of himself as a seller and of the capitalist as a buyer, just like other buyers and sellers in the midst of petty commodity production. In the same way, it is possible for Hegel's participant in the realm of contract and of the first universal to forget about his role in the realm of civil society and of the second universal.

Insofar as the worker does this and thinks of himself as participating in the world of petty commodity production, then he thinks of himself as belonging to the same realm of freedom and autonomy to which any petty commodity producer belongs. He also thinks of himself as reifying himself or objectifying himself in exchange value or money commodities. This reification is a result of the consciousness of equality, a consciousness which is not totally false when the buyer or seller is in the midst of simple exchange. However, in the world of capitalist production that objective basis for consciousness of equality does not exist, since it was generated by the universal form's abstraction from use value, an abstraction which is not accomplished when labor power is bought and sold.

So the worker can be subject to a consciousness which is doubly false: first, in that he falsely thinks of himself as existing primarily in the world of petty commodity production, and second, in that he is then subject to the same false consciousness as one who actually does exist in the world of petty commodity production. It is as though x believed that he was y and y believed that he was z. If x not only believes that he is y, but also is able to put himself in y's consciousness, then in believing that he is y he also believes that he is z. Similarly, the laborer under capitalism can believe that he is in petty commodity production. This is false consciousness. However, the ordinary petty commodity producer also believes that he is autonomous. This, too, is false consciousness. Thus, the laborer under capitalism is subject to a double false consciousness.[23]

Light is shed on this susceptibility of the laborer under capitalism to a form of double false consciousness, by noting another similarity between the surface/deep structure opposition in Marxist economics, and in Smith and Hegel. Both Smith and Hegel discussed labor as the measure of exchange and also as what produces goods in society. Thus, labor is connected both with the market and with production. The practice of buying and selling labor power also cuts across the two areas of the market and production. Labor power is bought and sold on the market like any other commodity, but as it is bought and sold, surplus value and new commodities are being produced. It is actually characteristic of alienation in capitalism that it arises out of the way in which the buying and selling of labor power to create new value affects production. Because the buying and selling of labor power also affects market relations, the consciousness of the laborer's alienation under capitalism can become distorted, and he falsely imagines himself to be alienated and reified in the midst of petty commodity production. It is the fact that the buying and selling of labor power straddles market and production relations that explains the possibility of a double form of false consciousness for the worker under capitalism. If the laborer concentrates primarily on the market aspect of the buying and selling of labor power, then he sees himself as primarily a commodity. It is, of course, true that labor power is a commodity and thus has an exchange value like any other commodity. Emphasis on this truth only leads to false consciousness when the laborer forgets that his commodity also has a peculiar use for which he is not paid, a use which is not expressible in market relations. That use is to constantly create surplus value and thus to constantly recreate, or keep going, the whole system of market relations, commodities, and values. Thus, there is a tension between the laborer's role as a commodity and his role as the creator of the world of commodities. Undue emphasis on the former causes him to forget his role in capitalist production and the alienation that he finds there, and instead to concentrate on his role as a buyer and seller like any other and the false consciousness of reification that goes along with this role.

As opposed to the alienation of petty commodity reproduction, alienation in the capitalist production and distribution of value is bound up with the buying and selling of labor power. The buyer of labor power and the tools that he owns become the objective conditions that allow the laborer to work. Thus, the laborer acts less and less because of his own principles. The analysis of capitalist alienation involves, first, the universality of labor power and of labor; second, the problem of how this universality comes about through capitalist social relations; and, third, Hegel's second type of universal and how it relates to the universality of labor and of labor power attained under capitalism.

The universality of labor power and of labor is much discussed in the *Grundrisse*. It has already been noted that the specificity of the use value of the commodity labor power is more significant for the form of exchange than the specificity of the use value of any other commodity. Paradoxically, however, one reason is that the concrete use of labor power is simply to be universal and thus to create new value. Thus, Marx talks of how it is a "purely abstract form, pure possibility of value positing activity, which exists only as a capacity in the body of the laborer"; and of how it is "capable of any determinateness."[24] This suggests that labor power attains its universality because of its end, its basic end being to create within the productive process more value than is embodied in it. It can only attain this end if it matches up with certain conditions outside of itself. Labor power derives its character of abstractness and universality from the fact that it must match up with these conditions, coupled with the fact that it is subjective, a capacity rather than an actuality. Thus it is unformed but is capable of taking on any number of forms: "the purely subjective form as opposed to its own conditions."[25]

The universality of labor power is also connected with the universality of labor. In the factory situation, a large amount of homogeneous labor is performed. This homogeneity requires that the work done on the job becomes more abstract and indifferent to any particular form. Labor which fits this mold is abstract as opposed to concrete labor. As capitalism develops, "work loses all its artistic character. Its particular skill always becomes more and more abstract and indifferent just as it more and more becomes abstract activity, completely mechanical, hence activity which is indifferent to its particular form."[26]

Labor power, then, has the universality of possibility. It can be used by the capitalist in many ways, and precisely because it can be used in so many ways it can have the specific use value of creating new value in the production process. New values in the form of new commodities represent new hours of labor time, and labor time must be homogeneous. Thus, the necessity of the universality of labor power is an effect of the necessity of the universality of labor. Labor, on the other hand, has the universality of actuality. It performs a multitude of activities, but its most important one is to be itself measured by time, i.e., labor time, or value when that time is embodied in commodities. And, of course, it is for the purpose of getting new value that the capitalist buys labor power.

In the *Grundrisse*, this analysis of universal labor and labor power is supplemented by an analysis of their genesis in the capitalist production of value. This points up a key difference between petty commodity production and the capitalist market. In petty commodity production, universality and alienation are connected to the actual market. In the capitalist market, they are connected primarily to the production of value for the market. It has been shown that that universality is closely connected with the end that labor power and labor serve. That end is, in part, to relate in a certain way to the conditions which face labor power or the conditions in which labor time is created. But these conditions are not identified with the tools with which labor power is to operate, as Marx makes clear when he notes that in capitalist production "not only the existence of those objective conditions of living labor are reproduced and newly produced, but their existence as autonomous values belonging to an alien subject opposed to this living labor power." These conditions "are opposed to the worker as alien property."[27] Thus, the end which labor power and labor serve is defined in terms of the relation between labor and capital. The proletariat acts in an alienated way because the conditions for the realization of its labor power through the creation of labor time are owned and controlled by the capitalist class. But the conditions of the realization of labor power through the creation of labor time are the conditions that allow both labor power and labor time to become universal. The objective conditions for their becoming universal, then, are outside themselves. They are the "objectivity of a subject which is different from living labor power and which stands opposed to it."[28]

Such a universality, which is attained through an external source, corresponds to Hegel's second type of universal. In the first type, individuals participated in the universal without transforming their individuality, or, in the special use that Marx makes of the theory, by even artificially emphasizing their individuality. This process was found in the universality associated with petty commodity production. In the second type, the individual elements are transformed, but alienation is still involved in that universality is attained through a force external to the individuals that are participating in it. Of this universality, Hegel had said it is "obvious at the outset that by existing only in this universal they [the individual elements] do not lie any longer apart from one another, but rather are in themselves self-cancelling sides and what is established is only their transition into one another."[29] This universality is an "abstract universality which stands outside and over against the individual."[30] In *The Philosophy of Right*, this universal describes the function of the property contract in bringing about the social distribution of good and the division into classes:

When men are thus dependent on one another and reciprocally related to one another in their work and the satisfaction of their needs, subjective self-seeking turns into a contribution to the satisfaction of the needs of everyone else. That is to say, by a dialectical advance, subjective self-seeking turns into the mediation of the particular through the universal, with the result that each man in earning, producing, and enjoying on his own account, is *eo ipso* producing and earning for the enjoyment of everyone else. The compulsion which brings this about is rooted in the complex interdependence of each on all.[31]

This passage brings out both the transformational and the compulsive aspects of the second universal. It transforms the nature of the individual's activities, but externally and compulsorily and is not in harmony with the individual.

Marx uses a similar concept of universality to show that alienation is no longer a matter peculiar to the individual, but rather true for all members of the working class. The working class as a whole is subject to alienation in the sense that the conditions for the activity of its members are outside of them in the form of alien property.

II. Alienation in the political whole

In the section on Marx's political economics, I argued that behind the alienation of being controlled by objective *(sachliche)* relations there is the alienation of being controlled by political coercion. This alienation is often discussed in the *Grundrisse* in relation to property and the division of labor. There Marx often stresses how the working class is controlled not only by alien relations but also by the alien will of the capitalist. Thus, he talks of how in the exchange relation between the buyer and seller of labor power, the objective conditions face the seller in such a way that they "confront him as alien property, as the reality of other juridical persons, as the absolute realm of their will."[32]

This political aspect of alienation is connected with how "private property in the product of one's own labor is identical with the separation of labor and property, so that labor will create alien property and property will command alien labor."[33] This separation between property and labor is connected with the buying and selling of labor power: "The worker's propertylessness, and the ownership of living labor by objectified labor, or the appropriation of alien labor by capital—both merely expressions of the same relation from opposite poles—are fundamental conditions of the bourgeois

mode of production and in no way accidents irrelevant to it."[34]
The identification of ownership with appropriation here suggests
again that the old modes of domination by armed bodies of men
found in precapitalist societies are present, but in a disguised form,
in capitalism. The exchange relations may dominate, but they do
not appropriate. Appropriation is done by men through relations.
That is why Marx talks of how the will of the capitalist is present in
the alienation of the worker, and of how "capital, therefore, appears
as the predominant subject and owner of alien labor."[35]

Finally, as we have seen, analysis of the division of labor shows
how the capitalist forces the laborer into the market in labor power.
Thus, Marx talks of the workers' "concentration at a single point
under the command of the capitalist," and of how "Their combination is not their being but the being of capital." Therefore,
the worker "relates to his own combination and cooperation with
other workers, as alien, as modes of capital's effectivenss."[36] Capital
now appears as "the concentration of workers . . . as a unity falling
outside of them. . . . Under capital the *association* of workers is
not compelled *(erzwungen)* through direct physical force, forced
labor, statute labor, slave labor; it is compelled *(erzwungen)* by the
fact that the conditions of production are alien property."[37]

III. Alienation in the relation between social
reproduction and value

The third type of alienation, having to do with the necessity of
bringing about social reproduction through value and the market,
is discussed in the chapter on fetishism in *Capital*. Fetishism is the
tendency to think of value as something material rather than something social. This fetishism does not arise out of confusion over use
values; nor does it arise out of the "content of the value determinations *(Inhalt der Wertbestimmungen)*. . . . Whence, then arises the
enigmatic character of the product of labor as soon as it assumes
the form of a commodity? Clearly it arises from this form itself."[38]

In discussing fetishism, Marx distinguishes between nonmaterial
objectivity and the false consciousness or fetishism that arises from
nonmaterial objectivity, and yet fails to recognize the objectivity
for what it is:

The determination of the magnitude of value by labour-time is therefore a secret hidden under the apparent movements in the relative values of commodities. Its discovery destroys the semblance of the merely accidental determination of the magnitude of the value of the products of labour, but by no means abolishes that determination's objective *(sachliche)* form.[39]

Thus, we make mistakes about the way in which abstract labor determines the prices of commodities. We come to think that prices are determined by material aspects of goods rather than by the amount of abstract labor necessary to create the commodities. This is fetishism. Yet, even if fetishism disappears, the nonmaterial objectivity associated with value relation will remain. "Its discovery—in no way alters its objective *(sachliche)* forms." Since, as we will see, nonmaterial objectivity is a way of speaking about alienation, this means that alienation is separable from fetishism and may remain after its disappearance. The converse, however, is not true, since fetishism has to do precisely with the misunderstanding of alienation.[40]

As we saw in the chapter on value, labor which creates the nonmaterial objectivity of value becomes opposed to individuals and thus alienated. Thus, Marx talks of how in exchange the product "must take this universal and yet external form *(äusserliche Form)*," and of how "the product of particular labor must prove itself as objectification of universal societal labor by taking the form of the thing, money, which is presupposed exclusively as the immediate objectification of universal labor." When universal labor must be objectified in this way, man's community must exist to the individual exchangers as "an independent subject opposing them, as something which is at the same time an independent, external, accidental, objective element *(Sachliches)*.[41] It is fetishism not to understand the alienation that occurs when social reproduction is brought about by the market. Yet, alienation may remain even if that fetishism were to disappear.

IV. Alienation in the relation between value and politics

The political and value wholes may be characterized as involving, respectively, direct and indirect domination, i.e., domination by political coercion and by objective relations. Marx seems to have thought that the relations of political coercion are semidissolved into market relations, at the same time keeping a life of their own:

> These external relations are very far from being an abolition of "relations of dependence"; they are rather the dissolution of these relations into a universal form; they are merely the elaboration and emergence of the general foundation of the relations of personal dependence. . . . These objective (*sachliche*) dependency relations also appear in antithesis to those of personal dependence . . . in such a way that individuals are now ruled by abstractions.[42]

In capitalism, people are still subordinated to other people; but this is not so obvious to them because they are also subordinate to relations which are in some sense independent of individual people.

Unfortunately, Marx did not complete this complex *Grundrisse* analysis. As a result, we are left with two separated images of exploitation and how to fight it: on the one hand, market exploitation and trade unionism (*Capital* and the First International); on the other hand, political exploitation and political revolution (in particular Marx's writings around 1848 on France and Germany). There is some mediation between the two in Marx's later political writings, but no work other than the *Grundrisse* tries even tentatively to show how both parts of exploitation, political and economic, work together as a whole, thus laying the groundwork for an account of how the exploitation of capitalist society as a whole can be overcome.[43]

In political alienation under capitalism, the worker does not act in terms of his own principles but acts more and more because of objective conditions outside of him. With alienation in the value whole, common elements connecting actions help bring about his own actions. The differences in alienation reflect the differences in the social wholes. The political whole and the common actions in it are more consciously created. The value whole and the common actions in it are more independent of conscious human plan. In the first case, which is closer to the Kantian model of alienation, the question is whether the individual's will is strong enough to allow him to act according to his own principles rather than because of external conditions. Thus, alienation is seen as a struggle between the subject and the object. In the second case, which is closer to the Hegelian model, the objective conditions simply come to conflict, as causes, with the individual's intentions, no matter how strong the individual's will is.

On the first analysis, the individual has to choose which will be the primary cause: subject or object. Thus, the subject/object dichotomy is prior. On the second analysis, the individual has a type of causal power, the external universal has another type, and the individual can do very little choosing about the matter. Thus, the conflict between causes becomes more central than the subject/ object dichotomy. Indeed, the subject/object dichotomy is broken down because the individual himself constantly recreates the common elements of his action as well as his own alienation. Thus, one aspect of the individual, the common elements of his action and his common relations, comes to be in conflict with another aspect, his subjectivity. He himself has created the objective conditions that confront him. Every time the individual recreates his own common relations, the subject/object dichotomy appears again to him, but in reality the demarcation between the subject and the object begins to be broken down. Thus, the subject/object dichotomy is not absolutely rigid, and the lines between them are not so clearly demarcated as they are in the political whole. Instead, as the individual recreates the common element of his action, he puts more of himself into it, and as he acts according to the common elements and relations, his sense of subjective self becomes broken down. The line between the subject and the object is constantly shifting.

Of this situation Marx notes:

The independent, for-itself existence of value vis-a-vis living labour capacity —hence its existence as capital—the objective, self-sufficient indifference, the alien quality *(Fremdheit)* of the objective conditions of labour vis-à-vis living labour capacity, which goes so far that these conditions confront the person of the worker in the person of the capitalist—as personification with its own will and interest—this absolute divorce, separation of property, i.e., of the objective conditions of labour from living labour capacity— that they confront him as alien property, as the reality of other juridical persons, as the absolute realm of their will—and that labour therefore, on the other side, appears as alien labour opposed to the value personified in the capitalist, or the conditions of labour—this absolute separation between property and labour, between living labour capacity and the conditions of its realization, between objectified and living labour, between value and value-creating activity—hence also the alien quality of the content of labour for the worker himself—this divorce now likewise appears as a product of labour itself, as objectification of its own moments.[44]

Alienation arises, then, out of the act of exchange between the buyer and the seller of labor power. This must be understood as a synchronic account of what happens as the buying and selling of labor power is constantly recreated. Each time labor power is bought and sold, it becomes easier to accomplish the buying and selling again. Thus, alienation refers to the confrontation between the worker who has nothing to sell but his labor power and the capitalist who gives the worker money for that labor power and then allows him to work using the tools of the capitalist. It refers also to the process of creating this confrontation. It is not only the objectivity and externality of their relation that is alienating, but also the fact that the worker keeps reproducing those objective and external relationships. The alienation of the worker causes the continued alienation of the worker.

The more the worker recreates his own alienation, the more he creates the necessity of relating as a subject to the objective conditions for his labor. There are no absolutely fixed boundaries between the subject and object, since the subject himself, the worker, constantly reproduces the relationship between his subjective capacity to work, his labor power, and the objective conditions that allow him to work: "Living labor therefore now appears from its own standpoint as acting within the production process in such a way that, as it realizes itself in the objective conditions, it simultaneously repulses this realization from itself as an alien reality." Since the line between subject and object is constantly shifting in the relation between labor and capital, labor therefore "posits itself as insubstantial, as mere penurious labor power, in the face of this reality alienated from it, belonging not to it, but to others; . . . it posits its own reality, not as a being for it but merely as a being for others." This opposition between "being for it" and "being for others" even reflects the terminology that Hegel uses to discuss the opposition between object and subject:

It [labor] posits itself objectively, but it posits this, its objectivity, as its own not-being or as the being of its own not-being—of capital. . . . As a consequence of the production process, the possibilities resting on living labor's own womb exist outside its realities—but as *realities alien* to it, which form wealth in opposition to it.[45]

I argued earlier that a primary problem with Kant's ethic was that he makes an arbitrary distinction between the self and the objective conditions that the self followed. For him, the realm of economic institutions such as property and exchange tend to be neutral. By themselves they are neither identified with the self nor with external conditions. The Hegelian analysis is different. Exchange relations are both external to the self and part of the self, and the degree of their externality changes constantly; the subject and the object change according to the way relations are recreated. Thus, the exchange relationship is not neutral as Kant thought, but is both part of the self and of the external relations of the economy. Since Kant did not recognize this, he continued to try to deduce an account of action from the a priori self, even though in fact he was not able to do so. He was not able to completely cut off his account of self from common economic actions; yet, Kant never realized the implications of this failure. His rationalistic philosophy could not accommodate the value paradigm in which a whole series of actions occur without being based on conscious acts of will.

Hegel's accomplishment was that he was able to fully integrate the value paradigm into his philosophy. For him, the actions of civil society arose out of the conflict between particular intentions and social wholes that individuals constantly reproduced. Of course, it is true that ultimately the autonomy of the market is subordinated to state intervention. But Hegel's state intervention, although supposedly ending the alienation of civil society, is never really shown to accomplish that task. Thus, the realm of politics and value are not really integrated. Marx's analysis of the relation between politics and the market is very different.

For Marx, relations are unconsciously reproduced within the realm of value. Furthermore, there are political institutions, potentially backed up by armed bodies of men, which make sure that those value relations will continue to be reproduced. The second point does not simply reveal the first to be an illusion. There is room in the Marxist analysis for the political paradigm of the despot consciously forcing people to do something. It is just that the political despotism has to be related to the more unconscious despotism of the market. By penetrating through the recreation of relations, the worker is able to move from an understanding of how he produced his own alienation to an understanding of how the capitalist class forces him to produce it.

Thus, Marx cannot completely follow Hegel's account of the holism of the market. Hegel's account of value, as a process whereby people are forced to do things by structures that they do not understand or control, too often becomes simply the inversion of the Kantian analysis. Whereas in the Kantian account some individuals must be named as doing the forcing, Hegel sometimes suggests that no one can or should be named. It is simply the fault of objective relations beyond one's control. Marx, too, often follows Hegel in falling into a mass of phrases about the nonmaterial objectivity of the value relation, without indicating that such objectivity is not a magical force that totally dissolves responsibility.

When Marx asks in *Capital* why this content takes this form, i.e., why is social reproduction achieved through the market, he seems to be asking for a return to a causal analysis, of why the proletariat is forced to reproduce the value whole. His answer to that question, like Smith's in his unpublished statements, is that political relations of violence and domination are partly responsible for the fact that social reproduction is achieved through the market.

Thus, Marx resolves the problem of the relationship between the value paradigm (classical British political economy) and the paradigm of political economics (mercantilism), at the same time that he resolves the problem of the relationship between a Hegelian analysis and a Kantian analysis. Politics is the realm where dominated actions are forced directly on the proletariat, and in the realm of value actions are indirectly forced on them. The whole of value-creating actions is made necessary because of the political whole. Yet, no particular value-creating action is forced on an individual by the special bodies of armed men of the political realm.

CHAPTER TEN

Holism and Explanation

I have now analyzed alienation in connection with the various social wholes, showing how the self is divided from its own unity, i.e., its own community and common actions. But how can community and common actions be divided from men? Answering this "how" involves deepening a concept without which the Marxist argument for alienation cannot succeed: social holism as an explanatory tool. However, we have seen so many different versions of this concept: Quesnay's, Smith's, Kant's, Hegel's. Where would a Marxist account stand? At this point, a synthesis must be made, drawing on the best parts of Marx, his predecessors, particularly Hegel, and his later Hegelian interpreters, especially Georg Lukács and Lucien Goldmann.[1] The Hegelian, Marxist account of epistemological holism reflects three positions: (1) that the universal helps explain the action; this is shared with Hegel and Kant; (2) that the universal is not simply internal but external as well; both Hegel and Kant have tendencies that push them in this direction, but neither arrives at a consistent view on this; (3) that it is possible to find the truest universal description, truth being defined in terms of basicness, which in turn is defined in terms of which description best explains why the act is repeated. This third element is not found in Kant and only embryonically in Hegel.

As we have seen, the Hegelian, Marxist version of holism holds that some actions must be explained in relation to other common actions. This is opposed to individualism, which holds that all actions can be explained without relating them to other common actions.[2]

If we start from this broad definition, there are several ways to delimit the claims of the Hegelian, Marxist version of holism. One limitation is that holism will not deal with actions that are similar everywhere. There is evidence that the action of producing for the market, for example, although general, is nevertheless historically specific. Barrington Moore has argued that the market did not exist in a general way in French farming before the French Revolution. Marcel Mauss has argued that those actions in Melanesia and the northwest coast of the United States, thought to be associated with the market, were really associated with giving gifts.[3] This specificity of market actions, as actions susceptible to holistic analysis, is important to establish because it means that human nature cannot be used to explain them. Appeal to human nature cannot explain the diverse types of human action. Rejection of the human nature explanation does not prejudice the case for holism versus individualism, since the human nature explanation may either concentrate on the relation of the individual to a larger whole or on the individual motive. Thus, it may explain the individual action in terms of the general human propensity to perform such actions, or it may argue that this human propensity translates into individuals always acting for their own good. Looked at from the one side it is more holistic, and from the other side, more individualistic. It is very difficult to choose which to stress as long as the argument remains on the issue of human nature. It is only with actions that are not only general but also specifically general that my version of holism can be tested out.

A second limitation is to avoid the problem of historical change or teleology in general. One way of confounding holism is to argue that it has to defend teleology or explain historical change. However, at least within certain limits, one can analyze market actions without referring to either history or teleology, and thus see them in their synchronic perspective.[4]

Holism could be connected with teleology by claiming that whereas the cause of an action, as the event preceding it, is atomic and separated from the action itself, the aim or telos of the action, as that which pulls the individual toward the action, is not atomic and not separated from the action. In this view, cause and action are two individual parts which do not make a whole. End or telos and action are individual parts which together do make a whole. But it is not with this concept of whole, however it be characterized, that I am dealing. My version of Hegelian, Marxist holism is only concerned for now with wholes that unify common elements. I am not concerned to define or defend another kind of whole, such as the whole which may tie together end/action as opposed to cause/action. Furthermore, holism, as I am defending it, does not entail that ends, as opposed to prior causes, bring about action.[5]

How can explanatory holism be connected with historical change in general? The changing of a society might involve holism either in the sense in which I am willing to defend it, the necessity of explaining certain actions in reference to other common actions, or in the sense in which I am not willing to defend it, teleology. If holism in the former sense were involved, then it might be argued that societal changes can be explained only by explaining individual actions in terms of the creation of new types of common actions. If, however, holism were being used in the latter, teleological sense, then it may be claimed that society as a whole changes for certain ends. I am not concerned with this latter link between holism and historical change for reasons that I have already indicated, since this notion of whole does not involve common elements. Nor am I concerned with the former link between historical change and holism. It is true that this connection between holism and historical change is not inconsistent with my view of holism. It is also true that it seems to present a more powerful case for the necessity of holistic analysis. However, this is partly a fact about the psychology rather than the logic of explanation. After living in a situation for a while, it might seem that we can explain our action simply on its own, whereas when the situation changes, often without our will, we now begin both to describe and to explain our action in terms of common actions. However, that certainly does not prove that action in a stable situation is more explicable individualistically than action in a more unstable situation. It might only seem to be. On the other hand, it may be that it is only in times of change that the more general features of our action come to the fore and are conceived by the individual as something to be considered when explaining his particular action. Still, Hegelian, Marxist holism must first be defended in its simplest form, and its simplest form is with as little attention to historical change as possible. The situation without change can be analyzed, within limits, without bringing in change, whereas the analysis of change depends upon an analysis of stability.[6]

A third limitation on Hegelian, Marxist holism is that only the common aspects of actions can be explained by it. For example, those actions that produce for the market have many concrete aspects that differentiate them from each other. Each person in certain societies may produce for the market, and all these actions may be similar in that respect, but it is also true that each person may produce for the market in different ways. Holism does not consider the particular, but only the general, aspect of action.[7]

Let us examine again, then, the various ways that holism and universals, or common elements, have been connected.

In Kant, common structures were given by the mind to a world that lacked them. Thus, the dependence of the particular on the universal was bound up with a dualism between mind and externality, along with a stress on what the mind contributed to knowledge. Hegel's account was also mentalistic but lacked Kant's dualism. Common elements were analyzed as mental, but this was because the world external to the human mind was conceived to be ultimately mind-like. Thus, the same common structures were found in the human mind and also in the world.

Marx's final position is somewhat ambiguous. It is obvious that he cannot completely accept the Hegelian position on the nature of common elements. Marx has to reject the Hegelian idea that social forms such as property or the state are mental, but not humanly mental. If social forms are mental, then it is too easy to make the move that Hegel himself makes in *The Philosophy of Right:* to argue that there is no ultimate difference between the inner mental principle that individuals follow and the social mental principle that they follow. It is true that Hegel admits in the civil society section that there is an apparent dichotomy between the two. The inner mental principle may be a moral one, whereas the socially mental principle may be the amoral principle of profit. In the long run, however, for Hegel, when this disharmony is examined from the standpoint of the notion, i.e., the state, then it disappears.

Both as economist and as theoretician of alienation, however, Marx wants the common social form to be in some sense distinct from the inner mental principle. As economist, he wants this because otherwise the laws of value become reduced to the consciously held principles of the human mind as in subjective value theory, or else to the consciously held laws of the state as in in mercantilism or in Hegel. He also wants this as theoretician of alienation because otherwise the social forms will only seem to be opposed to the inwardly mental principle of action, and thus a good argument for believing that there is division between what the social form contributes to action and what the individual contributes to action disappears.

Marx, then, cannot simply adopt the Hegelian interpretation of holism and universals. Does he, then, as some people have thought, accept Hegel's theory that the mind and the world are not qualitatively distinct, but do so by stressing the material nature of mind rather than the mental nature of what we call the physical? This view is the traditional dialectical materialist one. Our analysis of value and objectivity refutes such an interpretation, since the objectivity of value relations is often stated by Marx to be a nonmaterial objectivity.[8] At this point, the nature of that objectivity must be examined more critically.

Earlier, we saw how Marx criticized Proudhon for holding that social relations are subjective. We noted that, on the one hand, Marx could be implying that they are not subjective because the mental apprehension of the common element in the social relation is not unique for each individual. Rather, each individual would comprehend the same common element, which implies that the common elements as mentally apprehended cannot be abstracted from particular mental apprehensions. In this account common elements are mental, but they are not abstracted from particular mental apprehensions. On the other hand, Marx could be implying that common elements are not subjective for another reason: that they are not mental but characterize the world independent of the mind and are not abstracted from particular occurrences in the world. The first, what we might call the Kantian interpretation, comes to the fore when Marx stresses that these relations and common elements have nonmaterial objectivity; the second interpretation, the Hegelian or inverted Hegelian one of the dialectical materialist variety, is suggested when Marx talks of how in exchange people are ruled by objective (sachliche) relations. He then rephrases this notion and says that people are ruled by abstractions, which he once again rephrases to say they are ruled by ideas: "The abstraction or idea, however, is nothing more than a theoretical expression of those material relations *(materiellen Verhältnisse)* which are their lord and master."[9] This is one of the few instances in all of Marx's writings of this phrase, "material relations." Yet, it does not have to imply the materialistic interpretation. Rather, Marx's uncertainty here probably expresses an oscillation between something like a Kantian or Hegelian idealist view and something like a materialist view. That is why he first says that we are dominated by ideas and then that we are dominated by material relations.

We can see how Marx would want something from both materialism and idealism.[10] However, in each case what he would want also entails something that he would not want. What Marx would want from the Hegelian or Kantian interpretation is the ontological reality of common elements. He needs this to argue against the view that the individual controls or understands his action. However, in both Kant and Hegel, common elements, although they can stand against individuals, can never stand against mind. Thus, in the long run the human will, extended as it is by Kant and Hegel into a communal will because of its relation to universals, cannot be dominated by external universals but only by internal mental universals. In Kant and Hegel, however, the mentalism goes along with the universality.

What would Marx want from the materialistic interpretation? Exactly what he could not get from the idealistic interpretation. He wants to show how common elements dominating men are distinct from their minds. Materialism would allow Marx to do this except that it takes away with one hand what it grants with the other. It would allow the common elements to be external, but it would not allow them to be other than abstracted from particulars and to have an ontological reality of their own. It is probably more accurate to say that materialism had not yet succeeded in giving common elements ontological reality at the time Marx was constructing his theory of society than that it could not do this. French and English materialism of the eighteenth century had been empiricistic in its resolute attachment to the view that universals were only abstractions from particulars. This empiricism was often the main argument for their materialism. The sensuous thing, the particular, was what they appealed to in order to establish the power of nature. Furthermore, the materialism which had most influenced Marx, that of Feuerbach, himself influenced by French materialism, had also wound up by attacking the ontological reality of universals. Marx had even accepted this attack in his early writings.[11]

Thus, Marx does not have at hand any characterization of the material world that would allow him to characterize the ontological reality of universals. Still, he wants to utilize some form of materialism because at least material entities could be said to cause other entities, even though in the materialism of his day they caused them not because of common structures connecting them but through particular efficient causes. Marx is in a dilemma. He wants to say that the individual act is caused, but if it is caused by matter then it is caused by particulars. If the individual act is caused partially by common elements, Marx does not know how to characterize these elements in such a way that they have an objectivity which is not merely mental. The more they are simply mental, the more stress on these common mental elements conflicts with Marx's account of how it is not only ideas that bring about social events, but also forces and relations of production external to the mind.

All these points place Marx in a peculiar perspective in relation to Kant and Hegel. Marx cannot accept Kant's view that common elements such as causality are mentalistic.[12] Nor can he accept Hegel's subject-object identity, with its implied certainty about the correspondence between the common elements found in the mind and those found in the world. Marx gives an analysis of common actions in economic society: individual value-producing actions cannot come about without other actions of the same type. His analysis of material objects is so different from this analysis of value-producing actions that he sometimes insists that the latter have nonmaterial objectivity. However, his characterization of this objectivity is no more a full-scale rejection of materialism than his discussion of men being ruled by material relations is a full-scale rejection of idealism. Neither mind nor matter, as currently analyzed, can account for the existence of value-producing actions. Marx's ultimate relation to Kantianism, or to Hegelian idealism, or to materialism, must be viewed in this light. Since Marx has not shown that holism exists in the realm of material objects, for the time being he cannot say that material objects and exchange value-producing actions can be analyzed in the same way. This does not mean that, in principle, they could not be analyzed in the same way.[13]

These methodological points may underlie Marx's use of Hegel against Kant. Marx cannot accept, as we have argued Kant did, that the common structures of reality are mentalistic. Hegel's subject-object identity also implies a rejection of this Kantian view. But whereas Hegel claims to know exactly what the common structures are, Marx only claims that they operate in society. Ultimate characterization of what they are is left open. This open-ended part of Marx's philosophy could be said to place him closer to Kant. However, in the very process of showing that holism operates in society, Hegelian Marxism is able to give a new definition of society. That definition allows Hegelian Marxism to take the elements that it wants from idealism and materialism, rejecting the elements that it does not want. This is quite a trick, since, as noted earlier, the characteristics wanted from both idealism and materialism seem to imply elements that are not wanted. Thus, in order to avoid getting what it does not want from materialism and idealism, Hegelian Marxism must reformulate the interconnections between what it does want.

What it wants from idealism is the reality of the common aspects of action, but that commonness must not be just internal to the mind. Only if it has an element of externality can it both cause individual action and be alienated from individual action. We now see the connection in the Hegelian, Marxist version of holism between the idea that common elements help explain action and the idea that they are not simply external. An external commonness that could cause action is never arrived at in Kant.[14] In Hegel, it is almost achieved with Essence and civil society. Yet, it is always taken back by the Notion, because as philosopher Hegel held that mind dominated the world and as economist he held that the state dominated the economy. Thus, the external universal of civil society is always shown as illusory in the light of state and mind. The state and mind alienate themselves in civil society, but they always find their way home again. That is why at a certain point Hegel always starts pulling punches in his description of the externality of the principles operating in civil society. Civil society has to be described increasingly as something that has only secondary reality as compared to the state.

For Marx, it is important to keep the cutting edge of that sense of externality in his description of capitalism. Only by doing so and by constantly contrasting that externality with the internal universals of the mind can Marx come up with an account of community which truly is divided from individuals and is thus alienated. Marx could not achieve a theory of divided community and external universality by first stressing external universality, as in Hegel, and then downplaying it. Of course, neither could he achieve it by stressing inner mental universals as Kant did. In some ways, however, there is more real alienation described in the Kantian system than in the Hegelian. The reason is simply that, since in Kant the deep problems, of connecting the self with the economy and thereby the inner universals of the mind with the external universals of society, are not fully grasped, they are therefore laid on the table in a naive form. Kant's system shows the pathos of beginning with a theory of the self and of the mental universal, and then being forced to eventually include domination of the self by the economy. As Hegel sees it, this domination could be described only with the concept of the external universal. However, precisely because as philosopher of alienation Hegel sees this, as philosopher of reconciliation he wants to soften it. Since Kant does not see the domination as clearly, when it is presented it is not softened.

Still, even though the externality of Hegel's universal turns out to be only apparent, the concept, before it is softened, does allow him to approach the problem of truth as applied to action in a different manner from Kant. The concept of truth shows the inner connection between all three aspects of Hegelian, Marxist holism: (1) that the common element helps explain action, (2) that the common element must not be merely internal, and (3) that there must be a search for the most basic common element. We noted earlier that Kant did not adequately face the problem of how true a given description of action is. He seemed to have thought that the description of an action was unproblematic and that only the question of whether the description could be universalized was of interest. Hegel, however, in his doctrine of universals grapples with the question of the

truth of descriptions. In *The Philosophy of Right,* the description of
the action as following contract and the first universal is the most
illusory and has the least truth. The description of the action as
following the laws of capitalism and the second universal is the next
most illusory and has more truth. The description of the action as
following the rules of the state is the least illusory and has the most
truth. The problem, however, is that Hegel utilizes his mentalism
in order to assign the most truth to the state description. Thus,
although he recognizes the problem of the truth of the description
of action, he certainly does not solve it.

I have said that Hegel attempts to deal with the question of the
truth of descriptions of action. We must further analyze this concept
of truth by relating it to causal explanation. This connection between
truth and causal explanation ultimately reveals the difference between subjectivist accounts of the relation between subject and
object, such as is found in many representatives of post-classical
German philosophy, and objectivist accounts of the type offered by
the Hegelian, Marxist tradition. For the subjectivist accounts,
subject-object identity is often a matter of identity of meaning,
whereas for the objectivist accounts the subject is only partially
identical with the object, and this is shown by an analysis of causality.

The basic connection between subject-object identity and meaning
is that subject-object identity does entail some sort of homology
between meaning in the subject and meaning in the object. Thus,
the meaning of a tool transformed by legal system would have
some of the same characteristics as the meaning of the mental ideal
that gave rise to the creation of the tool. Similarly, the meaning of
the act as defined by a social law and as defined by the subjects
performing it may be very close. However, in the Hegelian, Marxist
theory, subject and object, although identical in one way, are also
different. The tool may have meanings that the idea in the mind
would not have. The act defined by the social law may have meanings that the subject did not foresee. In addition to analyzing the
tool and the action in terms of their meaning, the tool must be
analyzed as a material object and the action must be given a causal
explanation.

If, however, one were to stress that meaning is the basic ontological
category here, then one might be better able to assert total identity

of subject and object. It is easier to establish that the same meaning is found in subject and object than to show that material objects or socially caused actions are the same as mental acts. But often, subject-object identity as found in post-classical German philosophy, particularly phenomenology, primarily asserts homology of meaning between subject and object. This meaning, since it is not sullied by questions about material objects or the social causes of actions, can be reconstructed by the mind. On the other hand, precisely because for Hegelian Marxism subject-object identity involves identity and difference between the subject and object, all aspects of subject-object interaction must be studied in order to understand the meaning of a given activity. The person must analyze all the social forms that influence his action. Only in this way can the truth of the action be grasped as well as the meaning. For the person is defined by many meanings, his own and those coming from society. He must penetrate into all the strands of descriptions that can be found, using science, economics, or any other tool. For some meanings of his actions are causally imposed by an alien society.[15]

This insight into how meanings are sometimes imposed by society, which is both identical to and different from the subject, results in the possibility of distinguishing between basic and nonbasic meanings of actions. One must get at truth by asking not just what is the meaning of action but what is the meaning which, when grasped, best causally explains the action, what I call the basic meaning. It is the basic meaning that explains why x's action is repeated. When the concept of the truth of the description of action is arrived at by deciding which description best gets at the cause of the repetition of the action, the result is a concept of basicness which connects Marx's base/superstructure theory to Hegel's and Kant's theories of action. Applying these concepts to Hegel, we can say that the aspect of the action defined by civil society is more basic than that defined by contract, and that the aspect defined by the state is yet more basic. The more basic aspects do not by themselves give us the truth but allow us to look at the totality of descriptions and their ranking in terms of basicness, all of which then gives us the truth. Thus, for Marx the act of working in a factory is repeated not primarily because of the religious connotations given to it (the superstructural aspect), but because the act produces surplus value (the basic aspect). The truth of the action is given by understanding both of these aspects as well as the relation between them, i.e., understanding which is more basic relative to the other.[16]

For Marx, the base is made up of the mode of production which consists primarily of the realm of value as it brings about social reproduction. The superstructure, on the other hand, is made up primarily of the state and actions within the political whole. Marx argued that the superstructure is determined by, caused by, or, in our language, less basic than, the base.[17]

For our purposes, we consider the base/superstructure metaphor only as it expresses a relation between the actions in the base and the actions in the superstructure. As soon as we concentrate on the way the doctrine applies to actions rather than things, then certain of its metaphorical connotations must be stripped away, primarily those suggesting that the superstructure is built on the base in the way that one thing is built on another thing. This suggests that first the base is built and that then the state happens on top of it. But the actions which reproduce the social wholes of the base and superstructure are not necessarily separate actions. One action could produce and reproduce the realm of value, social reproduction, and the realm of politics all at the same time. Therefore, if we were to stick too closely to the base/superstructure metaphor, we would have to say that one part or aspect of a given action is determined by or is built upon another. But how can one part of the action cause or determine the other part? Certainly not in the sense that one is the efficient cause of the other.

Of course, it might be easier to apply the base/superstructure metaphor when talking about a situation where the action of individual *a* causes the action of individual *b*. An example might be that *a*'s action within the value whole causes *b*'s action within the political whole. The former could conceivably be the efficient cause of the latter. But the value aspect of *a*'s action could not in the same way cause the political aspect of his own action. Thus, there would be an asymmetry between the way in which *a*'s market action would be connected with his own political action and the way it would be connected to *b*'s political action. But the fact that market or political actions are common as defined by a social whole works against such an asymmetry. Any action should be analyzable in the same way as any similar action. Thus, the metaphorical interpretation of the base/superstructure doctrine does not seem consistent with Marx's account of actions being defined as common within social wholes.

An alternative approach, as we have seen, would be to hold that using characteristics from the base to define the action would give a truer description of the action than using the language of the super-structure. This would tie the whole problematic of base and super-structure to the opposition between Hegel and Kant on the problem of finding out the truth or basicness of the action. In this case, by giving multiple descriptions of actions and using various universals corresponding to various social or economic stages, both Marx and Hegel would oppose the more illusory description of the action to the truer description of the action. It should be kept in mind here that for Marx, even more than for Hegel, the truth is found in the whole series of descriptions when they are ordered in terms of their ability to explain why the action is repeated. It is not that x's non-basic action is caused by a single basic action, either his own or someone else's; rather, all the nonbasic actions are caused by all the basic ones.[18]

Only such an account is consistent with Marx's theory of aliena-tion or division from the common aspects of actions. That account involves holding that as actions become homogeneous, then one is just as alienated from the actions of others as they are from their own. One might say that (1) the base/superstructure theory becomes more personalized to the degree that (2) the theory of alienation becomes less personalized. The first happens because it must be possible to give an account of base/superstructure where the basic part of x's own personal action does in some sense cause the non-basic part, and the second happens because alienation is not just a matter of alienation from one's own personal actions, but rather from all actions that follow the same rules and have the same com-mon elements.

On this account, then, Hegelian Marxism offers a resolution to the problem raised by Kant's ethics of how to relate the self to the basic description of action. But the difference between Marx and Hegel still needs to be stressed. Even though they use the same method of moving from the less basic to the more basic description, they certainly do not see the same economic and social structures or their corresponding universals as the most basic, one stressing the state and the other the mode of production. This difference would not be that important if Marx were to cling to the mentalism of Hegel, but Marx's subtle theoretical rejection of Hegel's mentalism complements the difference of content.

We have now seen how the Hegelian, Marxist account of social holism, then, reflects three positions: (1) that the universal helps explain the action; (2) that the universal is not simply internal but external as well; and (3) that it is possible to find the truest universal description, truth being defined in terms of basicness, which in turn is defined in terms of which description best explains why the act is repeated.[19]

Conclusion

This book began with a general account of alienation in terms of arguments for division in the self. Among the many possible types of arguments, those were stressed which centered on opposition between social and individual aspects of the self. It was claimed, however, that these arguments could develop in two different ways: through a concept of moral holism, where the ethical self must sometimes justify itself within the context of social rules; and through an epistemological concept of explanatory holism where individual actions must sometimes be explained within the context of society and social rules. Both moral and epistemological holism were seen to lead to a conception of a social self which could sometimes be said to be in tension with or in opposition to an individual self.

The result of linking alienation to these two types of holism, moral and epistemological, was to broaden the tradition of alienation theory to include thinkers like Kant, Smith, and Quesnay, who might ordinarily not be said to use the concept of alienation. New themes became linked with alienation, such as Kant's conception of community, Quesnay's epistemological use of Malebranche and Smith's moral use of natural law. At the same time, alienation and both moral and epistemological holism were linked to the economic doctrines of Smith, Quesnay, and Kant.

By the time this study arrives at Hegel and Marx, familiar theorists of alienation, the concept of alienation has been fructified so much by including unfamiliar themes within it that Hegel's and Marx's concepts of alienation also appear in a new light. This impression is perhaps strengthened by the fact that, in order to link up with the economic traditions of Smith and Quesnay, a very detailed economic account of alienation in Hegel and Marx is given. Hegel is analyzed in relation to both the mercantilists and free-enterprise theorists in economics, and his theory of alienation is seen to emerge partly out of the juncture of these two theories. In the case of Marx, this is, I believe, the first account of Marx's theory of alienation to be based entirely on his economic plan first sketched in the *Grundrisse* in 1857 and repeated, with various modifications, until the end of his life. Both Marx and Hegel are thus seen in the context of German idealism and classical political economy and the theories of holism and the self that arise from them. The leading difference between the accounts of alienation in Smith, Kant, and the Physiocrats and the account in Marx and Hegel is that for the former alienation is clearly bound up with both epistemological and moral holism, whereas for the latter I have presented it as primarily bound up with epistemological holism. It might be asked, where is the corresponding moral holism in Marx's and Hegel's account of alienation? To answer this question, I must once again refer to the tradition of Hegelian Marxism in which I am writing.

Throughout the book, it is stressed that although alienation rests on the concept of division, it also rests on the concept of lack of division or order. In social theories of alienation, the social order of the self is in tension with the individual order. That social order is either a holistic ethical ideal related to the self, or the holistic working of society on the self. In both cases, the individual is in tension with his own social action. But whereas in Kant, Smith, and Quesnay this idea is approached morally as well as in terms of epistemological holism, with Hegel and Marx there is a tendency to deny the validity of the purely moral approach. In Kant, Hegel, and Marx, the alienated self with its ambiguous communal nature, out of its control, is contrasted to a nonalienated self which has firmly controlled its own communal nature. In Kant, this moral and communal self is posited as an abstract ideal as over and against the actual self. In contrast, with Hegel and Marx, the moral content of Kant's communitarian theory becomes transformed into an account of the difference between the actual alienating relation between the self and its communal nature and the potential nonalienating relation between them. There is no doubt that the account of alienation in Hegel and Marx is an attempt to eliminate the concept of a purely moral claim located outside the self, and to oppose to it the concept of a potential/actual self. The actual self is divided between a social self, explained by the social whole, and an individual self in tension with that social self. In the potential self, the social and individual aspects of the self are in harmony.

Now it may be that it is primarily the opposition to a language of pure morality which explains the growth of the theory of alienation in both Hegel and Marx. However, just as I have stressed the affinity of moral accounts of the self, as in Kant and Smith, with concepts of alienation, in a parallel way I also want to stress the affinity of the paradigmatic theories of alienation of Hegel and Marx with some of the elements of moral theory in thinkers like Smith and Kant. Although the moral theory of the communal self may have become transformed in Hegel and Marx into an account of the potential self, the potential self theory still retains some of the original moral theory in it. First, both the moral account and the potential/actual self account rest on the notion of a true self which has attained freedom, as the ultimate human value. Second, what we ascribe to the potential self may owe much to our prior understanding of the moral self. What in Kant was a moral theory of man may, in Hegel and Marx, have become more a method of studying society. Yet, it is unclear whether Hegel and Marx would have seen holistic man in society if they were not familiar with holistic man in the realm of moral theory. The problem is that too often Marx's and Hegel's rejection of a purely moral way of analyzing man has been assimilated to a kind of positivism, where the moral has been displaced by the factual. However, if Marx and Hegel have attempted to break down the fact/value dichotomy, then they are concerned neither with the factual alone nor with the moral or valuational alone, but with something that synthesizes them.

In sympathy with the idea of breaking down the fact/value dichotomy, I would add that when moral values as a whole are given to man and when his epistemological standpoint is also given as a whole, then the individual perhaps does not make a sharp division between fact and value. However, let me also add a word of skepticism about overcoming the fact/value dichotomy: it seems that in the present state of affairs it is necessary to make moral judgments about socialism, democracy, and the nature of a just society. There is now renewed interest in these questions among Marxists. A task for the future would be to present a fuller explication of the parallels between the languages of alienation and of morality.

Having introduced the idea that contemporary economic man lacks a sense of the whole, we can consider some ramifications of this work for future developments in the relation between economics and philosophy. It is no accident that this book traces the theme of economy and self only up to the debates over subjective value theory after 1871. Subjective value theory was the most extreme form of individualism economics had faced, much more extreme than the individualism Quesnay and Smith represented. This book shows that individualistic elements in Quesnay and Smith were always in tension with holistic elements. Mercantilism, physiocracy, classical British political economy, Marxism—all tried to place the economic self in the larger context of society as a whole. Within this social context the economic self attempted to achieve knowledge and value. An aim of this book is to show how the holistic view of economy and self paralleled some of the eighteenth- and nineteenth-century philosophical systems: Quesnay's and Smith's natural law theories, and Kant's, Hegel's and Marx's classical philosophy. The twentieth century is often seen as one of fragmentation—a fragmentation that perhaps proceeds in parallel lines: in economics with the advent of subjective value theory, in philosophy, art, literature, sociology. If this is true, there are countervailing tendencies. From the start, for example, the individualism of subjective value theory was criticized by such diverse elements as the German historical school and religious efforts to humanize economics. Some of this opposition was primarily moral in nature, which explains some of its limitations. Holistic opposition to excessive individualism must not only present moral aspirations, but also delineate the individual's distance from and integration into economic society. I agree with Lukács and Goldmann that Marxism is distinguished by its methodological stress on knowledge of the whole. To delineate how that knowledge might be achieved, however, is again, a task for the future.

Notes

Introduction

1. For the history of the concept of alienation, see István Mészáros, *Marx's Theory of Alienation*, pp. 27-65. The definition of alienation in the glossary to Karl Marx, *Early Writings*, trans. Rodney Livingston and Gregor Benton, pp. 429-430, seems to center around the split between the subject and the object. However, I would include subject-object division within the general category of division within the self. If the self did not partially identify with the object and oppose it to the more subjective parts of itself, then division between subject and object would not be alienation. I must add that the aim of my characterization is to cover as many aspects of alienation as possible and to allow themes to be included under alienation which have previously remained outside the Marxist and existentialist arena of alienation theories.

2. I do not adopt Lucien Goldmann's position, *Recherches Dialectiques* (Paris: Gallimard, 1959), pp. 293-294, that the fact/value dichotomy can be completely overcome. Nevertheless, that position has guided me in opting for a closer relation between fact and value than is usually adopted.

3. For alienation in modern art, see Herbert Read, *Art and Alienation* (New York: Viking, 1970). For an interpretation of Greek tragedy which could lend itself to this analysis of alienation, see Jan Kott, *The Eating of the Gods* (New York, Random House, 1971).

4. I follow the terminology in George Lukács, *Zur Ontologie des gesellschaftlichen Seins: Hegels falsche und echte Ontologie* (Neuwied: Luchterhand, 1971), p. 4.

5. For a discussion of social and individual accounts of alienation, see Adam Schaff, *Marxism and the Human Individual* (New York: McGraw-Hill, 1970).

6. For an account of economic thought in Germany at the end of the nineteenth and beginning of the twentieth centuries, the period of Tönnies, Simmel, Schmoller, and Weber, see David Frisby, "Introduction" to Theodore Adorno, et al., *The Positivist Dispute in German Sociology*, pp. xvii-xix; T. W. Hutchinson, *A Review of Economic Doctrines, 1870-1929*, pp. 130-196. For the relation between German economics and philosophy, see Frisby. For the German philosophy of the time, see Lucien Goldmann, *Lukács et Heidegger*, pp. 59-66. Among Hegelian Marxists, Goldmann and Lukács managed to combine some classical German philosophy with some trends found in the late nineteenth and early twentieth centuries, such as *Verstehen* philosophy. However, for Goldmann and Lukács, classical German philosophy always predominated in the end. Lucien Goldmann, *Marxisme et Sciences Humaines*, pp. 263-264, argues that Frankfurt School Hegelian Marxism sometimes let other currents, such as existentialism, triumph over the elements of classical German philosophy.

7. W. Stanley Jevons, *The Theory of Political Economy*, p. 44.

8. G.W.F. Hegel, *Hegel's Logic*, pp. 47-53.

9. Lucien Goldmann, *The Hidden God*.

10. For a survey of the controversy over the young and old Marx, see Ernest Mandel, *The Formation of Marx's Economic Thought*, pp. 164-184. For a discussion of the young and old Hegel, see Charles Taylor, *Hegel*, pp. 51-75. Marcel Xhaufflaire, *Feuerbach et la Théologie de la Secularisation*, has analyzed how the notions of species essence and alienation gradually disappear from Feuerbach's work. For the two Lukács, compare Georg Lukács, *The Theory of the Novel* (Cambridge: MIT Press, 1971), originally published in 1920, and the new preface, written in 1962.

11. Plato, *The Republic of Plato* (Oxford: Oxford University Press, 1945), trans. Francis MacDonald Cornford, pp. 283-286.

12. See Georg Lukács, *Soul and Form*, pp. 152-155.

13. Friedrich Nietzsche, *Beyond Good and Evil* (New York: Boni and Liverwright, n.d.), p. 264, was one of the first to analyze this aspect of ethics.

14. Ludwig Feuerbach, *The Essence of Christianity*, pp. 1-12; Karl Marx, *The Economic and Philosophic Manuscripts of 1844*, p. 187.

15. See Karl Löwith, *From Hegel to Nietzshce*, pp. 50-51.

16. For the left Hegelians, see Goldmann, *Lukács et Heidegger*, pp. 171-172. The incident about Marx rejecting the papers is in Maximilien Rubel and Margaret Manale, *Marx Without Myth*, p. 26.

17. For the discussion of Borgia, see Friedrich Nietzsche, *Ecce Homo*, in *Complete Works* (Edinburgh: T. N. Foulis, 1911), Vol. 17, p. 58.

18. Jean Paul Sartre, "Materialisme et Révolution," in *Situations*, Vol. 3, p. 222.

19. For further discussion of social contract theory, see Wilmoore Kendall, *John Locke and the Doctrine of Majority Rule*; John M. Dunn, *The Political Thought of John Locke* (London: Cambridge University Press, 1969); C. B. Macpherson, *The Political Theory of Possessive Individualism* (Oxford: Oxford University Press, 1962).

20. Karl Marx and Frederick Engels, *Selected Correspondence*, pp. 198-199.

Chapter 1

1. James Bonar, *Philosophy and Political Economy*, p. 131.

2. Eli Heckscher, *Mercantilism*, Vol. 2, pp. 14-15. However, see Ronald Meek, *Studies in the Labor Theory of Value*, pp. ii, 295-296, and *Economics and Ideology*, pp. 200-201, for a discussion of the thesis of continuity between medieval political economy and mercantilism.

3. All these points are discussed at length in Heckscher, *Mercantilism*. The criticisms of Heckscher in D. C. Coleman, ed., *Revisions in Mercantilism*, are not directed against his attribution of these policies to the mercantilists. For the identification of money and wealth, see J. Marcus Fleming, "Mercantilism and Free Trade Today," in Thomas Wilson and Andrew S. Skinner, eds., *The Market and the State*, p. 165.

4. For a criticism of Heckscher's failure to adequately grasp this point, see D. C. Coleman, "Eli Heckscher and the Idea of Mercantilism," in Coleman, ed., *Revisions*, pp. 100-102.

5. Heckscher, *Mercantilism*, Vol. 2, pp. 337-338.

6. See Franz Neumann, *The Democratic and the Authoritarian State*, pp. 28-31, for a discussion of the relation of modern law to capitalism.

7. See Chapter 3.

8. See Chapter 5.

9. Antonio Gramsci, "The Revolution Against 'Capital'," in *Selections from Political Writings 1910-1920*, pp. 34-38.

10. W. Stanley Jevons, *The Theory of Political Economy* is an example.

11. For Schmoller and *Katherersozialismus*, see William Henry Spiegel, *The Growth of Economic Thought*, pp. 425-426. See also S. R. Sen, *The Economics of Sir James Steuart*, and Gunnar Myrdal, *The Political Element in the Development of Economic Theory*.

12. A. V. Judges, "The Idea of a Mercantile State," in Coleman, ed., *Revisions*, pp. 59-60. Jacob Viner's essay is "Power Versus Plenty as Objectives of Foreign Policy in the Seventeenth and Eighteenth Centuries," in Coleman, ed., *Revisions*.

13. Karl Polanyi, "Aristotle Discovers the Economy," in Karl Polanyi,

Conrad M. Arensberg, and Harry W. Pearson, eds., *Trade and Market in the Early Empires*, p. 68.

14. Sir Henry Maine, *Ancient Law*, pp. 6-7; Ferdinand Tönnies, *Community and Society*, pp. 46, 75.

15. Paul Chamley, *Économie Politique et Philosophie chez Steuart et Hegel*, p. 213.

16. Of interest here is the discussion by Neumann, *The Democratic and The Authoritarian State*, pp. 61-65, of how certain forces in Germany attempted to oppose community to the impersonal market. But the communal corporatism that they opposed to the market only exacerbated the political inequalities that existed in the already embedded German economy.

17. See J.G.A. Pocock, *The Machiavellian Moment*, p. 425, for a clear statement of what are in fact mercantilist themes.

18. Ibid., p. 333.

19. Ibid., p. 440. Also see Albert O. Hirschmann, *The Passions and the Interests*, pp. 56-63.

20. Pocock, *The Machiavellian Moment*, p. 447.

21. Ibid., p. 452.

22. Ibid., p. 455.

23. It is a fact often overlooked, for example, that for Mandeville, the state helped to turn private vices into public benefits. See Hirschmann, *Passions*, pp. 18-19.

24. Ibid., pp. 83, 86.

25. Pocock, *The Machiavellian Moment*, p. 462.

26. Ibid., p. 464.

27. Ibid., p. 433.

28. Ibid., p. 465.

29. Ibid., p. 487.

30. Another use of the work of Hirschmann and Pocock would be to apply it to the period of mercantilism proper, when the flood of free-enterprise theory was much smaller—how much smaller is still open to question.

Chapter 2

1. For the concept of social reproduction in Quesnay, see Ronald Meek, *The Economics of Physiocracy*, pp. 227-286; Jean Benard, "Marx et Quesnay," in Francois Quesnay, *Francois Quesnay et la Physiocratie*, Vol. 1, pp. 108-114; Michael Lutfalla, "Preface" to *Francois Quesnay: Tableau Économique des Physiocrates*, pp. 19-22.

2. The anecdote is recounted in S. K. Srivastava, *History of Economic Thought*, p. 75. For the relation of politics to economics in physiocracy, see Guillaume (Wilhelm) Hasbach, "Les Fondements Philosophiques de L'Éco-

nomie Politique," pp. 771-772; H. Baudrillart, "La Philosophie des Physio-crates," pp. 12-13; Elizabeth Fox-Genovese, *The Origins of Physiocracy*, pp. 202-245.

3. For a detailed discussion of the various versions of the *Tableau*, see Ronald Meek in Marguerite Kuezynski and Ronald Meek, eds., *Quesnay's Tableau Économique* (London: Macmillan, 1972), pp. ix-xx.

4. There is not just a conceptual connection between Harvey and Quesnay. There is also a historical connection in the person of the Dutch physician Boerhaave. Boerhaave was a follower of Harvey, and Quesnay was a close disciple of both. See Jean Sutter, "Quesnay et la Médecine," in *Francois Quesnay et la Physiocratie*, Vol. 1, pp. 201-202. For more on the relation between economics and medicine in Quesnay, see Lutfalla, *Francois Quesnay*, pp. 22-23, and Vernard Foley, *The Social Physics of Adam Smith*, pp. 122-125, 128-131.

5. For a discussion of the problems in dating the *Tableau*, see Meek, *Quesnay's Tableau Économique*, pp. ix-xx.

6. Sutter, *Francois Quesnay et La Physiocratie*, Vol. 1, p. 202.

7. Quoted in Akiteru Kubota, "Quesnay, Disciple de Malebrance," in *Francois Quesnay et La Physiocratie*, Vol. 1, p. 193.

8. Hasbach, "Fondements," has argued against the claim that Male-branche influenced Quesnay very much. One of his arguments (p. 768) is that for Malebranche order is in God, whereas in Quesnay it is in the world. However, Pierre-Maxim Schuhl, "Malebranche et Quesnay," pp. 313-314, has argued that both Quesnay and Malebranche stress the order of the world. Hasbach's attempted refutation of the importance of Malebranche for Quesnay is partly bound up with his assertion (p. 769) that Quesnay was influenced more by the inductive method of English philosophy than by Cartesianism. However, he by no means establishes this point; indeed, he admits in the same context (p. 769) that Quesnay may have been influenced by Malebranche's metaphysics.

9. Quoted in Kubota, "Quesnay, Disciple de Malebrance," Vol. 1, p. 194; Francois Quesnay, "Évidence," in *Francois Quesnay et La Physio-cratie*, Vol. 2, p. 419.

10. Quesnay, "Évidence," p. 419.

11. O. H. Taylor, "Economics and the Idea of *Jus Naturale*," p. 217, discusses the issue of animism in physiocracy.

12. For a discussion of Mach on Berkeley, see Karl Popper, "A Note on Berkeley as Precursor of Mach and Einstein," in C. B. Martin and D. M. Armstrong, eds., *Locke and Berkeley* (Garden City, N.Y.: Doubleday, 1968), pp. 44-447. There is also a discussion of Malebranche in relation to late nineteenth-century positivism in Jean Wahl, *Tableau de la Philosophie Française*, pp. 39-40.

13. Quesnay, "Évidence," p. 419.

14. Ibid., p. 423.

15. However, Kubota, "Quesnay, Disciple de Malebrance," pp. 183-185, holds that as a physiologist Quesnay was somewhat opposed to Malebranche.

16. The role of empircial sensation is stressed very much in Quesnay, "Évidence," pp. 409, 411. One can still defend the Malebranchian influence on Quesnay without deemphasizing the empiricistic influence as strongly as August Oncken, ed., *Oeuvres Économiques et Philosophiques de F. Quesnay*, p. 745.

17. Hasbach, "Fondements," p. 776, argues that whereas for Smith there is a preestablished harmony among men which is psychological and ethical, for the Physiocrats there is no preestablished harmony, but harmony must be worked for through political laws.

18. Francois Quesnay, "Natural Law," in Meek, ed., *The Economics of Physiocracy*, p. 53; *Quesnay et la Physiocratie*, Vol. II, p. 734.

19. For a discussion of this "physicism," see Edgard Allix, "Le Physicisme des Physiocrates."

20. Quesnay, "Natural Law," p. 46.

21. Baudrillart, "La Philosophie des Physiocrates," p. 17.

22. Quesnay, "Évidence," p. 423; Francois Quesnay, *Essai Physique sur L'Économie Animale*, excerpted in Oncken, ed., *Oeuvres Economiques et Philosophiques de F. Quesnay*, p. 751. By giving man some freedom, Quesnay revises Malebranche in the same direction that Berkeley did. For a discussion of Berkeley and Malebranche on this issue, see A. A. Luce, *Berkeley and Malebranche*, p. 89.

23. Quesnay, *Essai Physique*, p. 755; "Évidence," p. 484.

24. See Jean-Jacques Rousseau, *The Social Contract*, pp. 19-21; Otto Gierke, *Natural Law and the Theory of Society*, pp. 293-295, gives an excellent bibliographical discussion of views on property both before and after the Physiocrats.

25. For an interesting discussion of these issues, see Adam Smith, *Lectures on Jurisprudence*, pp. 17-18.

26. Quesnay, "Natural Law," p. 52 (translation amended).

27. Ibid., p. 45.

28. Ibid., p. 55; p. 54 (translation amended).

29. Ibid., p. 47.

Chapter 3

1. Adam Smith's abstraction from politics is only relative, as shown by his definition of economics as "a branch of the science of a statesman or legislator" (*The Wealth of Nations*, p. 428). The abstraction was partly a

matter of separating subject matters that were later to be brought back together. Thus, W. R. Scott, *Adam Smith as Student and Professor* (1937; reprinted New York: Augustus M. Kelley, 1965), p. 319, talks of Smith's "epoch making decision to separate it (economic material) completely from the treatment of Jurisprudence in which it had been previously embedded."

2. Exchange value is most fully discussed in Chapters 5 and 7 of *The Wealth of Nations*.

3. Smith, *The Wealth of Nations*, pp. 74-75.

4. The term "invisible hand" appears in the context of a discussion of trade between nations in *The Wealth of Nations*, p. 456. The concept of reattaining equilibrium between supply and demand is discussed on pp. 74-75. For a discussion of exchange value in relation to supply and demand, see Maurice Dobb, *Theories of Value and Distribution Since Smith*, p. 44.

5. Claudio Napoleoni, *Smith Ricardo Marx*, pp. 31-32, analyzes the relation between petty commodity production and capitalism. He argues that the stress on petty commodity production is a remnant of the type of thought found in Smith's Glasgow *Lectures on Jurisprudence*.

6. The extent to which Smith had a labor theory of value at all has become a topic of much controversy. The discussion of the point in Dobb, *Theories of Value and Distribution*; Napoleoni, *Ricardo und Marx*; and E. K. Hunt, "Value Theory in the Writings of the Classical Economists, Thomas Hodgskin, and Karl Marx," centers around Sraffa's account in *The Works and Correspondence of David Ricardo*, 10 vols., ed. Piero Sraffa. The controversy turns partly on Smith's comment in *The Wealth of Nations* that the "value of any commodity . . . is equal to the quantity of labor which it enables him to purchase or command" (p. 47). According to Sraffa, Ricardo interpreted this statement to mean that "commodities exchanged according to the amount of labor required for their production" (p. xxxvi). Dobb also thinks (p. 48) that Smith sometimes holds a labor theory of value in the sense that the value of the commodity is analyzed in terms of the labor necessary to produce it. However, Dobb then finds it surprising that Smith could ever state this in terms of the idea that the commodity is equal to the amount of labor that it can purchase or command (p. 490). Hunt also holds that it is only in some odd sense that "labor alone creates value" (p. 332). Napoleoni (pp. 60-61) offers the interesting theory that the concept of commanded labor reflects a capitalist as opposed to a noncapitalist market.

7. See Ernest Mandel, *The Formation of the Economic Thought of Karl Marx*, p. 45.

8. Smith, *The Wealth of Nations*, p. 67.

9. Ibid., p. 25.

10. Ibid., pp. 65, 67.

11. Adam Smith, "Early Draft of Part of The Wealth of Nations," in *Lectures on Jurisprudence*, p. 563.

12. This assumes, of course, that he did hold in some sense that the value of the commodity is equal to the labor necessary to produce it.

13. "Early Draft," pp. 563-564.

14. Ronald L. Meek and Andrew S. Skinner, "The Development of Adam Smith's Ideas on the Division of Labour," pp. 1102-1103, discuss the dating of the relevant material.

15. This point is in opposition to Gary Wills, "Benevolent Adam Smith," pp. 41-42, who argues that the extent of the market, although primarily geographical, strengthens Adam Smith's human nature explanation for exchange. Wills also argues that the human nature explanation is based on the cooperative elements of human nature just as much as on the competitive elements.

16. There are passages in both sets of the lectures in Smith's *Lectures on Jurisprudence*, pp. 340-341, 490, which parallel the violence and law passage from the "Early Draft."

17. Smith, *Lectures on Jurisprudence*, p. 492.

18. Smith, *The Wealth of Nations*, pp. 28-29, "The difference between the most dissimilar characters, between a philosopher and a common street porter, for example, seems to arise not so much from nature as from habit, custom, and education."

19. Smith, "Early Draft," p. 564.

20. Smith, *The Wealth of Nations*, pp. 781-782. See especially the last chapter of Joseph Cropsey, *Polity and Economy: An Interpretation of the Principles of Adam Smith*.

21. Eli Halévy, *The Growth of Philosophic Radicalism*, pp. 100-102, gives as evidence for Smith's realization of this inequality the fact that he holds that in some countries profits and rent devour wages; that there is a natural monopoly in land; that masters have an edge over workmen in contracts.

22. Smith, *Lectures on Jurisprudence*, pp. 404, 208-209.

23. Adam Smith, "A Letter to the Editors of the *Edinburgh Review*," in *The Works of Adam Smith*, Dugald Stewart, ed., p. 578.

24. Smith, *Lectures on Jurisprudence*, p. 401.

25. Ibid., pp. 397, 398.

26. Ibid., p. 13.

27. Ibid., p. 17.

28. Ibid., p. 5.

29. Joseph Cropsey, *Polity and Economy: An Interpretation of the Principles of Adam Smith*, p. 93.

30. Lucio Colletti, *From Rousseau to Lenin*, pp. 205-206.

31. Smith, *The Wealth of Nations*, pp. 26-27.

32. Adam Smith, *The Theory of Moral Sentiments*, in *Works*, p. 146.

33. Ibid., p. 147.

34. For Harvey, too, the circulation of the blood could be analyzed in terms of purposiveness and final causes. See O. H. Taylor, "Economics and the Idea of Natural Laws," p. 17.

35. Quoted in Jacob Viner, *The Long View and the Short*, p. 219.

36. Smith, *The Wealth of Nations*, p. 456.

37. Viner, *The Long View and the Short*, p. 224; H. J. Bitterman, "Adam Smith's Empiricism and the Laws of Nature."

38. Smith, *The Wealth of Nations*, p. 28.

39. Guillaume (Wilhelm) Hasbach, "Les Fondements Philosophiques de L'Économie Politique," p. 776.

40. However, we still must answer Jacob Viner's claim *(The Long View and the Short*, pp. 227-228) that although Smith needed providence or the invisible hand in *The Theory of the Moral Sentiments*, he did not need it in *The Wealth of Nations* because political laws replaced the guidance of the invisible hand. One aspect of Viner's objection can be cleared up immediately. It is not true that there is some inconsistency between stress on a natural market guided by providence and the use of political laws. As Eli Heckscher, *Mercantilism*, Vol. 2, p. 318, points out: "If every social phenomenon is regarded as the working out of fundamental forces, this does not necessarily mean that those same forces bring about a favorable result for society." Thus, there *could be* a combination of invisible hand analysis and political analysis. To answer Viner any further, we must show that there is such a combination, but it seems that we have already shown this in the passages demonstrating the compatibility of the extent of the market principle with the "violence or the more orderly oppression of law" principle.

41. Halévy, *The Growth of Philosophic Radicalism*, p. 97; Bitterman, "Adam Smith's Empiricism and the Laws of Nature"; Skinner, "Adam Smith: Philosophy and Science."

42. Bitterman, "Adam Smith's Empiricism and the Laws of Nature," p. 498.

43. Quoted in Skinner, "Adam Smith: Philosophy and Science," pp. 309-310.

44. Skinner, "Adam Smith: Philosophy and Science," pp. 315-316.

45. Adam Smith, "A Letter to the Editors of the *Edinburgh Review*," p. 570.

46. A. A. Luce, *Berkeley and Malebranche*, pp. viii-ix, discusses the relation between Berkely, Hume, and Malebranche.

47. Howard Becker and Harry Elmer Barnes, *Social Thought from Lore to Science*, 3 vols. (New York: Dover, 1961), Vol. 1, pp. 366-388.

48. Quoted in Lucien Goldmann, *Immanuel Kant*, p. 63.

Chapter 4

1. The relation between epistemological and ethical community is embedded in a wider comparison between epistemological and ethical categories as revealed in the accompanying chart:

1. Quantity
   a. Subjective according to maxims . . .
   b. Objective according to principles
   c. Both subjective and objective . . .

2. Quality
   a. Commission . . .
   b. Omission . . .
   c. Exceptions . . .

3. Relation
   a. Relation to personality
   b. Relation to the situation
      (*Zustand*) of the person
   c. Reciprocally, relation of one person
      to the situation (*Zustand*) of another

4. Modality
   a. The permitted and the forbidden
   b. Duty and what is contrary to duty
   c. Perfect and imperfect duty

1. Quality
   a. Unity
   b. Plurability
   c. Totality

2. Quantity
   a. Reality
   b. Negation
   c. Limitation

3. Relation
   a. Substance
   b. Causality
   c. Community

4. Modality
   a. Possibility-impossibility
   b. Existence-non-existence
   c. Necessity-contingency

For more details about community in Kant's work on logic, science, etc., see Norman Fischer, "The Concept of Community in Kant's Architectonic," pp. 372-375.

2. Kant, *Critique of Pure Reason*, pp. 233-236.
3. Kant, *Metaphysical Foundations of Natural Science*.
4. Immanuel Kant, *Foundations of the Metaphysics of Morals*, p. 52; p. 50; p. 52.
5. For an opposite reading of Kant, however, see Peter Sachta, *Die Theorie der Kausalität in Kant's "Kritik der reinen Vernunft,"* pp. 1-8, where it is argued that Kant was concerned mainly with the structure of theories rather than the structure of reality. Sachta's argument is in the general tradition of neo-Kantian interpretation, which is discussed in Lucien Goldmann, *Lukács et Heidegger*, pp. 61-63.
6. Immanuel Kant, as quoted in Lucien Goldmann, *Immanuel Kant*, pp. 155-156. For a further discussion of subjective and objective aspects of

Kant's philosophy, see Norman Kemp Smith, *A Commentary to Kant's Critique of Pure Reason*, pp. 270-284, 312-315.

7. The main problem with both Arthur Melnick, *Kant's Analogies of Experience*, and A. C. Ewing, *Kant's Treatment of Causality*, is that they do not stress this adequately.

8. Immanuel Kant, *Prolegomena to Any Future Metaphysics*, in T. V. Smith and Marjorie Grene, eds., *Berkeley, Hume and Kant*, p. 310; ibid.; ibid., pp. 317-318; Kant, *Foundations of the Metaphysics of Morals*, p. 64.

9. Kant, *Foundations of the Metaphysics of Morals*, p. 55; p. 52.

10. For Kant's discussion of the universal moral law, see *Foundations*, p. 39. Much of the English discussion of Kant's ethics has concentrated on the idea that every action must be universalizable as the basic element of the categorical imperative, even though Kant's statement in the third forumulation is more inclusive, containing the idea of the universal moral law along with the idea that it is made by a community.

11. Claude Lévi-Strauss, *Le Cru et le Cuit*, and Fernand Braudel "La longue Durée," in *Ecrits sur l'Histoire*.

12. Kant, *Religion*, p. 93. Lucien Goldmann, *Immanuel Kant*, p. 178, quotes part of this passage as evidence that Kant sometimes stresses the we or the community as the originator of action. However, he gives no detailed analysis of it. Community is discussed here, as elsewhere, under the category of relation. See note 1.

13. Kant, *Religion*, p. 85.

14. Ellington, appendix to Kant, *Metaphysical Foundations*, p. 37.

15. Immanuel Kant, *Metaphysical Elements of Justice*, p. 217.

16. Kant, *Foundations*, pp. 51, 64.

17. See the discussion of Hegel's criticism of Kant in Georg Lukács, *The Young Hegel*, pp. 148, 154-155. Bernard Edelman, "La Transition dans la Doctrine du Droit," pp. 39-61, has expanded Hegel's point by suggesting that the lack of content in Kant's philosophy of law leads to simply adopting the content at hand, as in the case of Kant's examples of domestic law. The criticism made by Sir David Ross, *Kant's Ethical Theory*, pp. 32-33, that Kant does not seem to realize that most actions reveal several different aspects, really speaks to the same point.

18. For Reinhardt Brandt, *Eigentumstheorien von Grotius bis Kant*, p. 167, this is the major account of property in Kant's writings. Brandt also gives references to Kant's other scattered passages on property.

19. Immanuel Kant, *The Metaphysical Elements of Justice*, p. 66.

20. Cf. Adam Smith, *Lectures on Jurisprudence*, p. 19. For a comparison of Smith and Kant, see Donald G. Rohr, *The Origins of Social Liberalism in Germany*, p. 3.

21. For a discussion of the relation of the more individual to the more

universal concept of property, see Brandt, *Eigentumstheorien*, pp. 181-182.

22. Kant, *Elements*, p. 52.

23. To say, as does Susan Shell, "Kant's Theory of Property," pp. 78-80, that the combination of communalism and privacy in Kant's theory derives from the fact that there is a common ego, which is yet individual, seems somewhat farfetched. Lucio Colletti, *From Rousseau to Lenin*, pp. 206-207, has argued that Kant's theory of unsocial sociability found in his philosophy of history is a culmination of the Smithian doctrine of the dichotomy of individual and social. However, Paul Chamley, *Économie Politique et Philosophie chez Steuart et Hegel*, pp. 195-197, has argued that the theory of unsocial sociability is more likely to have come from Sir James Steuart than from Smith.

24. Kant, *Elements*, p. 64.

25. Kant, *Foundations*, pp. 64, 80.

26. Kant, as quoted in Goldmann, *Immanuel Kant*, p. 179.

Chapter 5

1. See the discussion in Georg Lukács, *The Young Hegel*, pp. 148, 154-155.

2. These two options reflect right- and left-wing Hegelianism. See Georg Lukács, "Moses Hess and the Problems of Idealist Dialects," in *Tactics and Ethics*, for a fuller discussion of these movements.

3. Paul Chamley, *Économie Politique et Philosophie chez Steuart et Hegel*, intermingles early and late Hegel, although his concentration is on the early writings. Chamley, "Les origines de la Pensée Économique de Hegel," and Georg Lukács, *The Young Hegel*, concentrate almost exclusively on the early writings.

4. From G.W.F. Hegel, *Hegel's Philosophy of Right*, pp. xiii-xiv. I have added the references to aspects, topics, and the like. Throughout, when I quote from the English translation of this work, I sometimes do not follow the practice of the translator of capitalizing nouns. Since all German nouns are capitalized, to capitalize them in English often tends to turn a fact about the German language into a fact about Hegel's philosophy.

5. See Sir James Steuart as quoted in Karl Marx, *Werke*, Vol. 26, part I, p. 7; Thomas Hobbes, *Leviathan*, ed. C. B. Macpherson, p. 299.

6. Hegel, *The Philosophy of Right*, pp. 126-127, 130.

7. The police had the task of keeping cleanliness, security, and good prices *(nettété, sûreté* and *bon-marché)*. See the editor's introduction to Adam Smith, *The Wealth of Nations*, ed. Edwin Canaan (New York: Modern Library, 1937), p. xxix.

8. For a discussion of the corporations, see Rolf Hocevar, *Hegel und der Preussische Staat*, pp. 37-40; also see Hegel's discussion in Homeyer's lecture notes in G.W.F. Hegel, *Vorlesungen über Rechtsphilosophie*, p. 322.

9. Hegel, *The Philosophy of Right*, p. 278.

10. Ibid.

11. Hegel, *The Philosophy of Right*, p. 184; p. 154; and G. Heiman, "The Sources and Significance of Hegel's Corporate Doctrine," in Z. A. Pelczynski, ed., *Hegel's Political Philosophy: Problems and Perspectives*, p. 125.

12. Hegel, *The Philosophy of Right*, p. 205.

13. Ibid., p. 126.

14. Ibid., p. 200.

15. Ibid., pp. 198-199. For a further discussion of classes and politics in Hegel, see Manfred Riedel, "Der Begriff der 'Bürgerlichen Gesellschaft' und das Problem seines Geschichtlichen Ursprungs," in *Studien zu Hegel's Rechtsphilosophie*. For an account of Hegel's politics that attempts to rescue him from the myth of being scholar valet to the Prussian king, see Jacques D'Hondt, *Hegel en son Temps*. One chapter of this book is called "Hegel, Lawyer for the Oppressed." For a short discussion of the combined effect of the reading of Hegel in D'Hondt and Ilting, see the introduction by Jean-Pierre Lefebvre to G.W.F. Hegel, *La Société Civile Bourgeoise*. See Ilting's preface to Hegel, *Vorlesungen über Rechtsphilosophie*.

16. My stress on the synchronic aspect of Hegel's means that I do not accept the judgment in Louis Althusser and Étienne Balibar, *Reading Capital*, pp. 125-126, that Hegelianism can only deal with the genesis of societal forms and never with their stability within a given synchronic time period.

17. Hegel, *The Philosophy of Right*, p. 122.

18. Ferdinand Tönnies, *Community and Society*, cf. Chapter 2 of this book.

19. Hegel, *The Philosophy of Right*, pp. 151-152.

20. See Emil Fackenheim, *The Religious Dimension in Hegel's Thought*. *The Young Hegel* was written in Moscow.

21. G.W.F. Hegel, *Hegel's Logic*, is part 1 of the *Encyclopedia of the Philosophical Sciences* and is sometimes known as the lesser logic; G.W.F. Hegel, *The Science of Logic*, is sometimes known as the large logic.

22. For further discussion of subject-object identity, see George Lukács, *History and Class Consciousness*, p. 206, and throughout the section "Reification and the Consciousness of the Proletariat."

23. For Lucien Goldmann, *Lukács et Heidegger*, p. 123, the Hegelian Marxist tradition needs the concept of partial subject-object identity.

24. Hegel, *Hegel's Logic*, p. 37; p. 37; p. 31. Also see Hegel, *The Philoso-*

phy of Right, p. 31, where Hegel talks of the universal of the "common characteristic," and G.W.F. Hegel, *The Phenomenology of Mind*, p. 182, where he talks about the universal that is "passive" and "indifferent."

25. Hegel, *Hegel's Logic*, p. 182.

26. Hegel, *The Philosophy of Right*, pp. 38; p. 59; p. 64 (translation amended).

27. Ibid., p. 31; Hegel, *The Phenomenology of Mind*, p. 182 (translation amended).

28. Hegel, *The Philosophy of Right*, p. 123.

29. Ibid., p. 124.

30. Ibid., p. 31.

31. Ibid., p. 156.

32. Ibid., pp. 156-157.

33. Ibid., pp. 160-161.

34. Hegel, *Hegel's Logic*, p. 155.

35. Hegel, *The Philosophy of Right*, pp. 35-36.

36. Ibid., p. 139.

37. See Z. A. Pelszynski, introduction to G.W.F. Hegel, *Hegel's Political Writings*, pp. 87-88.

38. Hegel, *The Philosophy of Right*, pp. 126-127.

39. Ibid., pp. 278, 147.

40. Ibid., p. 156. One aim of my analysis of the relation between the state and civil society is to bring together in a coherent whole both the insights of Lukács, *The Young Hegel*, and Chamley, *Économie Politique et Philosophie chez Steuart et Hegel*. In general, Lukács stresses the importance of Smith for Hegel and deemphasizes the purported influence of Steuart (pp. 171-172). In contrast, Chamley's tries in almost every case to show that what may appear to have come from Smith actually comes from Steuart, who, according to Chamley, was, like Hegel, neither a liberal abstentionist in economics nor a collectivist but something in between: a proponent of liberal interventionism. However, as I suggested in the chapter on mercantilism, there are many types of possibilities between an economy outside the state and one totally controlled by the state. The interest of Hegel's system for the theme of this book is that he first develops a holism of the autonomous forces of the market far beyond anything Smith ever did and then, having given this holism an ontology, connects it to the holism of the state. Hegel's system is Janus-faced according to which side is stressed most.

Chapter 6

1. As quoted in the "Introduction" to Karl Marx, *The Grundrisse*, trans. and ed. David McClellan, p. 7.

2. Marx, in Karl Marx and Frederick Engels, *Selected Correspondence,* p. 100.

3. Everything that Marx wrote will appear eventually in the original language in Karl Marx and Frederick Engels, *Gesamtausgabe* (Berlin: Dietz Verlag, 1975-1979).

4. Ernest Mandel, *The Formation of the Economic Thought of Karl Marx*, pp. 163-176, discusses how most theorists who have stressed the importance of alienation in Marx have concentrated on the early writings, whereas the later writings have been favored by those who have deemphasized alienation. However, the first major account of alienation in Marx, George Lukács, *History and Class Consciousness*, was based primarily on *Capital* and was written before many of the early writings were discovered. In my account, I want to stress the achievement of Marx's later economic synthesis, and at the same time show how it is bound up with alienation.

5. This plan for *The Philosophy of Right* follows, apart from the fourth and fifth categories, what I have called the synchronic structure of the book. Marx's plan is in the *Grundrisse*, pp. 28-29, repeated several times in the "Introduction." For the concept of *bürgerliche* society, which, following common practice, will be translated as civil society for Hegel and capitalist or bourgeois society for Marx, see Manfred Riedel, "Der Begriff der 'Bürgerlichen Gesellschaft' und das Problem seines Geschichtlichen Ursprungs," in *Studien zu Hegel's Rechtsphilosophie.* I first presented this comparison between *The Philosophy of Right* and the *Grundrisse* in "Alienation, Reification and the Labor Theory of Value," (Ph.D. Dissertation, University of Washington, 1975), p. 148. There are similarities between my comparison and that of Joseph O'Malley, "Marx's 'Economics' and Hegel's *Philosophy of Right:* An Essay on Marx's Hegelianism," *Political Studies* (March 1976), p. 52. O'Malley, however, does not draw the connection between contract and petty commodity production, nor does he stress the synchronic nature of the plans. O'Malley records his debt to two authors to whom I am also indebted: Schlomo Avineri, *The Social and Political thought of Karl Marx*, and Maximilien Rubel's "Introduction" to Karl Marx, *Oeuvres*, Vol. 2. Avineri had stressed Marx's general indebtedness, particularly in the early writings, to *The Philosophy of Right* (pp. 41-64). Rubel had stressed the importance of the original plans for Marx's economics, written around the time of the *Grundrisse*, and had argued that that plan did not go through any fundamental change (pp. xci-cxvii).

6. Marx, *Grundrisse*, trans. Martin Nicolaus, p. 108 (translation amended).

7. Ibid., p. 227 (translation amended).

8. Karl Marx, *Grundrisse der Kritik der Politischen Ökonomie*, pp. 172, 177.

9. Marx, *Grundrisse*, trans. Martin Nicolaus, pp. 83, 100.

10. Ibid.

11. This analysis of relations necessitates a comment about my relation to Ollman's well-known thesis about the centrality of internal relations in Marx's thought. See Bertell Ollman, *Alienation.* This book has been very important in breaking the dominance of the empiricistic interpretation of Marx in Anglo-American scholarship. However, I am not convinced that internal relations are as central to the Hegelian Marxist tradition and political economy in general, as the opposition between universal and particular, which may take the special form of an opposition between relations or internal relations and atomistic particulars. Unfortunately, there is an unclarity in Marx's discussion of those who begin with population and isolated individuals. When Marx delivers his attack on those who begin with individuals, he specifically charges Smith with this fault—even though he sets up in opposition to those who begin with population those who, like Smith, begin with abstract forms such as exchange value (Marx, *Grundrisse*, trans Martin Nicolaus, pp. 83, 104). This may have led people to assume that there is a lack of homology between the two critiques: the critique of those who begin with isolated individuals and of those who begin with population. Marx criticizes Smith in the one case and praises him in the other. Yet, Marx's point is consistent. Those who begin with individuals and those who begin with population lack a sense of the whole. Marx thought that in one sense Smith lacked this sense of the whole and in another sense did not.

In his attack on those who begin with individuals, Marx notes that "individuals producing in society—hence socially determined individual production—is, of course, the point of departure. The isolated hunter and fishermen, with whom Smith and Ricardo begin, belongs among the unimaginative conceits of the eighteenth century Robinsonades" *(Grundrisse*, p. 83). Thus, Smith is castigated for not assuming that people produce socially. Yet, Smith's conception of beginning with abstract forms is seen as beginning with relations among people rather than using isolated individuals. The double attitude reflects two different topics. Smith is castigated for not dealing with social production; he is praised for stressing exchange relations that unite individuals. For Marx, Smith's attitude toward production is individualistic, and toward exchange more holistic.

Marx characterizes as vulgar economy that variation on the economics of Smith and Ricardo which began to dominate English political economy after 1850, and which gives an individualistic account of exchange as well as of production. The vulgar economists deny that there are any general regularities in price, but hold that price is wholly determined by demand (Roman Rosdolsky, *The Making of Marx's Capital,* pp. 28-31). This is the kind of economics most subject to Marx's critique of beginning with isolated individuals without consideration of social relations.

12. See Rosdolsky, *Making*, p. 56. Rosdolsky's lines display the similar features of the two plans. Both deal with (1) the production process of capital, and (2) the circulation process of capital. (3) The original plan deals with profit and interest, competition, credit and share capital, the changed plan, with profit and profit rate, merchants, capital, credit and interest. (4) Both deal with wage labor. (5) The original plan deals with landed property, and the changed plan with ground-rent, which is basically the same thing. Furthermore, it can be shown that both deal with petty commodity production. This is explicitly for the changed plan, and it is also true for the original plan, for "Capital in general" always includes a discussion of petty commodity production. (*Capital*, p. 89, *Critique*, p. 19).

It is quite clear that the controversy over Marx's plan for his economics will not be satisfactorily resolved until the whole second part of the new *Gesamtausgabe* is available and assimilated. However, it does seem clear at this point that the early view associated with Henrik Grossman, "Die Änderung des ursprunglichen Aufbauplans des Marxschen 'Kapital' und ihre Ursachen," that there was a fundamental change between the writing of the *Grundrisse* and the writing of *Capital*, was distorted by not having the texts now available. The Russian Marxist W. S. Wygodski, *Wie 'Das Kapital' Entstand* (Chapters 4, 5, and 6) talks of three different layers of Marx's economics: the first is the *Grundrisse*, the second, written in 1861-1863, contains the *Theories of Surplus Value* and another version of *A Contribution to the Critique of Political Economy;* and the third, written in 1863-1865, contains the sixth, unpublished chapter of *Capital*, known as the *Resultate des unmittelbaren Produktionsprozesses*, the only manuscript version of the third volume of *Capital* and one manuscript version of the second volume of *Capital*. The other manuscript versions of the second volume were written after 1867. Neither the *Grundrisse* nor the sixth chapter were available to Grossman, not to speak of the layers described above which are now being made available through the new *Gesamtausgabe*. Furthermore, based on the preliminary evidence, it is quite unlikely that the new manuscripts will uphold the Grossman thesis. Wygodski, who has worked extensively with all the manuscripts and who is hardly a Hegelian Marxist, has argued for a considerable amount of continuity between the two plans (pp. 91, 109).

13. See Franz Mehring, *Karl Marx: The Story of His Life* (London: George Allen and Unwin, 1936), pp. 370-380.

14. Karl Marx, *Capital*, trans. Samuel Moore and Edward Aveling, Vol. 1, p. 8.

15. "Along the first path the full conception was evaporated to yield an abstract determination; along the second the abstract determinations lead towards a reproduction of the concrete by way of thought. . . . the simplest economic category, say e.g. exchange value, presupposes population, moreover a population producing in specific relations. . . . It can never exist other than as an abstract one-sided relation within an already given, concrete living whole *(Ganzen)*. . . . But do not these simpler categories also have an independent historical or natural existence predating the more concrete ones? That depends. Hegel, for example, correctly begins *The Philosophy of Right* with possession *(Besitz)*, this being the subject's simplest juridical relation. But there is no possession preceding the family or master-servant relations, which are far more concrete relations. However, it would be correct to say that there are families or class groups which merely possess *(besitzen)*, but have no property *(Eigentum)*. The simple category therefore appears in relation to property as a relation of simple families or clan groups. In the higher society it appears as the simpler relation of a developed organization. But the concrete substratum of which possession is a relation is always presupposed. One can imagine an individual savage as possessing something. But in that case possession is not a juridical relation" *(Grundrisse*, pp. 101-102).

Our discussion so far prepares us for this praise of Hegel since we have seen the close connection between the structure of *The Philosophy of Right* and the structure of Marxist economics. Furthermore, Marx believes Hegel's method of beginning with possession is homologous with his method of beginning with exchange value. This is shown by the fact that Marx moves back and forth between the two when discussing the advantages of beginning with the abstract forms. While his discussion is slightly elliptical, it can be understood easily against the background of our account of *The Philosophy of Right*.

There, property, though originally not discussed as a juridical relation, was later seen to be just that. Marx compresses Hegel's account somewhat by simply calling possession a juridical relation, although for Hegel property *(Eigentum)* was usually the juridical relation and possession *(Besitz)* a nonjuridical relation. Marx correctly grasps Hegel's methodology, however, of delineating a realm of illusion in his discussion of possession: "But there is no possession preceding the family." Later, Marx returns to the more strictly Hegelian terminology when he notes that "one can imagine an individual savage possessing something. But in that case possession is not a juridical relation." Imagining an individual possessing something is exactly what Hegel does in the first section of *The Philosophy of Right*. For Marx, Hegel is correct not because he begins with the nonjuridical category of possession, but because he begins with possession as a juridical category. Marx simply has an incorrect grasp of Hegel's terminology. What he must be referring to when he says that Hegel begins with the abstract relation of possession as a juridical category is Hegel's discussion of the alienation of goods on the market through contract, where possession has become more like property. It is only here that the individual has a socioeconomic relation with others. With brute possession he simply has a physical relation with a good.

Thus, the intended homology must be between Marx's account of exchange value and Hegel's account of contract. For both, the realm of contract and the realm of exchange value are "abstract one-sided relations within an already given, concrete totality." They can, however, predate the concrete living totality, but only as "dominant relations of a less developed totality."

16. Marx, *Critique*, p. 14.

17. Ibid.

18. This fact was most puzzling to Marx's readers and perhaps contributed to the Smithian myth of petty commodity production.

19. See Marx's note to the first chapter of the first German edition of *Das Kapital* (quite different from the later editions on which all English translations are based), as reprinted in Karl Marx and Frederick Engels, *Studienausgabe*, Vol. 2 (Frankfurt: Fischer, 1966), p. 274.

20. Marx, *Selected Works*, p. 212.

21. Marx, *Grundrisse*, trans. Martin Nicolaus, p. 651.

22. Marx, *Grundrisse der Kritik der Politischen Ökonomie*, p. 901.

23. Ibid., p. 907.

24. Marx, *Grundrisse*, trans. Martin Nicolaus, p. 101.

25. Ibid., p. 102 (italics mine).

26. Ibid., pp. 103, 105.

27. For further discussion of the Marxist analysis of precapitalist societies, see Eric Hobsbawm's "Introduction" to Karl Marx, *Pre-Capitalist Economic Formations*.

28. Galvano Della Volpe, *Rousseau et Marx et Autre Écrits* (Paris: Bernard Grasset, 1974), pp. 233-258, is not willing to admit the possibility that the "Introduction" to the *Grundrisse* could contain an acceptance of part of Hegel's doctrine and a rejection of other parts. This same intransigent attitude characterizes the otherwise very illuminating book by his pupil, Lucio Colletti, *Marxism and Hegel*.

29. Marx, *Grundrisse*, trans. Martin Nicolaus, p. 100.

30. This seems to be the interpretation followed by Della Volpe, *Rousseau et Marx*, pp. 233-258.

31. By stressing the relative independence of the social wholes or totalities, I am closer than one might expect to the position of Louis Althusser and Étienne Balibar, *Reading Capital.*

32. The concrete here does not include the rules of petty commodity production, insofar as they presuppose individuals producing for themselves. For this is an illusory realm.

Chapter 7

1. Ronald Meek, *Studies in the Labor Theory of Value*, p. 310. For more on the concept of paradigms in economics, see the remarks by G. N. Reynolds in an unpublished paper called "A Bibliography on Sraffa's Standard Commodity and Post-Keynesian Economic Theory."

2. For more on subjective value theory, see chapter 1, notes 6 and 7. Also see Paul Sweezy, Introduction to Böhm-Bawerk's *Karl Marx and the Close of His System*, xii-xiii. According to Oscar Lange, *Political Economy*, p. 227, the term "classical political economy" was first utilized by Marx. Subjective value, or what Lange called subjectivism, or what is sometimes called neo-classical theory, is usually thought to be fully ushered in with the work of Jevons, Menger, and Walras in the early 1870s. Lange argues, p. 229, that what Marx criticized as vulgar economy was not full-blown subjective value theory but the beginnings of it. For a short history of what Joan Robinson calls the neo-classical school, see her "The Relevance of Economic Theory," pp. 30-33. Meek, *Smith, Marx and After*, p. 166, refers to the new school as marginalism, although he admits that in certain respects Lange's subjectivism is a better term. It is common to hold (see Lange, p. 229, Meek, *Smith, Marx and After*, p. 166, and Sweezy, *The Theory of Capitalist Development*, pp. 5-6) that classical political economy does, and subjective value theory does not, stress class relations in production.

3. Lucio Colletti, *Marxism and Hegel*, p. 274.

4. I. I. Rubin's *Essays on Marx's Theory of Value* originally appeared in Russian in 1924, and was published in English in 1972 and in German in 1973. For Rubin and the Soviet Union, see Roman Rosdolsky, *The Making of Marx's "Capital,"* p. 570.

5. Rudolph Hilferding, "Böhm-Bawerk's Criticism of Marx," p. 191.

6. Franz Petry, *Der Soziale Gehalt der Marxschen Werttheorie*, pp. 7-10.

7. Georg Lukács, *History and Class Consciousness*; Karl Korsch, *Marxism and Philosophy*; Sweezy, *The Theory of Capitalist Development*, pp. 20, 25, 26. Rosdolsky, *Making*, p. 118, also utilizes the quantitative, qualitative distinction.

8. Lukács, *History*, p. 183; Rancière, "Le Concept de Critique et la Critique de L'Économie Politique des Manuscrits de 1844 au Capital," in *Lire le Capital*, Vol. 2, p. 134; Rubin, *Essays*, p. 135.

9. Good examples are Otto Bauer, as quoted in Rosdolsky, *Making*, p. 569, and Joan Robinson, *Economic Philosophy*, p. 37, who object to Marx's language in describing value as "metaphorical" and "metaphysical," respectively.

10. For a somewhat specialized survey of interpretations of Marx's labor theory of value, see Carlo Benetti, Claude Berthomieu, and Jean Cartelier, *Économie Classique, Économie Vulgaire*, pp. 93-136.

11. Lucien Goldmann, *Lukács et Heidegger*, pp. 59-66. Also see Norman Fischer, Review of *Lukács et Heidegger*, *New German Critique*, No. 14 (Spring, 1978): 186-187.

12. See Rubin, *Essays*, pp. 133-134. Here it is interesting to note that the Neo-Kantian whole was closer to Smith's interpretation of the whole (on Hasbach's account), whereas the Hegelian account was closer to the physiocratic conception of the whole. See Chapter 2, note 17.

13. Karl Marx, *Grundrisse der Kritik der Politischen Ökonomie*, p. 111.

14. Karl Marx, the first chapter of the 1867 edition of *Capital*, reprinted in Marx, *Studienausgabe*, Vol. 2 (Frankfurt: Fischer, 1966), p. 242. The first chapter and the appendix, "Die Wertform," of the first, 1867 edition are very different from the later German editions.

15. Lukács, *History*. The Frankfurt School followers of Lukács inherited his failure to develop a political economy to the extent that eventually Habermas, in *Theory and Practice*, pp. 221-235, gave an account of the labor theory of value much more positivistic than that given by those supposed heirs of anti-Hegelianism, Colletti and Rancière.

16. Marx, "Randglossen zu Adolph Wagner's *Lehrbuch der Politischen Ökonomie*," in Karl Marx and Frederick Engels, *Werke*, Vol. 19, p. 375; Marx, *Capital*, trans. Ben Fowkes, Vol. 1, pp. 125-126, 177; "Randglossen," p. 375. The opposition between natural and social objectivity suggests that Marx approaches nature and society using different epistemological tools. For the controversy over the relation between Marx's analysis of nature and his analysis of society, see Colletti, *Marxism and Hegel*, pp. 40-51.

17. Marx, *Theories of Surplus Value*, Vol. 2, pp. 242-243.

18. This does not mean that Hegelian Marxism, by stressing action, therefore cannot achieve a realistic analysis of the external world. The question of the compatibility of stress on action and realism has been complicated by Lukács' self-criticism of his views in *History and Class Consciousness* in the 1967 preface to that work (p. xxxvi). Yet it is clear

from the same preface (p. xx) that even in 1967 Lukács was still trying to combine realism with the Hegelian heritage.

19. Marx, first chapter of the 1867 edition of *Capital*, p. 245.

20. Marx, in Karl Marx and Frederick Engels, *Selected Correspondence*, pp. 198-199; Marx, *Grundrisse der Kritik der Politischen Ökonomie*, pp. 24-25.

21. Marx, *Grundrisse der Kritik der Politischen Ökonomie*, p. 25; Marx, *A Contribution to the Critique of Political Economy*, p. 55 (translation amended).

22. Marx, *Capital*, trans. Ben Fowkes, Vol. 1, p. 142.

23. Marx, *Selected Works*, p. 323 (translation amended).

24. Marx, *Das Kapital*, in Karl Marx and Frederick Engels, *Werke*, Vol. 23, p. 61; Rancière, "Le Concept de Critique," p. 131.

25. See Marx, "Die Wertform," reprinted in Marx, *Kleine Ökonomische Schriften*, p. 275. Also, in *Capital*, trans. Ben Fowkes, Vol. 1, pp. 164-165, Marx talks of the "mysterious" and "mystical" nature of the commodity, and of how the value relation has "absolutely no connection with the physical nature of the commodity." He also talks of the "ghostly objectivity" of value *(Das Kapital*, p. 52). It has been a favorite tack of anti-Hegelian Marxists to stress that the "mature" Marx began with the commodity, i.e., with something solid rather than something abstract. See W. S. Wygodski, *Wie "Das Kapital" Entstand*, p. 126; Athar Hussain, "Marx's Notes on Adolph Wagner: An Introduction," *Theoretical Practice*, No. 5 (Spring, 1972): 26. Louis Althusser, Introduction to Karl Marx, *Le Capital* (Paris: Garnier-Flammarion, 1969), p. 17, apparently recognizes the Hegelian aspects of Marx's comments on the commodity, and thus warns readers to put the first chapters on commodities and money to the side for the time being.

26. Marx, *Werke*, Vol. 13, pp. 16, 18, 32.

27. Ibid., Vol. 23, p. 74; "Die Wertform," p. 275; the first chapter of the 1867 edition of *Capital*, p. 227.

28. Marx, *Grundrisse der Kritik der Politischen Ökonomie*, pp. 59, 78, 79, 80.

29. Rubin, *Essays*, p. 117.

30. Marx, the first chapter of the 1867 edition of *Capital*, p. 274.

31. Rubin, *Essays*, pp. 67-68.

32. Marx, "Randglossen," p. 375. Also see the discussion by Athar Hussain, "Marx's Notes on Adolph Wagner; An Introduction," pp. 18-35. Hussain does not pay adequate attention to the various concepts of form.

33. Marx, *Werke*, Vol. 32, p. 553.

34. Marx, *A Contribution to the Critique of Political Economy*, p. 55 (translation amended).

35. There is, however, a problem in textually interpreting Marx in terms of the concept of the form and content of value. Marx sometimes identifies the form of value, not with the general form of a commodity society, which involves value before it appears in the market, but with exchange value, which involves actual comparing of commodities on the market. In order to distinguish the two uses of "form," Rubin suggests that exchange value might be called the "form of value" and that the concept of the form of value in general might be called "value as form" (*Essays*, p. 112).

36. Rubin, *Essays*, pp. 107-114. Rubin argues that Marx's critics always stress the method that begins with value and then asks for its substance. The fact that Marx himself stresses this side of the question in the opening pages of *Capital* has made it all the easier for his critics to misinterpret him.

37. Rubin, *Essays*, p. 141.

38. Marx, *A Contribution to the Critique of Political Economy*, p. 34. Two other types of labor have also been confused with social labor and abstract labor. Petry, *Der Soziale Gehalt*, p. 22, contrasted the concept of abstract universal labor with (1) that of simple as opposed to complicated labor and (2) that of socially necessary labor. The concept of simple labor and complicated labor is taken up by Rubin in his chapter on qualified labor, which is the same as what Petry calls complicated labor. Simple labor is labor which does not require the special training that complicated or qualified labor does. The concept of socially necessary labor holds that the value of a commodity is equal not to the labor time necessary to create it, but rather to the labor time socially necessary to create it. For example, in the shoe-making industry, there is some average labor time needed for the making of shoes, and it is this time that determines the value of shoes. This refinement in the labor theory of value is necessary, for without it the conclusion would follow that the person who does not make shoes as fast as the average would produce more value than someone who works as fast as the average, since he would take more time to produce the commodity. The concept of socially necessary labor implies that the abstract labor time connected with a given commodity is constantly subject to change, since the socially necessary labor time may change even after a commodity has already been produced. Thus, the time socially necessary for making shoes may change over a period of time. This fact implies that the objectivity of value is subject to a fluctuation which is certainly not associated with the physical properties of the commodity.

39. Rubin, *Dialektik der Kategorien* (Berlin: V.S.A. 1975), p. 13. Rubin's

claim to take a middle road on this issue is somewhat misleading and probably represents a prudent political silence. For the debates in the Soviet Union about the continuance of value relations under socialism, see J. L. Dallemagne, "Justice for Bukharin," *Critique*, No. 4 (Spring, 1975): 43-61; Donald Filtzer, "Preobrazhensky and the Problem of the Soviet Transition," *Critique*, No. 9 (Spring-Summer, 1978): 63-85. The distinction between the form and content of value appears in Marx's scattered discussions of value under socialism. The value form, the market, is one way of relating individual and social aspects of action; and the value content, physiocratic social reproduction, is another way of doing this. The content remains in socialism but not the form. It is true that several texts seem to support opposite positions about the existence of value under socialism. Marx notes that in socialism "the labor which has been transformed into a product does not appear as the value of that product, as an objective *(sachliche)* quality possessed by it." *(Selected Works*, p. 323, translation amended). This seems to suggest that under socialism there will be no object to be studied by the labor theory of value. But Marx also says that, "after the abolition of the capitalist mode of production, but still retaining social production, the determination of value *(Wertbestimmung)* continues to prevail in the sense that the regulation of labor time and the distribution of social labor among the various production groups, finally the bookkeeping encompassing all this, becomes more essential than ever." *(Capital*, Vol. 3, p. 851, translation amended). This seems to suggest that value will continue to exist in socialism.

Yet the seeming opposition between the two texts is removed if we argue that the disappearance of value in socialism refers to value as form, whereas the endurance of value in socialism refers to value as content. Here close reading of the original German text is important. Marx notes that the determination of value *(Wertbestimmung)* will remain in socialism. This term appears again in the first volume of *Capital* when Marx inquires about the source of alienation and fetishism. He argues that these characteristics do not come from the content of the vaue determinations *(Inhalt der Wertbestimmungen)* but from the form of value. *(Capital*, trans. Ben Fowkes, Vol. 1, p. 163).

40. Marx, *Grundrisse*, trans. Martin Nicolaus, p. 157.

41. Marx, *Selected Works*, p. 323 (translation amended).

42. Marx, *Grundrisse*, trans. Nicolaus, pp. 171-172 (translation amended).

43. Marx, *Capital*, trans. Ben Fowkes, Vol. 1, p. 164 (translation amended).

44. Marx, *Grundrisse der Kritik der Politischen Ökonomie*, p. 909.

45. Rubin, *Essays*, p. 95.

46. Marx, *Capital*, trans. Ben Fowkes, Vol. 1, pp. 166-167 (translation amended); Rubin, *Essays*, p. 100.

47. See note 35.

48. Rubin, *Essays*, p. 148. As Rubin notes, the French edition of 1875 was meant by Marx to be a correction of the second German edition. Engels tried to incorporate the changes in the French edition into the third and fourth German editions. See Frederick Engels, "prefaces" to the third and fourth editions of *Capital*, in Marx, *Capital*, trans. Ben Fowkes, Vol. 1, pp. 106, 114.

49. Marx, the first chapter of the 1867 edition of *Capital*, p. 227.

50. Rubin, *Essays*, p. 129.

51. Ibid., pp. 125-126.

52. Marx, *Capital*, trans. Ben Fowkes, Vol. 1, pp. 125-137.

53. See note 35.

54. Marx, *Theories of Surplus Vaue*, Vol. 3, pp. 140-141.

55. Marx, *Theorien über den Mehrwert*, in *Werke*, Vol. 26.3, pp. 140-141.

56. Ibid., p. 144.

57. Ibid., p. 147.

58. We now know why Louis Althusser warned readers of Marx away from the first chapters of *Capital*, dealing with the commodity. See note 28.

59. Marx, *Theorien über den Mehrwert*, in *Werke*, Vol. 26.3, p. 130.

60. Ibid., p. 144.

61. Marx, "Die Wertform," p. 271.

62. See the section of "Die Wertform" called "The Peculiarities of the Equivalent Form." The equivalent form is simply one type of value form. Its first peculiarity is that "use value becomes the manifestation of its opposite, value; the second is that "concrete labor becomes the manifestation of its opposite, abstract human labor." Both peculiarities are clearly laid out in a parallel way. Yet, examination of the first peculiarity reveals that it is clearly not parallel to the second, for if the parallel had been carried out, then we would have expected Marx to say also that it is of the essence of use value to be value, just as he had said that it is of the essence of concrete labor to be abstract labor. The whole passage from "Die Wertform" has been analyzed by two of the leading opponents of the Hegelian interpretation of Marx: Lucio Colletti and Jacques Rancière (in an essay written before Rancière turned against Althusser). Colletti, *Marxism and Hegel*, pp. 281-282, argues that the fact that abstractions are taken seriously in the passage shows that the mystical world of Hegel has some application to the mystical world of capitalism. Since Colletti had been arguing through-

out the book that Hegel is too idealistic to be of any help in understanding capitalism, this admission on Colletti's part is rather damning for his anti-Hegelian theory. Since then, Colletti has been increasingly forced to admit the existence of Hegelian elements in Marxist thought. See Lucio Colletti, "Contradiction and Contrariety," *New Left Review*, No. 93 (September-October 1973): 28-29. Rancière, "Le Concept de Critique," pp. 137-138, also discusses the passage with a curious ambivalence. He admits that it is Hegelian, but seems to forget for a moment that it is part of his task to attack the Hegelian interpretation of Marx.

63. Marx, *Selected Correspondence*, p. 198.

64. Marx, *Grundrisse*, trans. Martin Nicolaus, p. 449.

65. Ibid., pp. 264-265 (translation amended).

66. Marx, *Capital*, trans. Ben Fowkes, Vol. 1, p. 187 (translation amended). Franz Petry, *Der soziale Gehalt der Marxschen Werttheorie*, pp. 16-17, takes a stand against a subjective, psychological account of social relations. Nevertheless, Petry is too much under the influence of Neo-Kantian epistemology to be able to see how relations could stand against individuals.

67. Marx, *Grundrisse*, trans. Martin Nicolaus, p. 585.

Chapter 8

1. V. I. Lenin, *State and Revolution* (Peking: Foreign Languages Press, 1965), p. 10. For a further discussion of violence and the capitalist state, see Lucio Colletti, *From Rousseau to Lenin*, pp. 103-108.

2. Such realistic assumptions may also underlie Quesnay's use of the concept of natural law. See the discussion in Chapter 3.

3. For further discussion of the Marxist concept of class in relation to labor, see Balibar in Louis Althusser and Étienne Balibar, *Reading Capital*, pp. 214-215.

4. Karl Marx, preface to *A Contribution to the Critique of Political Economy*, p. 19.

5. Marx, in Karl Marx and Frederick Engels, *Selected Correspondence*, p. 69.

6. Marx, *Capital*, trans. Ben Fowkes, Vol. 1, p. 90.

7. Karl Marx, *The First International and After*, p. 395.

8. Karl Marx, *Anarchism and Anarcho-Syndicalism*, p. 73.

9. Marx, *Capital*, trans. Ben Fowkes, Vol. 1, p. 178.

10. Karl Marx, preface to *Critique*, p. 21 (translation amended).

11. For further discussion of the interpenetration of the political and the economic, see Louis Althusser and Étienne Balibar, *Reading Capital*, p. 129;

Antonio Gramsci, *Selections from the Prison Notebooks* (New York: International Publishers, 1971).

12. Karl Marx, *Grundrisse*, p. 493.

13. Marx, *Capital*, trans. Ernest Untermann, Vol. 3, p. 818.

14. Marx, *Pre-Capitalist Economic Formations*, pp. 102-103.

15. Marx, *The First International*, p. 80.

16. Karl Marx, *Grundrisse*, trans. Martin Nicolaus, p. 88.

17. Ibid., p. 164 (translation amended).

18. Ibid., pp. 156-157. Martin Nicolaus, "The Unknown Marx," p. 93, pointed this out.

19. Karl Marx, *Grundrisse der Kritik der Politischen Ökonomie*, p. 951.

20. Marx, *Grundrisse*, trans. Martin Nicolaus, p. 238.

21. Ibid., p. 514.

22. See the discussion of the division of labor in Chapter 3.

23. Marx, *Grundrisse*, trans. Martin Nicolaus, p. 586.

24. Ibid.

25. Marx, *Grundrisse der Kritik der Politischen Ökonomie*, p. 965.

26. *Capital*, like *The Philosophy of Right*, contains a very specific pattern of synchronic analysis.

27. Marx, *Capital*, trans. Ben Fowkes, Vol. 1, p. 450 (translation amended).

28. Marx, *Grundrisse*, trans. Martin Nicolaus, p. 585.

29. Ibid., p. 586.

30. Ibid., p. 587 (translation amended).

31. Marx, *Capital*, trans. Ben Fowkes, Vol. 1, pp. 173-174.

32. My stress on special bodies of armed men as the ultimate backup force for capitalist power is not to deny the Gramscian stress on more subtle means for the capitalist class to keep power. See Gramsci, *Selections from the Prison Notebooks*, pp. 238-239.

Chapter 9

1. For another statement of the theory of the "two" Marx's," see Louis Althusser, *For Marx*.

2. Marx, in Karl Marx and Frederick Engels, *Selected Correspondence*, p. 100.

3. Although originally, in *For Marx*, Althusser held that the concept of alienation was dropped after 1845-1846, he eventually wound up admitting that there are only two works which are free of Hegelian categories: the "Critique of the Gotha Program," 1875, and the "Marginal Notes on Adolph

Wagner's *Lehrbuch der Politischen Ökonomie*," written in 1879 or 1880, three or four years before Marx's death. See Louis Althusser, "Preface" to Karl Marx, *Le Capital* (Paris: Garnier-Flammarion, 1969), Vol. 1, p. 21.

4. My work differs from other accounts of Marx's theory of alienation that I know of, in that it concentrates exclusively on those works and often the very themes that have been stressed by the opponents of the concept of alienation. In this respect, as in many others, it resembles the works of the early theorists of the Marxist concept of alienation, I. I. Rubin and Georg Lukács.

5. It must be admitted that there may be elements of the economics (such as the explanation of prices) and elements of the theory of alienation (such as the purely moral aspect) which fall outside of this common ontological basis.

6. Marx, in Karl Marx and Frederick Engels, *Werke*, Vol. 32, p. 52.

7. For a fuller discussion of this issue, see Norman Fischer, "Lucio Colletti on Socialism and Democracy," in Louis Patsouras and Jack Thomas, eds., *Varieties and Problems of Twentieth Century Socialism* (Chicago: Nelson-Hall, forthcoming).

8. See Georg Lukács, *History and Class Consciousness*, pp. 46-81, for a discussion of earlier forms of political power which were not mediated through the market. For a discussion of later forms of political power which are not mediated through the market, see H. H. Ticktin, "Soviet Society and Prof. Bettelheim," *Critique*, Vol. 6, pp. 17-44.

9. See Antonio Gramsci, *Selections from the Prison Notebooks*, pp. 238-239, for another perspective which I do not consider inconsistent with mine.

10. Marx, *Das Kapital*, in Karl Marx and Frederick Engels, *Werke*, Vol. 23, p. 12; *Kapital*, Vol. 3, p. 818. My stress on synchronicity suggests that, like Lucien Sebag, *Marxisme et Structuralisme*, pp. 15-57, I do not regard structuralism and Hegelianism as being inconsistent on all points.

11. See Chapter 2.

12. Here I am not using reification in the broad sense utilized by Lukács, "Reification and the Consciousness of the Proletariat," *History and Class Consciousness*, pp. 83-222. I have used Lukács' concept throughout in arriving at my own concept of alienation. When I talk of reification, however, I have in mind a very limited form of alienation, whereas in Lukács, reification is really coextensive with alienation.

13. Karl Marx, *Grundrisse der Kritik der Politischen Ökonomie*, p. 153.

14. Ibid., p. 156.

15. Ibid.

16. Karl Marx, *Grundrisse*, trans. Martin Nicolaus, p. 84 (translation amended).

17. Marx, *Grundrisse der Kritik der Politischen Ökonomie*, p. 186.

18. Ibid., p. 185.

19. Ibid., p. 196.

20. Ibid., pp. 195, 408-409.

21. Karl Marx, *Capital*, Vol. 3, p. 797; *Capital*, trans. Ben Fowkes, Vol. 1, pp. 433, 421-422.

22. For further discussion of the surface-deep structure opposition, see Norman Geras, "Fetishism in Marx's 'Capital'," pp. 70-71.

23. For the theme of false consciousness, see Karl Marx, *The German Ideology* (New York: International Publishers, 1970), 64-68.

24. Marx, *Grundrisse der Kritik der Politischen Ökonomie*, pp. 204, 205.

25. Ibid., p. 306.

26. Ibid., p. 204.

27. Ibid., pp. 306, 356.

28. Ibid., p. 306.

29. G.W.F. Hegel, *The Phenomenology of Mind*, p. 183 (translation amended).

30. G.W.F. Hegel, *Hegel's Philosophy of Right*, p. 31.

31. Ibid., pp. 129-130.

32. Marx, *Grundrisse*, p. 452.

33. Ibid., p. 238.

34. Ibid., p. 83.

35. Ibid., p. 471.

36. Ibid., p. 585.

37. Ibid., p. 590.

38. Marx, *Capital*, trans. Ben Fowkes, Vol. 1, p. 164 (translation amended).

39. Marx, *Capital*, trans. Ben Fowkes, Vol. 1, p. 168 (translation amended).

40. I am using the word "fetishism" to refer to a certain type of false consciousness, and not, as Lukács and Rubin sometimes do, to alienation itself. See Rubin, *Essays*, pp. 5-12, and Lukács, *History and Class Consciousness*, pp. 83-92.

41. Marx, *Grundrisse der Kritik der Politischen Ökonomie*, pp. 908, 909.

42. Marx, *Grundrisse*, trans. Martin Nicolaus, p. 164 (translation amended).

43. Again, the works of Antonio Gramsci are seminal for understanding this problem in a twentieth-century perspective.

44. Marx, *Grundrisse*, trans. Martin Nicolaus, p. 452 (translation amended).

45. Ibid., p. 454.

Chapter 10

1. I am also particularly indebted to the works of Henri Lefèbvre, Herbert Marcuse, and István Mészáros.

2. For discussions of the individualism, holism controversy from an Anglo-American perspective, see John O'Neill, ed., *Modes of Individualism and Collectivism* (New York: St. Martin's Press, 1973).

3. Barrington Moore, *The Social Origins of Dictatorship and Democracy* (Boston: Beacon Press, 1966); Marcel Mauss, *The Gift* (Glencoe, Ill.: Free Press, 1954).

4. Only, however, within certain limits. See Karl Marx, *Capital,* trans. Ben Fowkes, Vol. 1, p. 103.

5. For a discussion of Hegel's concept of natural science which has relevance for his notion of teleology, see Lucio Colletti, *Marxism and Hegel,* pp. 40-51.

6. For an analysis of the importance of change and movement in Hegel and Marx, see Herbert Marcuse, *Reason and Revolution,* pp. 8-11, 309.

7. This caveat differentiates my account both from phenomenology and from some aspects of the version of Hegelianism attacked in Colletti, *Marxism and Hegel.*

8. For dialectical materialism, see Colletti, *Marxism and Hegel,* pp. 40-51.

9. Karl Marx, *Grundrisse,* trans. Martin Nicolaus, p. 164.

10. I define materialism and idealism loosely for the purpose at hand as views which tend, respectively, to reduce everything to matter or to mind. For some of the ambiguities in the concept of matter in Marx, see Alfred Schmidt, *The Concept of Nature in Marx* (London: New Left Books, 1971), pp. 19-61.

11. Karl Marx, *The Economic and Philosophic Manuscripts of 1844,* pp. 171-173.

12. For a less mentalistic account of Kant by an anti-Hegelian Marxist, again see Colletti, *Marxism and Hegel,* pp. 106-112, where Colletti adopts the views on Kant espoused by the neo-Kantian Ernst Cassirer. For the relation of Lukács and Goldmann to the neo-Kantian interpretation of Marx, see Norman Fischer, Review of Lucien Goldmann, *Lukács et Heidegger, New German Critique,* No. 14 (Spring 1978): pp. 186-187.

13. Thus, Marx could be interpreted as a materialist in the tradition of Spinoza, a view which, certainly for very different reasons, Louis Althusser, *Reading Capital,* p. 102, also seems to adopt.

14. To approach the point from another perspective, Kant ultimately cuts man off from the world. See Lucien Goldmann, *Immanuel Kant,* p. 15.

15. See Lucien Goldmann, *Lukács et Heidegger,* pp. 102-105, for the multidimensional ways of recovering meaning.

16. Thus, Hegel's concept of knowledge is much less tied to the concept of the absolute spirit than Colletti *(Marxism and Hegel,* p. 72) argued.

17. For the ambiguities in Marx's account of base and superstructure, see

Melvin Rader, *Marx's Interpretation of History* (New York: Oxford University Press, 1979).

18. Unlike the *Verstehen* school, I hold that one can use the concept of causality in explaining human action without thereby becoming a positivist. For a short note on the *Verstehen* or *Geisteswissenschaft* school and its relation to Marxism, see Lucien Goldmann, *Marxisme et Sciences Humaines*, pp. 28-30.

19. These three concepts distinguish Marxism from Verstehen-type economic thought. For the economic and philosophic debates in Germany around the time *Verstehen* philosophy was developing, see David Frisby's introduction to Theodore Adorno, et al., *The Positivist Dispute in German Sociology*.

Bibliography

Adorno, Theodore, et al. *The Positivist Dispute in German Sociology.* New York: Harper and Row, 1976.

Allix, Edgard. "Le Physicisme des Physiocrates." *Revue D'Économie Politique* 25 (1911): 563-586.

Althusser, Louis. *For Marx.* New York: Vintage, 1970.

————, et al. *Lire le Capital.* 2 vols. Paris: Maspero, 1966.

————, and Balibar, Étienne. *Reading Capital.* London: New Left Books, 1975.

Avineri, Schlomo. *Hegel's Theory of the Modern State.* London: Cambridge University Press, 1972.

————. *The Social and Political Thought of Karl Marx.* London: Cambridge University Press, 1969.

Bartoli, Henri. *La Doctrine économique et sociale de Karl Marx.* Paris: Éditions du Seuil, 1950.

Baudrillart, H. "La Philosophie des Physiocrates." *Journal des Économistes* 19 (May 1851): 1-17.

Bigo, Pierre. *Marxisme et Humanisme.* Paris: Presses Universitaires de France, 1953.

Bitterman, H. J. "Adam Smith's Empiricism and the Laws of Nature." *Journal of Political Economy* 8 (1940): 487-520, 703-734.

Böhm-Bawerk, Eugen von. *Karl Marx and the Close of His System,* ed. and with an introduction by Paul Sweezy (New York: Augustus M. Kelley, 1966).

Bonar, James. *Philosophy and Political Economy.* London: George Allen and Unwin, 1922.

Bosch, Günther, ed. *Folgen einer Theorie.* Frankfurt: Suhrkamp, 1967.

Brandt, Reinhardt. *Eigentumstheorien von Grotius bis Kant.* Stuttgart: Frommann-Holzboog, 1974.

Braudel, Fernand. "La longue Durée." In *Écrits sur l'Histoire*. Paris: Flammarion, 1969.

Calvez, Jean. *La Pensée de Karl Marx*. Paris: Éditions du Seuil, 1970.

Chamley, Paul. *Économie Politique et Philosophie chez Steuart et Hegel*. Paris: Librairie Dalloz, 1963.

_____. "Les origines de la Pensée Économique de Hegel." *Hegel-Studien* 3 (1965): 225-261.

Coleman, D. C., ed. *Revisions in Mercantilism*. London: Methuen & Co., 1969.

Colletti, Lucio. *From Rousseau to Lenin*. New York: Monthly Review Press, 1972.

_____. *Marxism and Hegel*. London: New Left Books, 1973.

Cropsey, Joseph. *Polity and Economy: An Interpretation of the Principles of Adam Smith*. The Hague: Martinus Nijhoff, 1957.

Della Volpe, Galvano, et al. *Moral und Gesellschaft*. Frankfurt: Suhrkamp, 1968.

Denis, Henri. *Histoire de la Pensée Économique*. Paris: Presses Universitaires de France, 1966.

D'Hondt, Jacques. *Hegel en son Temps*. Paris: Éditions Sociales, 1968.

De Saussure, Ferdinand. *Course in General Linguistics*. New York: McGraw-Hill, 1966.

Dobb, Maurice. *Theories of Value and Distribution Since Smith*. Cambridge: Cambridge University Press, 1973.

Dunayevskaya, Raya. *Marxism and Freedom*. New York: Twain, 1964.

Edelman, Bernard. "La Transition dans la Doctrine du Droit." *La Pensée*, No. 167 (February 1973): 39-60.

Emmanuel, Arghiri. *Unequal Exchange*. New York: Monthly Review Press, 1972.

Ewing, A. C. *Kant's Treatment of Causality*. 1924; reprint ed., n.p.: Archon Books, 1969.

Fackenheim, Emil. *The Religious Dimension in Hegel's Thought*. Bloomington: Indiana University Press, 1967.

Faure-Soulet, J. F. *De Malthus à Marx*. Paris: Gauthier-Villors, 1970.

Feuerbach, Ludwig. *L'Essence du Christianisme*. Translated and with an Introduction by J. D. Oisier. Paris: Maspero, 1968.

_____. *The Essence of Christianity*. New York: Harper and Row, 1957.

_____. *The Fiery Brook*. New York: Anchor, 1972.

_____. *Kleine Schriften*. Frankfurt: Suhrkamp, 1966.

Findlay, J. N. *Hegel: A Re-examination*. London: G. Allen and Unwin, 1958.

Fischer, Norman. "The Concept of Community in Kant's Architectonic," *Man and World*, Vol. 11, No. 4 (Fall, 1978): 372-391.

_____. "Lucio Colletti on Socialism and Democracy." In Lou Patsouras and Jack Thomas, eds. *Problems of Twentieth Century Marxism* (Chicago: Nelson Hall, 1979).

_____. "Review of *Lukács et Heidegger*." *New German Critique*, No. 14 (Spring 1978): 185-192.

Foley, Vernard. *The Social Physics of Adam Smith*. West Lafayette, Ind.: Purdue University Press, 1976.

Fox-Genevose, Elizabeth. *The Origins of Physiocracy*. Ithaca, N.Y.: Cornell University Press, 1976.

Fromm, Erich. *Marx's Concept of Man*. New York: Unger, 1966.

Geras, Norman. "Fetishism in Marx's 'Capital.'" *New Left Review*, No. 65 (January-February, 1971): 69-85.

Gierke, Otto. *Natural Law and the Theory of Society*. Boston: Beacon Press, 1957.

Goldmann, Lucien. *The Hidden God*. New York: Humanities Press, 1964.

_____. *The Human Sciences and Philosophy*. London: Jonathan Cape, 1969.

_____. *Immanuel Kant*. London: New Left Books, 1971.

_____. *Lukács et Heidegger*. Paris: Editions Denoël, 1973.

_____. *Marxisme et Sciences Humaines*. Paris: Gallimard, 1970.

Gramsci, Antonio. "The Revolution Against 'Capital'." In *Selections from Political Writings 1910-1920*. New York: International Publishers, 1977.

Greimas, A. J. *Sémantique Structurale*. Paris: Larousse, 1966.

Grossman, Henrik. "Die Änderung des ursprunglichen Aufbauplans des Marxschen 'Kapital' und ihre Ursachen." *Archiv für die Geschichte des Sozialismus und der Arbeiterbewegung* 14 (1929): 305-338.

Guiheneuf, Robert. *Le Problème de la Théorie Marxiste de la Valeur*. Paris: A. Colin, 1952.

Habermas, Jürgen. *Theory and Practice*. Boston: Beacon Press, 1973.

Halévy, Eli. *The Growth of Philosophic Radicalism*. Boston: Beacon Press, 1960.

Hasbach, Guillaume (Wilhelm). "Les Fondements Philosophiques de L'Économie Politique." *Revue d'Économie Politique* 7 (1893): 747-795.

Heckscher, Eli, *Mercantilism*, 2 vols. London: G. Allen and Unwin, 1935.

Hegel, G.W.F. *Hegel's Logic*. Oxford: Oxford Univesity Press, 1975.

_____. *Hegel's Philosophy of Right*. Trans. T. M. Knox. London: Oxford University Press, 1967.

_____. *Hegel's Political Writings*. Trans. T. M. Knox. Oxford: Oxford University Press, 1964.

_____. *The Phenomenology of Mind*. New York: Harper and Row, 1967.

_____. *Schriften Zur Gesellschaftsphilosophie*. Vol. 1. Jena: Fischer, 1927.

————. *The Science of Logic*. New York: Humanities Press, 1969.

————. *La Société Civile Bourgeoise*. Trans. Jean-Pierre Lefebvre. Paris: François Maspero, 1975.

————. *Vorlesungen über Rechtsphilosophie*. 6 vols., 1818-1831. Ed. Karl-Heinz Ilting. Stuttgart: Frommann-Holzboog, 1973.

Heilbroner, Robert. *The Worldly Philosophers*. New York: Simon and Schuster, 1961.

Heiman, G. "The Sources and Significance of Hegel's Corporate Doctrine." In Z. A. Pelczynski, ed. *Hegel's Political Philosophy: Problems and Perspectives*. Cambridge: Cambridge University Press, 1971.

Hilferding, Rudolph. "Böhm-Bawerk's Criticism of Marx," in Eugen von Böhm-Bawerk. *Karl Marx and the Close of His System*, ed. and with an introduction by Paul Sweezy (New York: Augustus M. Kelley, 1966).

Hirschmann, Albert O. *The Passions and the Interests*. Princeton, N.J.: Princeton University Press, 1977.

Hobbes, Thomas. *Leviathan*. Ed. C. B. Macpherson. Baltimore: Penguin, 1968.

Hocevar, Rolf. *Hegel und der Preussische Staat*. Munich: Wilhelm Goldmann, 1973.

Hunt, E. K. "Value Theory in the Writings of the Classical Economists, Thomas Hodgskin, and Karl Marx." *History of Political Economy* 19 (Fall 1977): 322-345.

Hutchison, T. W. *A Review of Economic Doctrines, 1870-1929*. Oxford: Oxford University Press, 1953.

Hyppolite, Jean. *Studies on Marx and Hegel*. New York: Basic Books, 1969.

Jevons, W. Stanley. *The Theory of Political Economy* Harmondsworth, Middlesex, England: Penguin, 1970.

Kamenka, E. *Marxism and Ethics*. New York: St. Martin's Press, 1969.

Kant, Immanuel. *Critique of Judgment*. New York: Hafner Publishing Co., 1951.

————. *Critique of Practical Reason*. Indianapolis: Bobbs-Merrill, 1966.

————. *Foundations of the Metaphysics of Morals*. Indianapolis: Bobbs-Merrill, 1959.

————. *Gesammelte Schriften*. Berlin: Georg Reimer, 1911.

————. *The Metaphysical Elements of Justice*. Indianapolis: Bobbs-Merrill, 1965.

————. *Metaphysical Foundations of Natural Science*. New York: Bobbs-Merrill, 1959.

————. *Prolegomena to Any Future Metaphysics* in T. V. Smith and Marjorie Grene, eds., *Berkeley, Hume and Kant*. Chicago: University of Chicago Press, 1957.

_____. *Religion Within the Limits of Reason Alone.* New York: Harper and Row, 1960.

Kendall, Wilmoore. *John Locke and the Doctrine of Majority Rule.* Urbana: University of Illinois, 1965.

Korsch, Karl. *Marxism and Philosophy.* London: New Left Books, 1970.

_____. *Three Essays on Marxism.* London: Pluto Press, 1971.

Lacroix, Antoine. *Actualité du Physiocrate.* Moulins: Éditions des "Cahiers Bourdonnais," 1969.

Lange, Oscar. *Political Economy,* Vol. I. Oxford: Pergamon Press, 1974.

LeFèbvre, Henri. *Dialectical Materialism.* London: Jonathan Cape, 1968.

_____. *The Sociology of Marx.* New York: Vintage, 1968.

Lekachman, Robert. *A History of Economic Ideas.* New York: Harper, 1959.

Lévi-Strauss, Claude. *Le Cru et le Cuit.* Paris: Plon, 1964.

Löwith, Karl. *From Hegel to Nietzsche.* Garden City, N.Y.: Doubleday and Co., 1964.

Luce, A. A. *Berkeley and Malebranche.* Oxford: Oxford University Press, 1967.

Lukács, Georg. *History and Class Consciousness.* Cambridge, Mass.: MIT Press, 1971.

_____. *Soul and Form.* Cambridge, Mass.: MIT Press, 1974.

_____. "Moses Hess and the Problems of Idealist Dialectics." In *Tactics and Ethics.* New York: Harper and Row, 1975.

_____. *The Young Hegel.* London: Merlin Press, 1975.

Mach, Ernst. *The Science of Mechanics.* La Salle, Ill.: Open Court, 1942.

Maine, Sir Henry. *Ancient Law.* New York: Henry Holt and Co., 1878.

Mandel, Ernest. *The Formation of Marx's Economic Thought.* New York: Monthly Review Press, 1971.

_____. *Marxist Economic Theory.* New York: Monthly Review Press, 1970.

Marcuse, Herbert. *Negations.* Boston: Beacon Press, 1968.

_____. *Reason and Revolution.* New York: Humanities Press, 1954.

_____. *Studies in Critical Philosophy.* London: New Left Books, 1972.

Marx, Karl, et al. *Anarchism and Anarcho-Syndicalism.* New York: International Publishers, 1972.

_____. *Auswahl aus den Schriften von Karl Marx.* Ed. Franz Borkenau. Frankfurt: Fischer, 1956.

_____. *Basic Writings on Politics and Philosophy.* Garden City, N.Y.: Doubleday, 1959.

_____. *A Contribution to the Critique of Political Economy.* New York: International Publishers, 1970.

_____. *Early Writings.* Trans. Rodney Livingston and Gregor Benton. New York: Vintage, 1975.

_____. *The Economic and Philosophic Manuscripts of 1844*. Ed. Dirk J. Struik. New York: International Publishers, 1964.

_____. *The First International and After*. New York: Vintage, 1974.

_____. *Fondements de la Critique de l'Économie Politique*. 2 vols. Trans. Roger Dangeville. Paris: Éditions Anthropos, 1967-1968.

_____. *The Grundrisse*. Translated and edited by David McClellan. New York: Harper and Row, 1971.

_____. *Grundrisse*. Trans. Martin Nicolaus. Harmondsworth, Middlesex, England: Penguin, 1973.

_____. *Grundrisse der Kritik der Politischen Ökonomie*. Frankfurt: Europäische Verlagsanstalt, n.d.

_____. *Das Kapital*. Hamburg: Otto Meisner, 1867; reprint ed., Tokyo: Auki-Shoten, 1959.

_____. *Capital*. 3 vols. Vol. I, trans. Samuel Moore and Edward Aveling. Vols. II and III, trans. Ernest Untermann. New York: International Publishers, 1967.

_____. *Capital Volume One*. Trans. Ben Fowkes. New York: Random House, 1976.

_____. "Die Wertform." In *Kleine Oëkonomische Schriften*. Berlin: Dietz Verlag, 1953.

_____. *Letters to Dr. Kugelmann*. New York: International Publishers, 1934.

_____. *Oeuvres*. Vol. 2. Ed. and trans. Maximillien Rubel. Paris: Gallimard, 1972.

_____. *Pre-Capitalist Economic Formations*. New York: International Publishers, 1964.

_____. *Resultate des unmittelbaren Produktionsprozesses*. Frankfurt: Neue Kritik, 1970.

_____. *Texte zu Methode und Praxis*. 3 vols. Ed. Günther Hillman. Hamburg: Rowohlt, 1968.

_____, and Engels, Frederick. *Briefe Über "Das Kapital."* Erlangen: Politladen, 1972.

_____. "Marginal Notes on Adolphe Wagner's Lehrbuch der Politischen Ökonomie." *Theoretical Practice*, No. 5 (Spring 1972): 40-65.

_____. *Theories of Surplus Value*. Moscow: Progress Publishers, 1971.

_____., and Engels, Frederick. *Werke*. Berlin: Dietz Verlag, 1959-1968.

McClellan, David. *Karl Marx, His Life and Thought*. New York: Harper and Row, 1973.

Meek, Ronald. *Economics and Ideology*. London: Chapman and Hall, 1967.

_____. *The Economics of Physiocracy*. Cambridge, Mass.: Harvard University Press, 1962.

———. *Smith, Marx and After*. London: Chapman and Hall, 1977.

———. *Studies in the Labor Theory of Value*. London: Lawrence and Wishart, 1973.

———, and Skinner, Andrew. "The Development of Adam Smith's Ideas on the Division of Labour." *Economic Journal* 83 (December 1973): 1094-1115.

Melnick, Arthur. *Kant's Analogies of Experience*. Chicago: University of Chicago Press, 1973.

Mészáros, István. *Lukács' Concept of Dialectic*. London: Merlin Press, 1972.

———. *Marx's Theory of Alienation*. London: Merlin Press, 1970.

Moore, Stanley. *Three Tactics: The Background in Marx*. New York: Monthly Review Press, 1963.

Myrdal, Gunnar. *The Political Element in the Development of Economic Theory*. Cambridge, Mass.: Harvard Univesity Press, 1954.

Napoleoni, Claudio. *Ricardo und Marx*. ed. Cristina Pennavaja. Frankfurt: Suhrkamp Verlag, 1974.

———. *Smith Ricardo Marx*. New York: John Wiley and Sons, 1975.

Naville, Pierre. *De l'Aliénation à la Jouissance*. Paris: Éditions Anthropos, 1970.

Neumann, Franz. *The Democratic and the Authoritarian State*. New York: Free Press, 1957.

Nicolaus, Martin. "The Unknown Marx." In Carl Oglesby, ed. *The New Left Reader*. New York: Grove, 1969.

Ollman, Bertell. *Alienation*. London: Cambridge University Press, 1971.

Petry, Franz. *Der soziale Gehalt der Marxschen Werttheorie*. Jena: Fischer, 1916.

Piettré, Andre. *Histoire Économique*. Paris: Editions Cujas, 1969. University Press, 1975.

Polanyi, Karl. "Aristotle Discovers the Economy." In Karl Polanyi, Conrad M. Arensberg, and Harry W. Pearson, eds. *Trade and Market in the Early Empires*. New York: Free Press, 1957.

Quesnay, François. *Francois Quesnay et La Physiocratie*. 2 vols. Paris: Institut National D'Études Démographiques, 1959.

———. *Francois Quesnay: Tableau Économique des Physiocrates*. Ed. Michael Lutfalla. Paris: Calmann-Levy, 1969.

———. *Oeuvres Économiques et Philosophiques de F. Quesnay*. Ed. August Oncken. New York: Burt Franklin, 1969.

Reichelt, Helmut. *Zur Logischen Structur des Kapitalbegriffs bei Karl Marx*. Frankfurt: Europäisches Verlagsanstalt, 1970.

Ricardo, David. *The Works and Correspondence of David Ricardo*. 10

vols. Ed. Piero Sraffa. Cambridge: Cambridge University Press, 1966.

Riedel, Manfred. *Studien zu Hegel's Rechtsphilosophie.* Frankfurt: Suhrkamp, 1969.

Robinson, Joan. *Economic Philosophy.* Chicago: Alpine, 1962.

_____. "The Revelance of Economic Theory," *Monthly Review,* Vol. 22, No. 8 (January 1971): 29-37.

Rohr, Donald G. *The Origins of Social Liberalism in Germany.* Chicago: University of Chicago Press, 1963.

Rosdolsky, Roman. "Der Esoterische und der Exoterische Marx." *Arbeit und Wirtschaft* (November 1957, December 1957, January 1958): 348-351, 388-390, 20-24.

_____. *The Making of Marx's 'Capital.'* London: Pluto Press, 1977.

Rosenthal, M. M. *Die Dialektische Methode der Politischen Ökonomie von Karl Marx.* Berlin: Dietz Verlag, 1969.

Ross, David. *Kant's Ethical Theory.* Oxford: Oxford University Press, 1954.

Rousseau, Jean-Jacques. *The Social Contract.* New York: Hafner Publishing Co., 1947.

Rubel, Maximilien. *Karl Marx, Essai de Biographie Intellectuelle.* Paris: M. Riviere, 1971.

_____, and Manale, Margaret. *Marx Without Myth.* New York: Harper and Row, 1976.

Rubin, I. I. *Essays on Marx's Theory of Value.* Detroit: Black and Red Press, 1972.

Sachta, Peter. *Die Theorie der Kausalität in Kant's "Kritik der reinen Vernunft."* Meisenheim an Glan: Verlag Anton Haim, 1975.

Sartre, Jean Paul. *Situations.* Paris: Gallimard, 1949.

Schmidt, Alfred, ed. *Beiträge zur Marxistischen Erkenntnistheorie.* Frankfurt: Suhrkamp, 1967.

Schuhl, Pierre-Maxim. "Malebranche et Quesnay." *Revue Philosophique de France et de L'Etranger,* Nos. 3 and 4 (1938): 313-315.

Sebag, Lucien. *Marxisme et Structuralisme.* Paris: Petite Bibliothèque, 1964.

Sen, S. R. *The Economics of Sir James Steuart.* London: G. Bell and Sons, 1957.

Shell, Susan. "Kant's Theory of Property." *Political Theory* 6 (February 1978): 75, 90.

Skinner, Andrew. "Adam Smith: Philosophy and Science." *Scottish Journal of Political Economy* 19 (November 1972): 307, 319.

Smith, Adam. *Adam Smith's Moral and Political Philosophy.* Ed. Herbert W. Schneider. New York: Harper and Row, 1970.

_____. *Lectures on Jurisprudence.* Oxford: Oxford University Press, 1978.

_____. *The Theory of Moral Sentiments* in *The Works of Adam Smith.*

Ed. Dugald Stewart. 5 vols. 1811-1812; reprint ed., Aalen: Otto Zeller, 1963.

_____. *The Wealth of Nations*. Eds. R. H. Campbell, A. S. Skinner, and W. B. Tood. London: Oxford University Press, 1976.

Smith, Norman Kemp. *A Commentary to Kant's Critique of Pure Reason*. New York: Humanities Press, 1930.

Spiegel, William Henry. *The Growth of Economic Thought*. Englewood Cliffs, N.J.: Prentice-Hall, 1971.

Srivastava, S. K. *History of Economic Thought*. Delhi: Atma Ram and Sons, 1965.

Sweezy, Paul. *The Theory of Capitalist Development*. Cambridge, England: Monthly Review Press, 1964.

Taylor, Charles. *Hegel*. Cambridge, Mass.: Cambridge University Press, 1975.

Taylor, O. H. "Economics and the Idea of *Jus Naturale*." *Quarterly Journal of Economics* 44 (February 1930): 1-39.

_____. "Economics and the Idea of Natural Laws." *Quarterly Journal of Economics* 44 (November 1929).

Tönnies, Ferdinand. *Community and Society*. New York: Harper and Row, 1963.

Tuscheerer, Walter. *Bevor Das Kapital Entstand*. Berlin: Akademie-Verlag, 1968.

Viner, Jacob. *The Long View and the Short*. Glencoe, Ill.: Free Press, 1958.

Wahl, Jean. *Tableau de la Philosophie Francaise*. Paris: Gallimard, 1962.

Wills, Gary. "Benevolent Adam Smith." *The New York Times Review of Books* 25 (February 9, 1978): 40-43.

Wilson, Thomas, and Skinner, Andrew S., eds. *The Market and the State*. Oxford: Oxford University Press, 1976.

Wygodski, W. S. *Die Geschichte Einer Grossen Entdeckung*. Berlin: Verlag Die Wirtschaft, 1967.

_____. *Wie 'Das Kapital' Entstand*. Frankfurt: Verlag Marxistische Blätter, 1976.

Xhaufflaire, Marcel. *Feuerbach et la Théologie de la Secularisation*. Paris: Éditions du Cerf, 1970.

Zelený, Jindřich. *Die Wissenschaftslogik bei Marx und 'Das Kapital.'* Frankfurt: Europäische Verlagsanstalt, 1969.

Index

Certain words, such as *self*, *economics*, and *capitalism*, appear so often that they have not been indexed.

About the Author

NORMAN FISCHER is assistant professor of philosophy at Kent State University in Kent, Ohio. He has contributed articles to *New German Critique, Man and World,* and the collection *Problems of 20th Century Socialism.*